Between Heaven And Hell

By Alan Rimmer

Text copyright 2012 Alan Rimmer
All Rights Reserved

ISBN 978-1-291-20928-0

To my wife Maryse for her loyalty, love and support.

TABLE OF CONTENTS

AUTHOR'S NOTE

INTRODUCTION
THE SMILING KILLER
TRINITY

BATTLEGROUND BRITAIN

ARMAGEDDON
THE WITCH'S CURSE
ON THE BRINK
ISLAND OF THE DAMNED
DITCHED
INTO THE JAWS OF DEATH
THE COVER UPS
NO WAY TO TREAT A HERO
THE LONG DEATH
SHIRLEY'S STORY
DID YOU KNOW HE WET THE BED?
NUCLEAR GUINEA PIGS
HUMAN EXPERIMENTS
DIRTY TRICKS
KEN AND ALICE
THE CORONER'S CLERK
MURDO'S STORY
CHILDREN OF THE BOMB
THE DARK TOWER
THE URINAL DIALOGUES
THE ROAD TO CHERNOBYL
BETRAYAL
SICK FAMILY SYNDROME
MARK OF THE BOMB THE DOG IN THE NIGHT-TIME
THE TRUTH OF CHRISTMAS ISLAND

AUTHOR'S NOTE

This book is dedicated to the thousands of nuclear veterans and their families whose selfless courage, dignity and kindness made it possible. I would like to acknowledge the contributions of Ken McGinley who has tirelessly campaigned on behalf of Britain's nuclear veterans; Mrs Shirley Denson, for her indomitable courage and determination; Archie Ross, whose Damascene conversion was an inspiration to all; Roy Sefton, New Zealand nuclear veteran, whose lone battle showed the way; Mrs June Charney and all the other widows of nuclear veterans who refused to allow their husband's memories to fade. I would also like to thank John Urquhart, statistician and epidemiologist, for his invaluable advice and encouragement, and John Large, nuclear scientist, for his technical expertise, and patience. I would like to pay tribute to the late Professor Michael Moore and Nobel Laureate Joseph Rotblat for their inside knowledge of Lord Penney and the men who built the atomic bomb; the late doctors Alice Stewart and Rosalie Bertell for their unceasing quest to expose the truth; and to the late Richard Stott, journalist and editor who never gave up on the nuclear veterans. But most of all, this book is for the children, grandchildren, and the children yet to be born who will be paying the price for mankind's folly unto the end of time.

INTRODUCTION

The small military convoy drove cautiously through the village of Wansford as it threaded its way to Bomber Command's Armament School at RAF Wittering in Cambridgeshire. It was snowing heavily and visibility was down to 50 yards. As the vehicles exited the village they faced a steep climb up Wansford Hill. Without warning a large Foden truck, its contents shielded by a black tarpaulin, began to fishtail as the wheels lost traction in the tightly-packed snow. The driver struggled to control the heavy vehicle but it slithered remorselessly to the side of the road mounted the kerb and toppled over into a ditch. The driver leapt from the cab and held his breath as he stared down at the stricken truck; the tarpaulin had been dislodged during the crash revealing a large packing case. Through the slats the man could make out the sinister outline of an enormous bomb.

Sir William Penney, Britain's master bomb-maker, was flown off the island at dawn, which was just as well because, as feared, something went badly wrong. The huge bomb, codename Grapple Y, was much bigger than expected. The blast wave scattered troops like leaves before the wind, and the fantastic heat of the explosion made the blood bubble beneath their skin, even at a distance of 30 miles. It also created a hellish thunderstorm that produced a curtain of sizzling radioactive rain. Thousands of men got caught in the downpour. Within hours many experienced nausea and vomiting; some coughed blood up; others were blinded and their skin erupted in blisters.

The scientists and military planners acted quickly to suppress the news. This was after all the Cold War, and with nuclear Armageddon just a heartbeat away, secrecy was paramount. Official observers specially flown in to view the event were assured there was no fallout, before being hastily removed from the island back to the safety of their base in Honolulu. Politicians in London announced the test was a success and that the results were "gratifying" to the scientists. The public was told in a routine statement that it was a "clean" bomb and that all the troops were safe.

No-one worried overmuch about the troops. None as far as is known was killed instantly by the blast, and their sudden afflictions were easily explained away as "coral poisoning". The real effects of the bomb in disease and death would not become apparent for many years, and the authorities knew it would be virtually impossible to make a connection.

Penney, the "Father of the British H-bomb" observed the crowning achievement of his career from the cockpit of a Dakota aircraft circling the island. He had a grandstand view of the explosion, the huge mushroom cloud that accompanied it, and the towering thunderclouds that formed in its wake. By the time the deadly rain came, he was on his way to safety to an island 400 miles to the south.

He would never make a bigger or better bomb. Grapple Y was a thousand times the size of the Hiroshima bomb and its awesome power ensured Britain's place at the top table of international politics alongside America and the Soviet Union. Penney was showered with honours, and after a distinguished academic career, retired to a chocolate-box cottage nestling in the heart of the Oxfordshire countryside. Grapple Y, his legacy, was allowed to disappear into the sealed archives of government, consigned to just a minor footnote in history.

Penney, a mathematical genius, was marked down as a high-flyer in World War II when his unique talents took him from backroom boffin at the Ministry of Supply, to America where he became one of the chief architects of the atomic bomb. He was a reluctant recruit to this apocalyptic venture and like all the other scientists had deep misgivings about the possible consequences.

But a capricious twist of fate guided one of Hitler's new terror weapons to Penney's modest home in Croydon, South London with disastrous results. Any doubts that he may have had disappeared along with the tragedy that befell his beloved wife.

THE SMILING KILLER

June 29, 1944.

Auckland Road, Croydon, London,

An eyewitness described it thus: "I saw a sphere of flame hurtling earthwards like a football on fire. This was followed by a bright flash and a frightful roar..."

It was a V1 flying bomb, the first of hundreds to rain down on London as Hitler unleashed a new blitzkrieg. The V1, with a 2,000 pound payload of high explosive, landed in the road outside 108 and 110 Auckland Road. Both houses were demolished in the blast and scores were damaged over a quarter mile radius. A local church was destroyed; shredded bibles and hymn books were discovered as far away as Streatham.

The raid had started at dawn. The official log states:-

04.23: A V1 totally demolished eight houses in Gibbs Close, not far from Auckland Road. More than 40 houses were severely damaged.

08.04: On the corner of Central Hill and Hermitage Road a V1 exploded in the air. Houses and Norwood Cottage Hospital were badly damaged.

11.07: V1 strikes the corner of Sylvan Hill and Auckland Road. Details of damage in this area were not released because of "military restrictions." One of the houses at the site, 159, Auckland Road, was the home of Mrs Adele Minnie Penney, wife of Dr William Penney. The extent of the damage to the house is unknown, but Mrs Penney was alone as the doodlebugs exploded all around.

There is no record of her physical injuries, but her mind couldn't cope with the horror and she suffered a breakdown. The news was broken to her husband in America and arrangements were made for him to be flown home under military escort. Meanwhile Mrs Penney, aged 31, was admitted to Warlingham Park Hospital in Surrey. Set in acres of lush grounds, it was listed as a hospital for nervous disorders, but to the locals it was the place where the mad people went.

Mrs Penney was put under the care of Dr William Shepley, the Deputy Superintendent, and Dr Joyce Martin, a leading

Freudian analyst. She was treated in a special complex called 'The Villas' where she received psychotherapy and electro-convulsive shock treatment.

When her husband finally arrived, Mrs Penney didn't recognize him; she was living in a twilight world. Her mental and physical condition was deteriorating rapidly. The doctors were not hopeful. They told the young husband with the tousled fair hair that everything possible was being done. Penney decided not to take up an invitation to view the "barrow squad", a collection of inmates in various chairs who were habitually wheeled about the grounds to show visitors the patients were getting some useful activity.

Penney's visit was short and afterwards he went to see his two young sons, who had been evacuated. Les Hogan who had married Penney's younger sister Muriel, recalled the change in his normally placid brother-in-law: "He was always a very secretive person, I suppose he had to be, but always very pleasant and approachable. I remember him before Adele's illness, his sense of humour and fun. I had a little dog and I used to hold this dog and rub a ruler across his tummy and he used to immediately burst into incredible sounds. Bill used to laugh like mad at that, he thought that was so funny. He was a very human person. But he changed after what happened to his wife. He didn't talk a lot about it, but we all knew he was hurting very much. But there was also anger; there was a lot of that."

Penney stayed only long enough to make the arrangements for the welfare of his children. Then he was off in the waiting car, back to what remained of his Croydon home which was still guarded by armed soldiers. He spent several hours inside, eventually emerging with a leather valise stuffed with papers. He handed his keys to an official and received a receipt.

A light blue RAF Hillman Minx staff car took him to an airfield where a two-seater Mosquito fighter-bomber waited, engines revving. Two hours later it deposited Penney at Shannon airport where a cumbersome, but reliable, converted Wellington bomber was ready for take-off. The old 'bone shaker' was the regular shuttle plane across the Atlantic for scientists taking part in secret work. On board already was a colleague from Liverpool, Professor Michael Moore, who was going to America for the first time. He was the personal assistant of the Nobel laureate Sir James Chadwick, 'discoverer of the neutron' and head of the British mission in America.

Both men sat huddled in the wind-whistling fuselage of the

Wellington, swathed in scarves and blankets. The plane rattled and creaked like an old cattle wagon. There were two security guards with them and there was little talk. Penney sat in his own world staring white-faced out of the window. Fifteen hours later, the plane touched down at an isolated, windswept airfield in the vast, featureless terrain of Newfoundland.

The weather closed in almost as soon as the aircraft bumped to a halt, and the two scientists were shown to a wooden transit room reeking of paraffin and damp. They spent a restless night wrapped in blankets and dozing fitfully as they waited for the sleet and rain to subside. They talked little, but Moore learned enough to understand the depth of his colleague's sadness.

A military transport plane of the US Air Force eventually flew Moore to Berkerley in California where his skills in precision engineering were needed. Penney, whose job was more important, went to Washington. General Groves, the man in overall charge of the project was waiting. He told Penney his expertise was urgently required as "the gadget" was almost ready for testing.

This time Penney didn't take the Santa Fe Chief, the famous Pullman train linking Chicago with Los Angeles, a distance of more than 2,200 miles, because of pressure of time. Instead a military plane took Penney across the continental United States to the scorched New Mexico desert. It landed at the Alburqueque air base where some unusual activity was taking place far out in the desert at a place called Alomorgordo. Dust clouds drifted across the horizon as heavy vehicles moved equipment to and fro. Penney knew what it was all about but, as always, he was close-mouthed.

An open-topped Ford sedan, a female chauffeur at the wheel, was waiting. They headed for Santa Fe, a large, bustling, dusty town sweltering 20 miles away in the middle of the desert. The car drew up outside an anonymous building at 109, East Palace Avenue. The clapboard property with peeling paintwork was in fact the business address for the most secret place on earth. Penney was welcomed back by Dorothy McKibbin, a young widow who was one of the first recruits to the top secret project. She presented him with his new white security pass. Penney and his chauffeur then set off up the treacherous, twisting roads towards the towering Jemez mountain range.

Early explorers examining the Jemez Mountains observed the huge circular shape in the centre of the 11,000-foot range and thought of it as merely a curious set of connected valleys. It was not until the 1930s that it was identified as the rim of an ancient and extinct volcano. Some thought it was the actual crater, but the favoured theory was that it was a caldera, the huge saucer left when the volcano collapses.

Lush, green alpine passes between the peaks give way to a vast sea of grass interrupted only by forested hills. In winter a blanket of snow fills the valleys and the stark peaks form a magnificent panorama. Next to all this glory is a long, narrow plateau extending along the eastern slope of the Jemez range overlooking the Rio Grande. This narrow bench is known as the Pajarito (Little Bird) Plateau. Lying at an altitude of 7,000 feet, it is covered with ponderosa pine, fir, aspen and oak. Where they can get a foothold, juniper and many varieties of scrub proliferate. Early hunters wandered into the narrow defile for deer, bear and elk that still abound there to this day. Beaver traps were set in the lower regions.

It was a landscape shaped for the American dream, and it was here in 1917 that a Michigan businessman called Ashley Pond opened the Los Alamos Ranch School for boys on a hill surrounded by a dense forest of pines. The school flourished and it was soon catering for more than 50 boys sent there for experience of the open air life. By the 1930s a 23-acre lake had been excavated with places for boating, swimming and ice skating in the winter. Vigorous outdoor life was the order of the day while entertainment was provided by local Indians who performed dances and sold their craftwork on blankets.

The idyllic lifestyle at the ranch ended in 1942 during the annual summer program when school officials noticed an increase in low-flying aircraft over the area. Cars, and all kinds of strange military vehicles began to appear on the approach roads to the ranch.

On December 7, 1942, the first anniversary of Pearl Harbour, Secretary of War Stimson gave an order requisitioning the school. School officials and parents were told the building was being closed, but they were not told why. But the owners were happy enough with the $450,000 cheque they received.

It was only after the destruction of Hiroshima that they and the world learned of the true purpose: Los Alamos ranch school, renamed Site Y, had been chosen as the top secret headquarters of the Manhattan Project, the billion dollar program to develop the atomic bomb.

At first, however, locals could only scratch their heads and wonder as teams of construction workers fell on the campsite and grounds like a huge army of worker ants frantically rebuilding a damaged nest. Laboratory buildings were thrown up and living quarters for at least 300 people prepared. Chalet-style wooden huts were erected overnight and a network of crude roads cut into the red soil. The old school buildings, which used to contain 27 rooms, were modified so there was room for 70 people. A protective cordon of barbed wire fencing was thrown around the whole site; the only way in and out was through two well-guarded frontier posts.

By early 1943 some of the most famous scientific brains in the world had arrived at the ranch which everyone now referred to as The Hill. First to arrive were scientists from the University of California under the scientific director J. Robert Oppenheimer. Others came from all over Europe and America. Academic giants like Enrico Fermi, Neils Bohr, Hans Bethe, Edward Teller, Otto Frisch and George Kistiakowski were in the vanguard. Toward the end of the year, the second wave arrived. Penny was included in the 20-strong contingent from England.

Penney was the son of William Alfred Penney, a sergeant major in the Royal Ordnance Corps, who could not afford to pay for an education for his son. In fact in the early years, young William had no formal education at all; for the first 12 years of his life he lived a nomadic existence in various outposts including Gibraltar, where he was born. His father was an explosives expert, and family rumour had it that during the First World War he helped train Lawrence of Arabia in the techniques of laying charges. On their return to England, the Penney family settled in Alexandra Road, a modest row of Victorian terraces in Queensborough on the Isle of Sheppey, Kent. Penney's mother Blanch had a head for figures and was chief cashier at the Co-op.

Penney was set for an unremarkable life until, almost by accident, his tutors at Sheerness secondary school discovered he was a mathematical genius. Exasperated teachers complained about the precocious boy who was shouting out the answers to mathematical problems almost before equations on the chalk board were finished. The tutors nurtured this unexpected savant and were not surprised when Penney obtained the highest results in all England when he sat for scholarships in mathematics and physics. His results were so spectacular they guaranteed him entry to the prestigious Imperial College London. From there he was awarded a Commonwealth scholarship, and spent two years in America at the University of Wisconsin.

On his return he was offered a place at Cambridge where he studied the magnetic properties of crystals and the structure of metals. He went back to Imperial College after obtaining a brilliant First, and picked up two doctorates on the way. Finally he was made a Professor of Mathematics at Imperial College. He was just 27 years old.

He married Adele, who lived next door but one in the tight huddle of terraced houses that formed a graceful perspective down to the sea at the bottom of the road. They married in Queensborough, had two children and eventually moved to Croydon. Adele's clever husband was set for a distinguished academic career, but the war intervened. Penney joined a loose collection of government scientific workers, and was "borrowed" by the Admiralty to investigate a subject about which little was known: the nature of blast waves. As part of that work he made a study of underwater blast effects which was eventually used in designing the floating 'Mulberry harbours' to be used later in the 'D' Day landings.

He also had another job: under cover of working as an air raid warden, Penney was tasked by the War Office with finding out the size of the Luftwaffe's bombs by studying the effects on the gutted remains of the buildings they destroyed. Penney's detailed calculations enabled Army ordnance chiefs to work out the probable performance of Britain's own bombs and missiles. There was a gruesome side to his work, however: he was required to work alongside the rescuers who brought the tragic victims of the bombings to the mortuaries. In this way Penney discovered among other things the extraordinary resistance of the human body to blast waves.

By the time that he was sent to Los Alamos the young scientist was the world authority on the effects of high explosives and blast waves on buildings and people. From backroom boy in an obscure government department, he was suddenly one of the foremost scientists of the times, and he was in distinguished company indeed. With him on his first trip to America on the converted luxury liner Andes which set off from Liverpool bound for America in late 1943, was a galaxy of scientific stars including James Chadwick, discoverer of the neutron, Rudolf Peierls, Egon Bretscher, George Placzek and Klaus Fuchs.

From New York the group, for security reasons, was separated and despatched by various modes of transport, first to Washington to be briefed on security by General Leslie Groves, the man in overall charge of the Manhattan Project. Groves (with good reason, as it turned out) deeply distrusted many of the British contingent. But for some reason he took an immediate liking to Penney. Physically they were very similar, both bulky figures with heavy facial features and a slightly rumpled look. In personality, however, they couldn't have been more different. Penney, quiet and unassuming, was the antithesis of Groves' bombastic deportment.

Groves appears to have recognised in Penney a kindred spirit. They both had an absolute commitment to their work and were impatient with colleagues who found the task distasteful. From their first meetings, Groves had marked Penney down as being only one of a handful of scientists he would allow into the bomb project's innermost councils.

Los Alamos with its alien landscape and dizzying altitude was in stark contrast to Britain's rain-soaked climate, and most of the scientists took to it with relish. Once comfortably billeted (they were overwhelmed by the plentiful supply of foodstuffs of all varieties) they threw themselves into intensive rounds of meetings and tutorials, punctuated by lively discussion groups. Music evenings and exuberant parties where alcohol and dancing flowed with equal verve were also a feature.

Christmas in Los Alamos brought with it a white blanket of snow turning the high desert shrub into a Hollywood movie set. Tinsel and other festive paraphernalia festooned every home while long icicles hung from rustic cabins giving everything a magical feel. The air was cold and crisp and the snow-capped mountains in the distance dazzled in the gorgeous sunsets. Poised as they were on the precipice of creating a monstrous, almost satanic force of nature, this outlandish and exquisite Christmas must have been a poignant counterpoint.

Penney seemed to come alive in the intellectually-charged climate and was a favourite among the American scientists for his easy-going manner and the quiet authority he showed when discussing the nature of blast waves. He stunned them with graphic descriptions of the worst effects of the bombings, all delivered in a matter-of-fact style, but with a glint in his eye and a gleaming smile. His audience was apparently so impressed that one scientist, Victor Weisskopf, nicknamed Penney "the smiling killer." It was a moniker that stuck.

It didn't go unnoticed that the quiet Englishman had a new, harder edge when he returned to Los Alamos after his compassionate trip to England. Gone was the shyness he displayed on first arrival, and his famous smile was not quite the same. His eyes had acquired a steely quality, and there was a firmer set to his shoulders.

Penney chose not to reveal his wife's mental trauma, saying only that she had been killed in an air raid (Mrs Penney in fact died from pneumonia on April 18, 1945 at Warlingham Hospital). Penney brought the reality of modern warfare home to the Americans at Los Alamos who had so far only viewed events from afar. And Penney's eyewitness account of the devastation wrought by Hitler's latest terror weapons the V1 and V2 bombs galvanised them more than anything. These futuristic weapons with a payload of 2,000lbs of high explosive arrived completely without warning and, as Penney was keen to point out, there was no defence against it. Imagine if it could be armed with an atomic weapon!

At one colloquium Penney announced the results of his calculations on the impact of an A-bomb. A hush descended on the room as Penney, with a beaming smile, described how a city of 300,000 people would be reduced to a sink for disaster relief, bandages and hospitals. One of the people most impressed by Penney's intensity was Philip Morrison, a 27-yr-old physicist. He described Penney's 'nervous smile' as he discussed casualty numbers. "It was reality," recalled Morrison. "We knew it, but we couldn't see it. But Penney could."

Just before Christmas 1944 Penney produced a memorandum in which he discusses in chilling detail the effects of the "blast resisting characteristics of German towns and those of Japanese towns." After calculating the relative heights for the most destructive results on civilian housing from the "Gadget", the code name for the atomic bomb, Penney moves briskly on to what is considered to be only two alternatives: a) complete destruction, or b) severe but not irreparable damage. He makes it clear in his memo, only recently declassified, which was the favourable option:

Opinion in England has recently changed from requirement b) to requirement a). This is a major change in policy...and details are being sought from England on the current opinion of the relative values of A and B damage caused in German towns by H.E. (high explosive) blast.

Penney then sets out the reason for the shift in policy: the V1 attacks on London, which of course were responsible for the devastating impact on his own life. Penney, who refers to the onslaught as "robot attacks", writes:

(these) have forced a large scale systematic repairing schedule, which has proved that B damage is more readily repairable than previously thought. This is confirmed by cover photographs of Hamburg and other cities showing that really large areas of B damage have been restored with incredible rapidity.

Total destruction, or A damage is Penney's preferred option, and he describes in grisly detail the effects of blasts on various structures ranging from three storey blocks of flats in Hamburg, to the wooden (but earthquake-resistant) structures of Yokohama. Calculations are made about how many pounds per square inch of blast pressure it would take to cause family homes to implode, tear concrete off the walls, collapse shelters (where people might be sheltering) and cause wooden structures to self-combust over varying distances. But where Penney really gets into his stride is in his calculations concerning the "fire producing" qualities of the bomb:

The explosion of a gadget either in Germany or Japan, causing large areas of A damage will almost certainly result in fires. The large number of casualties associated with A damage may well lead to such confusion that the critical incubation period of the fires is passed unobserved. Thereafter the fire guards are useless, and only the Fire Force counts.

In other words the more people you kill, the less people left to put out the fires. This, according to Penney, would leave only a handful of professionals (Fire Force) to deal with the resulting firestorm. But Penney had a plan to deal with them as well: lure the professional firefighters into the radioactive contaminated area and then firebomb them in a follow up attack to finish them off. "This is attractive and realistic", he writes. One can imagine the chill descending over the assembled scientists as Penney (probably with a smile) made his presentation.

When Neils Bohr later produced a sketch of what looked like a heavy water reactor and said it had been designed by the German Physicist Werner Heisenberg proving the Nazis were on to the possibility of nuclear fission, there was a ripple of panic, and thenceforth activity increased immeasurably. And as their work gradually bore fruit security became tighter than ever. Groves, who had his spies everywhere, was suspicious of everyone. Passes were checked daily and double banks of barbed wire surrounded the more sensitive areas.

Penney had become Groves' main intelligence source among the British group. Two scientists on the British team were later to complain about Penney's zeal in hunting down potential spies. Polish physicist Joseph Rotblat, who quit the Manhattan Project after it became clear the Nazis would be defeated, spoke of his bitterness about a large trunk containing his precious possessions which disappeared on his way home: he was convinced it had been taken by the Los Alamos security people.

The incident followed amazing rumours about Rotblat, who had aroused suspicions when he decided to take flying lessons on his days off. He had apparently talked to Penney and others about enlisting in the RAF and joining Polish Spitfire squadrons that had helped win the Battle of Britain. For some reason a bizarre idea went round that he was planning to parachute into Russia to help the communist cause. (Hitler's deputy Rudolph Hess's parachute drop into Scotland in the crazy hope securing a peace deal was big news at the time.) Rotblat was closely questioned before he was allowed to return to the UK.

Michael Moore, assistant to Sir James Chadwick, the leader of the British mission, complained he was also given a security grilling. Moore, who was born in Cork, said officials became suspicious after he had spoken to Penney and others, in nostalgic terms about his Irish roots. Later he was interviewed by security officials and shown documentary evidence, obtained from British police, that one of his distant relatives had been a member of the IRA. What upset Moore most was that members of his family back in Liverpool had been visited by police detectives and given a rough time as they quizzed them about their political affiliations.

The experience still rankled 40 years later when Moore discussed it for the first time during an interview at his home in St. Helens, a town 10 miles from Liverpool. "I always blamed Penney," he said ruefully. "I should never have confided in him. The experience left a bad taste in my mouth."

Whether Penney was responsible is debateable. But what is certain is that around this time he was moved up several tiers in the Los Alamos hierarchy to consultant to the Director of the atomic test programme, Kenneth Bainbridge. He was put in charge of measuring the blast waves from the test explosion, which was given the codename Trinity.

Penney was also afforded entry into the Manhattan Project's inner circle, the seven-man Target Committee set up to decide which Japanese cities to bomb after the successful completion of Trinity. He was given the task of deciding the height of the blast so as to afford maximum damage to Hiroshima, which was the primary target. Nagasaki would be drawn from a short-list of several other cities at a later date.

The youthful Englishman, still only 34, was also given the considerable accolade of being the only British scientist chosen to observe the combat use of the weapon. To prepare him for the role, arrangements were made for Penney to be given a grandstand view of the Trinity test explosion from one of the observer aircraft.

TRINITY

Monday July 16, 1945 was the day earmarked for the historic testing of the world's first atomic bomb. The huge spherical 'gadget' was hoisted to the top of a 100-foot tower in a remote corner of the Alomogordo air base, 230 miles from Los Alamos. The last minute checks were satisfactory; everything was ready for the show. But on Sunday night the skies darkened and thunder rolled in the surrounding mountains. Then it started to rain. There was no sleep that night for anyone.

By 2am the weather began to improve, but it was decided to postpone the shot from the planned 4am to 5.30. After receiving weather reports, the decision was made. Unfortunately for Penney the foul weather had moved to Albuquerque air base where he was waiting in full flying gear to take off in one of the observer planes.

As news flashed through that the shot would go ahead at 5.30am, a simultaneous decision was made to ground the bombers. It was a huge disappointment, especially for Penney who had been intimately involved in the last-minute preparations. But it was a wise move as there was a considerable risk of the observer aircraft becoming lost in the heavy cloud cover and straying over ground zero. A rueful Penney later admitted to Chadwick, "We wouldn't have had a chance."

At exactly 5.29 and 45 seconds the brightest light in the universe bathed the area in an unearthly brilliance. The steel tower that held the bomb didn't just vaporise – it vanished. In the command bunkers, the observers lay face down on the ground, their feet facing toward ground zero. As soon as the light went they stood and turned toward the explosion. Even at two miles distant, some were knocked off their feet by the shock wave. Witnesses to nuclear explosions, the 'destruction of the building blocks of the universe', have been moved to express it in almost religious terms. Oppenheimer forever now to be known as the 'Father of the Atom Bomb' remarked: "I am become death, the destroyer of world", a passage from the sacred Hindu text the Bhagavad Gita.

One of the military witnesses, Major General Thomas Farrell, clearly in awe of the moment, desperately tried to find the right words: "The effects could well be called unprecedented, magnificent, beautiful, stupendous, and terrifying," he wrote in his report to Groves. "The lighting effects beggared description...it was golden, purple, violet, grey and blue..." He continued in a like vein for some time. The more phlegmatic Groves replied with a single word: "noted."

Other observers and correspondents have been using equally florid language to describe the bubbling horror of nuclear explosions ever since. Those without quite the same literary bent, or foreknowledge of what to expect, reacted rather differently. A humble G.I. fled in terror from his dugout screaming: "The long-hairs have let it get away from them..." Scientists, technicians and other observers displayed varying degrees of fear and elation. As the shock wave rolled over their heads, many sprang from their bunkers and performed an impromptu conga beneath the spreading effulgence of the world's first mushroom cloud.

Others far away also noted the momentous event. The flash of light was seen in Santa Fe, Albuquerque, Silver City and El Paso. It was so intense a blind girl 50 miles away asked, "What was that?"

With secrecy still paramount, Groves issued a cover story to stop word of the new super-weapon reaching the outside world. The local Santa Fe radio announced there had been an explosion in an ammunitions dump; for chance observers further away, army intelligence prepared stories blaming the strange event on an earthquake or a plane crash. Groves manage to insert an item in the local paper about a fictitious rail passenger who described "the biggest firework display I have ever seen..."

But at Los Alamos, and very much against the wishes of Groves, there was uninhibited joy. As news of the success of Trinity started to filter through, people took to the streets gathering excitedly; when it was confirmed, the dancing and cheering began. A group of technicians' wives went out bashing pots and kettles; people sat on the hoods of cars drinking and laughing, while scores formed congas that snaked in and out of the houses. Parties sprang up all over town.

Later drunken revellers stood in swaying groups as they waited for the buses carrying the dishevelled scientists to return home from Alamogordo. When they arrived they were so exhausted many wished for nothing but a shower and bed. But others simply couldn't sleep. They barged into communal areas wearing huge grins and flashing 'V' for victory signs.

The mood of euphoria was replaced by more sober thoughts as the sheer scale of the explosion began to sink in. Early reports said it was equivalent to 20,000 tons of TNT and that it had caused a vast black cloud of radioactive fallout. This had drifted over the desert mesas and contaminated huge areas up to 100 miles away. The silent aftermath of the detonation was said to be punctuated by staccato gunfire as specially trained GIs fanned out into the desert to destroy a herd of antelope driven crazy by radiation burns.

Penney was one of the first to be taken into the still smoking blast area to check on vital monitoring instruments he had set up at varying distances from ground zero. Groves marvelled at the simplicity of some of the equipment the scientist had devised: wooden boxes with different sized holes drilled into them and covered with paper membranes; toothpaste tubes filled with differing amounts of water. From the way the membranes had been punctured, and the toothpaste tubes bent, Penney could calculate the force of blast wave and even its shape. His calculations were often more accurate than the expensive electronic equipment devised by American scientists.

With the success of the Trinity explosion, the military planners got down to deciding which of the cities on the Japanese mainland should join Hiroshima as the luckless recipient of this new and terrifying weapon. There was never any doubt in their minds that the A-bomb should be used on Japan. Reports of the fanatical and suicidal defence by Japanese soldiers on Iwo Jima and Okinawa were convincing proof of the level of opposition the Allies would be likely to face in the event of an attack on the mainland. Hundreds of thousands of American lives would be lost before Japan surrendered.

The use of the atomic bomb to subjugate Japan quickly and with a minimal loss of American lives was therefore a no-brainer for people like Groves. But by this time the tide of war had turned against Germany and many scientists, who had joined the Manhattan Project because of their fear of the Nazis, were uncomfortable about its use on Japan. To avoid huge loss of civilian life, some suggested the bomb should be exploded harmlessly over Tokyo Bay to demonstrate its power and force Japan to the negotiating table. This was dismissed by President Truman who believed Japan would never capitulate unless forced to. He told the hierarchy at Los Alamos to "get on with it."

Groves and his security detail decided to isolate what he called the 'dissidents' and excluded many of the scientists from involvement in further development. Penney was most definitely on the side of Groves and appears to have been part of what was called the 'goon squad', a group of scientists and security staff charged with investigating the backgrounds of those who objected to using the bomb.

Michael Moore marked down early on as a possible dissident said: "It's true I wasn't very happy about using the atom bomb on a city of defenceless people, and I remember signing a petition got up by some of the other scientists. Even though I wasn't a very important cog in the scheme of things, the goon squad arrived and put the thumb-screws on me to remove my signature. I refused. I argued that my primary objection was on moral grounds because I was horrified with what the bomb would do to people. But I was also very concerned about the long-term effects. The dangers from fall-out were very well known, even then, but that seemed to have no effect on plans for further bomb development which I knew were in the pipeline."

Moore was later sent back to Liverpool, where he was told his skills as a metallurgist were urgently required. It was a far less secretive task than his work in Berkerley and Los Alamos, and Moore always felt he had been sidelined. He was effectively barred from all future work on atomic projects.

It later turned out the 'goon squads' missed their targets completely. Neither Rotblat nor Moore was a security risk. That dubious honour fell to Klaus Fuchs one of of Los Alamos's most trusted scientists, who succeeded in handing Stalin the complete blueprints of the atomic bomb on a plate.

The plan to bomb Japan went ahead and Penney was set the task of deciding the height at which the bomb should be exploded to ensure maximum damage. Working alongside him was another British scientist and friend, Ernest Titterton. The two had been close ever since their university days and Penney was said to be mortified when Titterton's wife, who also worked at Los Alamos, gave birth to a child with spina bifida. Radiation exposure was accepted as being the cause, and it had a sobering effect on those enthusiastic about using the bomb. Penney never said what his thoughts were, but even though he was said to 'love children more than adults', he never had any more children, even though he remarried soon after returning from Los Alamos.

Penney as one of the elite of Los Alamos, joined 51 scientists, engineers and weapons experts who one morning was suddenly not there anymore. One by one they had left in the night; they didn't even bother to pack. Those left behind of course could guess what had happened: they were the ones chosen to complete the final phase of their work at Los Alamos.

It had taken just 28 months from the inception of the Manhattan Project to reach this point. It was a remarkable achievement. The 51, known simply as the 'destination team' later boarded one of several shiny new B-29 bombers, the first aircraft to have pressurized cabins, and set off for Tinian Island in the Marianas which was to be the launch pad for the nuclear attack on Japan.

Penney, who wore an American air force uniform at Groves' insistence, was head of the scientific team building a production line of atomic bombs that were being assembled on Tinian. A rare of picture of him at the time shows him smiling broadly as he sits with his team, dressed in their US Army uniforms, near the production shed.

Of course only two of the bombs were ever used: Little Boy, which had a uranium core and was dropped on Hiroshima, and Fat Man, the plutonium device used on Nagasaki. But at least a dozen bombs were assembled on Tinian, just in case the Japanese didn't surrender immediately. (These 'spares' were later abandoned and the remains of hundreds of tons of discarded ordnance material litter the crystal clear waters surrounding the island to this day.)

No British representative was allowed on the first historic flight. On August 6, 1945, at 08.15 am local time, a B-29 Superfortress called the Enola Gay with Colonel Paul Tibbets at the controls dropped the Little Boy uranium bomb on Hiroshima. 100,000 people died. A triumphal announcement was made by President Truman on board the cruiser USS Augusta a short time later.

Penney's big moment came on August 9 when he climbed aboard a superfortress called Big Stink, which was the observer aircraft for this mission. The lead B29 was Bock's Car and carried the Fat Man plutonium bomb destined for Nagasaki. At 11.02 am, the bomb was released and although it exploded a mile off course, 80,000 people perished.

Penney witnessed the annihilation of the beautiful Japanese port city (known as the Venice of the Orient) with the only other British observer, Group Captain Geoffrey Cheshire VC. Cheshire was horrified by what he witnessed. Later he became a pacifist and a life-long campaigner against nuclear weapons. Penney found the experience less appalling.

He was not surprised by what he saw, through welder's

goggles in the rear-gunner's position. He had spent months calculating its probable performance and had given lectures to air crew about what to expect. He knew only too well what would happen to the people of Nagasaki: first there would be the blinding flash with the 'brightness of a thousand suns.' Then there would be the huge, roaring sound like an approaching express train accompanied by an immense pressure wave, a howling wind and unbearable heat. He also had a very good idea of what would happen next: the hellish haze of rapidly darkening smoke that would rain lingering death down upon the luckless inhabitants.

Among those who died that momentous day was a young RAF engineer called Ronald Shaw who was on a "slave labour" detail at the Mitsubishi shipyard a couple of hundred yards from ground zero. He is the only known British victim of the Nagasaki bombing. He had been captured in Indonesia and sent by sea to Japan on the troop transports known as "hell ships". An allied torpedo sunk the ship, but Shaw survived and he was eventually sent to work in Nagasaki. The few known details of Corporal Shaw's life show he was an engine fitter at the RAF base at Kalidjati on the island of Java and was captured in Batavia, present day Jakarta, in 1942. After the torpedo attack he was rescued and taken to Kyushu, the southernmost of the Japanese islands and eventually found himself working in the Mitsubishi shipyard in Nagasaki. The force of the atomic bomb caused the entire building to collapse killing Corporal Shaw in the crush of falling masonry.

Penney doubtless would have been horrified, but by that time he had embraced the "total war" policy now favoured by the allies to bring the carnage to a swift end. He was a patriot with a deep and abiding love of his country. Later as he examined the smouldering ruins of the once great city he vowed to do everything in his power to avoid a British city suffering a similar fate. As he stared into the ashes of Nagasaki, he hoped it would not only end World War II, but perhaps end war itself. After all, what industrial country, knowing the destructive capacity of the atomic bomb, would deliberately embark upon another war in the face of such utter destruction?

When the Japanese surrendered, Penney was sent to rummage among the ruins of Hiroshima and Nagasaki to collect materials which would help to calculate the immense power that had been unleashed. He visited the makeshift hospitals and, with echoes of his grim task during the London blitz, examined the scorched bodies of the dead and barely living. With his task completed Penney returned home to write a detailed report on the blast effects of atomic bombs.

In summing up the British contribution to the Manhattan Project, General Groves singled out Penney for special praise; he was lukewarm about the rest of the British scientific contingent. No doubt his views were coloured by the exposure of Klaus Fuchs as a Russian mole. German-born Fuchs was a Jewish scientist who fled to England when the Nazis rose to power. Groves was furious when only later did he learn that the British had been informed by the Germans prior to the war that Fuchs was a communist. He felt let down by his British allies for not carrying out proper security checks on the scientists chosen to work on the Manhattan Project. Groves vented his spleen in his memoirs: "Since the disclosure of Fuchs' record, I have never believed that the British made any investigation at all. Certainly, if they had, and had given me the slightest inkling of his background, which they did not, Fuchs would not have been permitted any access to the project."

Postwar developments saw the US and the UK locked in discussions on cooperation over nuclear collaboration. The Americans were now reluctant to share their nuclear technology, but the British were insisting their ally adhere to promises made that nuclear know-how would be shared after the war. The Brits were suspicious about American insistence that it could not find the document on which the agreement was drawn. This document, referred to as the Hyde Park *aide-memoire*, supposedly summarized a conversation between President Roosevelt and Winston Churchill at Hyde Park on September 18, 1944. The Americans said they had no record of the document and was not therefore obliged to share its nuclear secrets with Britain. This intransigence persisted even when Churchill sent a Photostat copy of the agreement to the Americans.

General Groves, who was in the thick of the negotiations, commented: "While the mutual confidence which had prevailed throughout the war continued, we were completely mystified by the British references to this document. I am sure that on their part the British must have been annoyed by our insistence that we could find no copy of what they considered to be a valid and binding agreement. Where was it? Why had President Roosevelt never told any of us about this highly important document? This still remains a mystery."

It was of course convenient for Groves and the rest that Roosevelt wasn't around anymore to verify the agreement. The confusion was used to renege on the agreement, thus achieving a monopoly on nuclear weapons for the Americans. The Hyde Park *aide-memoire* eventually turned up in a file of papers pertaining to naval matters. According to Groves: "The misfiling was due, I suppose, to the fact that the paper referred to Tube Alloys, the British code name for the atomic project, and the file clerk must have thought it had something to do with ship boiler tubes."

While all this was going on, Penney slipped quietly away to resume his career in academia. But like the Sorcerer's Apprentice in Goethe's poem, he found it impossible to escape the elemental forces he had helped to unleash.

By this time it was now obvious to the British that America was determined to retain its monopoly over nuclear weapons for as long as possible. And of course the Soviets, who were perceived as the new threat to world peace, were by now throwing everything they had into acquiring its own atomic bomb. Way ahead of the game, American flexed its muscles and carried out a series of atomic tests in the Pacific in the summer of 1946. The British were excluded from this program, except for Penney. Groves thought so highly of him, he invited him to join the scientific team gathered in the Rongelap islands, Polynesia. Penney's political masters impressed upon him the vital necessity for him to attend; it could an invaluable experience if Britain was to have its own bomb.

Penney was welcomed back by Groves who allowed him a free rein to examine the arrangements. They were in the command bunker together when the huge atomic bomb was exploded 40-feet below the surface in a lagoon on Bikini atoll. A derelict flotilla of captured World War II Japanese warships was moored nearby to test the effects of the blast. Penney once again deeply impressed the Americans with the novel simplicity of measuring the blast wave using 300 old petrol cans and toothpaste tubes filled with varying amounts of water, strung around the atoll. Groves wasn't surprised when Penney's calculations proved to be more accurate than the immensely expensive electronic measuring devices used by the Americans (most of which, in any event, were destroyed by the blast).

On his return to Britain, Penney stock had now risen so high that he was seconded to take part in the first ever East-West discussions at the United Nations on the control of atomic energy. He was appointed scientific adviser to the British delegation. In a speech he announced that control over atomic energy was only possible provided nations allowed free access to observers. The Soviet Union, in the process of drawing an Iron Curtain across Europe, refused to cooperate.

In response, the USA decided to draw a curtain across its own scientific discoveries, especially those concerning atomic research. And in a surprise move the McMahon Act was introduced which specifically forbade Britain from a share in atomic secrets, despite the vital part played by British scientists in building the first A-bomb. It was a devastating blow for Britain which now had no choice but to go it alone if it wasn't to be shut out completely from the world stage. In 1947 Penney reluctantly accepted the post of Chief of Armament Research at the Ministry of Supply (forerunner of today's Ministry of Defense.) His job description was deliberately ambiguous to give the impression he was involved in conventional weapon research. In truth he had just one brief: "build an atom bomb."

BATTLEGROUND BRITAIN

Britain was in a perilous position in the 1950s. Both America and the Soviet Union were stockpiling atomic bombs at an alarming rate and the only thing preventing mutual destruction was that neither had aircraft with a long enough range to reach the other. But America had an ace in the hole: its heavily fortified air base at Lakenheath in Suffolk, which Britain had allowed them to build, despite the bad blood over the McMahon Act. The US had strike aircraft based at Lakenheath that could deliver A-bombs to Russian soil. The Soviets had no bases close enough for retaliatory action on mainland America. The only place they could effectively strike back at was America's closest ally, thus making Britain the likely starting point for World War 3.

The harsh reality galvanized the politicians into action. But building the atomic bomb was an enormous task and a huge drain on the resources of a country virtually bled dry by the ravages of five years of war. Nevertheless two reactors, both capable of producing plutonium, were constructed at enormous cost at Capenhurst near Windscale on the north west coast of Britain. In those days, the Cumbrian coastline between Barrow and Whitehaven was almost as remote as Los Alamos. Just to get there from London took all day and with construction workers arriving from all over the country, the area soon resembled the Klondyke.

But while Windscale was being built to make the plutonium for the bombs, it was decided to base Britain's 'Los Alamos', the bomb-making facility, at Aldermaston, near Reading in Berkshire. This was a former Ministry of Supply wartime armaments research facility which was not as remote as Cumbria and therefore more accessible for Penney and his staff. Harwell, an old RAF airfield, 60 miles from London was also requisitioned as a base for the scientists who devised the plans for the new super weapon.

Living accommodation at both centres was basic with many of the newly arrived staying in caravans or converted wartime hangars. The roads were rutted and unpaved, and there was a shortage of everything. Scientists were so short of equipment that some used milk bottles as beakers; the only 'luxury' items afforded them were extra milk rations because it was believed this could ward off the harmful effects of radiation.

Klaus Fuchs was taken on as a section head at Harwell, where all the theoretical work was done. Penney, who was based at Aldermaston, often met with him and the pair collaborated on every aspect of atomic research. It was a huge shock to Penney and his co-workers when in 1949, and against all expectations, the Soviet Union successfully exploded its first atomic bomb.

Penney was summoned to London for urgent talks as the politicians desperately tried to work out how the Soviets had so comprehensively beaten Britain to the punch. It had been thought it would be 1954 and probably later that Russia would have the expertise to build 'the bomb', so Penney had some awkward moments explaining the situation to his political masters.

Meanwhile panic swept America where this sudden development was regarded as a national humiliation. This quickly turned to outrage when Klaus Fuchs, who was critical to the development of Britain's bomb, was arrested in 1950 for espionage and confessed to being a communist spy. He admitted that while at Los Alamos he had provided the Soviets with the blueprints for the bomb.

The Americans were furious. Even Penney, the only British scientist with any access to United States nuclear technology was shunned by his erstwhile admirers in America. He was reduced, along with another Los Alamos scientist, the German-born theoretical physicist Rudolf Peierls, to visiting Fuchs regularly in Brixton prison to try to find out what secrets he might still have. It was a frustrating time for Penney.

Despite the setbacks, the development of Britain's bomb continued and in early 1951 prime minister Clement Atlee wrote to his Australian counterpart Robert Menzies with a request for Australia to be used as the site for Britain's first A-bomb. The anglophile Menzies agreed at once and the Monte Bello Islands, a small uninhabited archipelago off Western Australia, was earmarked as the site for the test.

By 1952, enough plutonium had been produced and the immensely precious and dangerous cargo was conveyed by saloon car to Aldermaston where Penney's first bomb was being assembled. But amid scenes that could have come straight out of an Ealing Studios comedy, the car broke down on the way and the ingot of plutonium (in a container about the size of a large can of beans) had to be left on the back seat while the driver looked for a telephone. Penney and his high-powered team sweated it out for hours while a local garage carried out repairs before the ingot was delivered into their safe keeping.

Based on the Fat Man design of the American bomb dropped on Nagasaki, Penney's bomb was an implosion device with about twice the destructive capacity. Penney's team, short of materials and the latest technical know-how, toiled for weeks to perfect the design before it was finally delivered into the hands of the Royal Navy for transportation to Australia.

In an operation codenamed Hurricane, a special task force of ships left London in August 1952 for their destination on the other side of the world. The flagship and leader of the squadron was the aircraft carrier HMS Campania. She was accompanied by the supply and landing crafts, HMS Tracker and Narvik. Guarding the little fleet was HMS Zeebrugge. A total of 1,075 men were aboard the four vessels. As the fleet nosed its way down the Thames, it was joined unobtrusively by another vessel, a battered old frigate called HMS Plym which had recently been salvaged from the breaker's yard. There was only a skeleton crew on board, together with a handful of scientists and technicians. In the hull of Plym was Britain's greatest secret, the atomic bomb.

The task force arrived at the Monte Bello islands in good order. Plym was anchored in a lagoon near Trimouille Island, the main one of the group. The rest of the squadron withdrew to safe positions about 12 miles off shore. An advance party of royal engineers had been laying cables and preparing the ground for weeks and everything was in readiness when Penney arrived by seaplane. He was welcomed aboard HMS Campania by the Commander of the Special Squadron, Rear Admiral Arthur Torlesse.

There were many delays caused by bad weather, and frustrating arguments over faulty equipment before Britain's first atomic bomb was detonated on October 3rd, 1952. It was exploded inside the hull of Plym which was anchored in 40 feet of water, 400 yards off-shore. It was a replica of the Bikini explosion witnessed by Penney in 1946. A dense cloud of mud and water rose 15,000 feet into the air, but the 'beauty' of the explosion was somewhat marred as the familiar mushroom shape was distorted by a series of cross-winds. Penney on the flight deck of Campania made no comment, but was said to be disappointed.

Penney's account of what he saw was broadcast around the world by the BBC. In his quiet, middle-England accent, he told his audience: "I was on the flight deck of HMS Campania with

Admiral Torlesse and most of the ship's company. We all faced away from the explosion as the last few seconds were counted over the loudspeakers. Suddenly there was an intense flash, visible all round the horizon. We turned to look. The sight before our eyes was terrifying...a great greyish-black cloud being hurled thousands of feet into the air and increasing in size with astonishing rapidity. A great sandstorm suddenly sprang up over the islands. It seemed ages before we heard the bang, but in fact it was less than a minute. Somewhat to our surprise a second bang, at least as loud as the first, followed a few seconds later. At the same time we felt a peculiar sensation in our ears such as one has in an aircraft losing height rapidly. We were feeling the suction of reduced pressure, which always follows a blast wave. All the time the cloud was getting higher and higher and assuming fantastic shapes as it was pulled about by the strong winds at different altitudes..."

Penney spoke at length about radiation, electronic gadgets, re-entry parties, contamination and how everyone had pulled together to make the test an outstanding success. He spoke soothingly about how the survey parties all wore protective clothing covering them from head to foot, and how they also wore gas masks to prevent inhalation of "foreign particles."

He continued: "The appearance of men in protective clothing, scrambling about on the white sand hills in the blazing sun and peering at their instruments every few seconds, was a weird sight. Everyone in the parties sweated profusely, and one man lost no less than 17 lb in weight in a single trip. However, on his return to the health control centre, a few long drinks of water, some salt tablets and a meal with lots of tea, quickly restored the loss of weight and nobody felt any the worse..."

It was all good Boys Own stuff delivered in the manner of a cosy fireside chat between old friends. The bomb had gone off without a hitch, everyone was safe, and 'our boys' had pulled it off and no damage done. Britain had a new hero who had restored its rightful place as a world power.

Rear Admiral Torlesse, listening to Penney's broadcast as he shepherded his little task force back to Britain, might have raised a somewhat quizzical eyebrow. As task force commander he had been involved in every stage of the operation. And although it had been an undoubted success, it had most assuredly not been without its problems.

For a start Torlesse and Penney's right-hand man Leonard Tyte, the operation's scientific director, had argued and bickered constantly. They fought royally over everything from lost messages, timings of rehearsals, accommodation, supplies; they even blamed each other for the capricious weather. At D-day minus two the relationship between the pair had deteriorated to such an extent they weren't even on speaking terms. It was only the prospect of international humiliation, not to mention the towering rage of Winston Churchill, newly returned to power after six years in Opposition, which pulled them back from the brink.

Even after the success of the mission, Torlesse remained a stickler for rules and procedure. He found the lack of discipline among the scientists a constant irritant. On one memorable occasion, Torless insisted on the scientists, who were famously bohemian in appearance, wearing ties for mess dinner. The scientists complied...the only problem was they "forgot" to put shirts on...

For his part, Tyte found the Rear Admiral an insufferable snob. It amused Tyte no end to see Torlesse's obvious irritation when Penney, who deferred to no man but Churchill, regularly plundered his personal cigarette stash.

Bickering apart, Torlesse had been greatly concerned about the safety of his men, especially those who had been sent in to some very dangerous areas to satisfy the scientists' insatiable thirst for knowledge. He later told in an interview how he was particularly concerned about radio communications from the pilots of two Shackleton aircraft who were tracking the mushroom cloud. At first Torlesse said he was irritated by the chatter, fed into main communications centre on the bridge of Campania, between the two pilots who were joking about who was the "hottest" pilot, when all of a sudden everything changed. One of the pilots was obviously in trouble.

Torlesse said: "I remember there was a hell of a flap about a chap in one of the planes who was flying through the cloud to collect samples. He was ordered back and I understand flown immediately to a hospital in Perth. I'm not sure what happened after that. It was all secret. No-one would tell me anything."

The Rear Admiral wasn't the only one to take a somewhat jaundiced view of Penney's cosy assurances. Thomas Wilson, a sapper in the Royal Engineers, scratched his head and wondered if he had been at the same bomb test as Penney when he heard the scientist talking about how the re-entry parties had been given head to toe protection from the radioactive fallout. And he should know: he was in the very first re-entry party that stepped ashore after the bomb was detonated. The only protective clothing he had on was an overall and bush hat.

This is how the former 19-yr-old squaddie remembered the event: "We went in on a little rubber dinghy and hit the beach on the run. As soon as we stepped ashore it was clear the whole place was crackling with radiation. I had a small hand-held Geiger counter and it was going crazy. I was wearing just a thin overall and a bush hat. Even I knew that wasn't enough. But being young we had this sort of couldn't-care-less attitude to the dangers and we just got on with the task in hand. We didn't think we were in any danger and enjoyed all the excitement."

For several hours Wilson and the other soldiers wandered around the scorched island collecting the scientific paraphernalia used to record the effects of the blast wave. They checked damaged buildings, and collected food stocks and other items for measurement back on the ship. They also had to bag and take back with them hundreds of dead seabirds that littered the island. It was all done beneath the blazing sun, and the smoke and heat from dozens of scrub fires ignited by the blast.

At last it was all over and Wilson and his band returned to their ship. Each man had to enter a special decontamination unit, and throughout the afternoon the clicking of Geiger counters were a constant feature. The men were ordered to strip, and their clothing was immediately consigned to the bottom of the sea encased in concrete. It was then into the showers where they were vigorously scrubbed down until the counters stopped ticking. Despite three scrub downs, Wilson remained radioactive for hours. A note in his Army paybook records: "1952 atomic tests. Radiation received 1.99 Roentigens."

Another serviceman who knew things hadn't all gone to plan was Royal Marine commando Frank Gray. Not long after the bomb went off, he and a small detachment of specially trained men were sent skimming in a dinghy across the highly-radioactive lagoon where Plym had been vapourised to rescue a group of scientists left in a forward area bunker. Mr Gray recalled: "We were told the scientists were in trouble because the fireball had finished very close to the bunker. We were dispatched to get them back. One thing I remember very clearly was the thousands of dead fish scattered all over the lagoon. And I remember we even had to avoid a sick whale that was thrashing about. When we got to the bunker which was built into the side of a hill we found it charred and smoking. The first thing I saw was two men in protective clothing and several others who were shaking and wrapped in blankets. They were only wearing sandals, shirts, stockings and shorts with no headgear. I was told they were scientists, but they didn't say anything and seemed to be in deep shock. We took them in two dinghies back to the ship. They had to be helped up the gangplank and a couple of them collapsed onto the deck. I believe they were taken from the ship later that night, and that was the last anyone saw of them."

Thomas Wilson and Frank Gray were to suffer terrible health problems in later life which they always blamed on their involvement in Operation Hurricane. Their complaints, however were dismissed as 'fanciful' by doctors, and disdained by politicians; the same depressing response was experienced by many hundreds of servicemen in the years to come.

But there was no doubting the technical success of Hurricane; it brought heady days for Penney who now found himself a national hero, feted and lionized wherever he went. His home-coming was pure Hollywood. He arrived back in Britain from the Monte Bello islands on October 15. The press and newsreels clamoured for news. They descended on the airfield at RAF Lyneham in Wiltshire after it was leaked that his plane was going to land there. They were herded into the airfield cinema and held for hours as the excitement mounted. At 4.20 and 4.25pm, two Hastings aircraft touched down. The press surged forward...

Was Penny on board? Officials said they couldn't say; it was secret.

Which plane was he in? That was a secret too.

What was in the other plane? That was also a secret.

As the press hubbub reached a crescendo, the object of all the excitement suddenly appeared round a corner. Penney was surrounded by RAF policemen and he looked stunned by all the attention.

The press swept forward. Penny managed a smile as he blinked into the combined light of scores of flash-bulbs. The cameramen wanted to know if he could be snapped by the aircraft he had arrived in? The answer was "no."

Penney kept smiling as his security detail cleared a path for him. After some whispered discussions, Penney was persuaded to move to a bank of microphones set up by the newsreel men. An official handed out a typed slip. It was a statement from Penney: "Naturally I am glad to be home. The test was most successful. I can say no more about it until I have made my report to the Government."

Would he speak about the atom test, they wanted to know.
No.
Would he say what it looked like?
No.
Would he say what the weather was like?
Emphatically, no.

Penney seemed relieved when asked what he did in his spare time: "What spare time I had in Australia I spent golfing. Golf is the complete relaxation. After completing my report I expect to be off on holiday...I should get some golf in."

After imparting this pearl of news, Penney was bundled into a waiting saloon car which roared off toward his tightly-guarded home in Idminster Road, Norwood, London. By this time Penney had remarried and his new wife Joan, a midwife, was a no-nonsense woman who ran the Penney household, and his two sons, with commendable efficiency.

A journalist who managed to get a word with Mrs Penney reported the following exchange (revealing that Mrs Penney was just as closed-mouthed as her famous husband):-

What had she cooked him for dinner?
"Brown stew," said Mrs Penney.
What was in it?
"Don't ask."
What did Dr Penney do after dinner?
"Why, the washing up of course. I washed, he dried. Being a great man doesn't excuse him from chores, you know."

Penney celebrated with a champagne lunch at his favourite Soho restaurant, the Pe're Auguste. Sitting on his left was his wife who kept a close eye on her husband's alcohol consumption. On his right sat General Sir Frederick Morgan, controller of atomic energy at the Ministry of Supply. A group of sharp-eyed special branch detectives had taken up strategic positions at nearby tables. A man with Penney's secrets was far too important to be left unguarded, even at lunch.

Newsreels showed him blinking owlishly behind his spectacles as the flash-bulbs popped around him. Observers noted 43-yr-old Penney looked the quintessential English boffin. He wore a rumpled old tweed suit with a tie knotted untidily round an ill-fitting shirt collar. His unruly hair flowed over his forehead in schoolboy style. A fountain pen was stuck carelessly in his breast pocket. He had 'a mischievous grin' and seemed to be perpetually amused as he talked brightly about atomic energy and how this new force could be harnessed for the greater good of humankind. His grin widened when he saw the menu specially prepared by the maitre d'hotel: Sole Monte Bello, Pommes de Bateau Vaporise, and Bombe Isotope.

As a scientific achievement, Penny undoubtedly deserved all the plaudits, and the champagne lunch. Almost single-handedly he had designed and built an atomic bomb with a fraction of the resources of America and the Soviet Union. In the finest traditions of British ingenuity, he was said to have confounded the Americans and nonplussed the Soviets by assembling the bomb with little more than "string and sticking plaster."

Penney had been to see Winston Churchill, and was still glowing with pride from the unrestrained praise he had received from the Great Man. In triumphal mood, Churchill had announced that the successful detonation of Britain's first atomic bomb was 'among the finest scientific achievements of the 20th Century.' Penney was hailed as the hero of the hour and Downing Street announced he was to be knighted.

ARMAGEDDON

The euphoria surrounding Penney's stupendous achievement lasted all of two weeks. On November 1st, 1952 the Americans exploded an awesome new weapon on a remote Pacific atoll. It wasn't a bomb in any conventional sense; it was basically a giant flask containing a liquid hydrogen isotope whose energy was released by an atomic bomb "trigger" in a process called fusion. There was no way of delivering the device which was so big it had to be housed in a 30-foot tall building. But the explosion was the equivalent to 1,000 Hiroshima bombs, and it was clear the hydrogen or "super" made atomic bombs obsolete even before they had left the production line.

This was the ultimate kind of weapon. It could destroy whole cities, kill millions of people at a stroke and end civilisation. It was glumly recognised that the Soviets would not be far behind, and Britain would have to play 'catch up' all over again. The order went out from Downing Street that Britain had to build weapons to match the superpowers. Failure to do so would lead to an inevitable loss of prestige and influence in the world.

In a momentous speech in the House of Commons Winston Churchill said the H-bomb placed Britain and mankind in a situation "both measureless and laden with doom." He went on: "I find it poignant to look at youth in all its activity and ardour and, most of all, to watch little children playing their merry games, and wonder what would lie before them if God wearied of mankind." Safety, he said, had to be the "sturdy child of terror," and Britain needed its own hydrogen bomb if it was to survive as a world power. Fine words by Churchill, but he knew he had to back it up with action and despite the risks and scarce resources everything was thrown into the project. To build and test the hydrogen bomb would be the biggest peacetime military operation Britain had ever undertaken. But there was no choice.

A chilling assessment of the likely fate awaiting the UK was contained in a 1955 report produced by the Joint Intelligence Committee whose function it was to bring together the intelligence flowing into the UK from overt and covert sources. Its chairman Sir Patrick Green set out the likely Soviet objectives which were: To knock out as quickly as possible those airfields from which nuclear attacks could be launched; to destroy the organization of government and control; and to render the UK useless as a base for any form of military operations. Sir Patrick warned the Russians would regard the UK as such a threat that, "they will aim to render it unusable for a long period, and will not hesitate to destroy great parts of the UK to achieve this aim."

Other reports give spine-chilling accounts of what, for example, would happen to a major city after a hydrogen bomb explosion at 20,000 feet: "A megaton delivery on a city such as Birmingham would render 'ineffective' 50% of the population within a radius of about 20 miles, including e.g. Coventry, where people would see, hear and smell what happened to Birmingham, and would either take to their cellars or get into their cars and drive to where they think they might be safe."

The intelligence assessors calculated it would take no more than 10 H-bombs to cause complete breakdown and destruction. And then, of course, there was the added agony of fallout. According to one Cabinet Office minute fallout presented: "New problems of an unprecedented kind...The effects of radioactive contamination create vast and novel problems for the medical services and for agriculture."

Penney was in full "smiling killer" mode when he was summoned to the Cabinet Office to "put the willies up" an assembled company of treasury ministers and officials who were kicking up a fuss at the enormous costs of thermonuclear warfare. In unvarnished terms he told the bean counters just what would be the effect of a hydrogen bomb on London:-

A bomb dropped on London and bursting on impact would produce a crater a mile across and 150-feet deep and a fireball of two and a quarter miles diameter. The blast from it would crush the Admiralty Citadel (a stone-clad World War 2 signals centre across Horse Guards Parade next to the Mall) at a distance of one mile. Suburban houses would be wrecked at a distance of three miles from the explosion, and they would lose their roofs and be badly blasted at a distance of seven miles. All habitations would catch fire over a circle of three miles radius from the burst.

Faced with this apocalyptic scenario the fiscal objections vanished, although the government agreed that spending on civil defence measures would be a waste of time and money. Only the threat of immediate retaliation would give the Russian Bear pause for thought. The only way to ensure survival was for Britain to build a nuclear deterrent of its own.

Penney's work load was prodigious. A stockpile of A-bombs for the RAF, based on the Monte Bello device, still had to be compiled as some kind of deterrent, and he had to make them small enough to be delivered by the new V-bomber strike force. But the top priority order Penney was given was: "put a union jack on a hydrogen bomb."

Australia was again chosen as the site to test the A-bombs that would be the triggers for the massively bigger H-bombs. Penney sent mushroom clouds billowing into the skies over the Outback, exploding 12 atomic devices, as he refined and perfected the techniques necessary for the super-bomb. But this took time, and that was a commodity in short supply in that mad decade. The Soviets, who had successfully exploded a hydrogen bomb just nine months after the Americans, had soon achieved nuclear parity. With both sides rattling their sabers Britain was again in a critically exposed position.

Britain's military planners were under enormous pressure as they tackled the logistical problems of preparing a remote Pacific atoll called Christmas Island for testing the H-bomb. The task was immense. And all the time America and the Soviet Union were forging ahead with bigger and better designs. With almost limitless resources they were constantly finding newer and more efficient bomb making techniques. The American's bulky liquid hydrogen device had quickly been replaced by a much smaller bomb which used 'dry' lithium deuteride which produced massive explosions with yields equivalent of many millions of tons of TNT. More importantly they were small enough to be delivered by aircraft.

Britain's beleaguered scientists at Aldermaston had to build and test a hydrogen bomb almost from scratch without the huge technical resources available to the superpowers. William Penney was in despair. He did not know how he was going to do it with what he had at his disposal. Denied access to the new super computers used by the Americans, the scientists had to make their calculations "on the back of fag packets" which sometimes took them weeks, rather than the seconds it would take using the new technology. Their task was likened by the great nuclear historian Lorna Arnold to blind men in a dark room looking for a black cat they knew was there, but unable to grasp.

Nevertheless at the Aldermaston bomb laboratory William Penney built up a small team of weaponeers willing to take on the enormous (and unfashionable) task of developing the weapon. Penney had been to America several times to pick the brains of former colleagues from Los Alamos who were now building the 'super.' But the Americans were still wary about giving up their secrets, and Penney was making little progress. With the few crumbs he did manage to get, he called his chief scientists to a meeting at Aldermaston in September 1955.

This occasion became known as the "Tom, Dick and Harry" meeting because Penney's H-bomb plan was a three part process that could be fired in one container. The first (Tom) would be an atomic (fission bomb) that would boost a further fission component (Dick); added together the pair would force the hydrogen fusion reaction (Harry). Penney made no secret of the enormity of the task facing them; their immediate challenge was to calculate without the help of computers how the incredibly high temperatures of an atomic explosion could be harnessed to bring about the even greater energy release through the fusion of hydrogen atoms. Privately some of his staff believed they were being asked to do the impossible, but they got on with it as best they could.

The atom scientists were now required to work under such demanding deadlines that even illness wasn't allowed to interfere with their mission. A flu epidemic laid much of the country low, and the Aldermaston scientists were not immune. However, many still found themselves roused from their sick beds by colleagues who wanted an answer to a particular problem. One scientist on coming out of the anaesthetic after an operation found a colleague waiting at the end of his bed with a problem he was unable to solve. Somehow they muddled through.

To add to the sense of urgency, public opinion across the world was hardening against the testing of H-bombs. But Penney was used to pressure and he put all his energies into the project. His small, but dedicated team responded in kind and gradually designs for their super-bomb began to roll off the drawing board. Their most pressing task was to test the new weapon before a proposed ban on atmospheric nuclear testing came into force.

But after a year, the prospect of failure still loomed large and in desperation the Conservative Government led by PM Anthony Eden visited Aldermaston in September 1956 and agreed a top secret plan with the atomic weapon scientists to fool the world into thinking Britain had a thermonuclear capability.

Given the problems of making an H-bomb and the pressure of time, they had to make sure that if the 'super' failed there was an alternative fail-safe method of ensuring a big bang at the forthcomings tests. Britain could not afford to lose face.

They decided to build a massively enlarged version of the existing A-bomb, which the scientists were much more confident about, and pretend it was an H-bomb. This wouldn't fool the Americans of course; cloud sampling aircraft would soon spot the ruse. But it would fool most of the international community and buy time for the scientists to sort out any production delays or design faults in the real H-bomb.

Penney and his team had come up with three designs, two were experimental hydrogen bombs which they knew could easily fizzle out; the third was the massive atomic device, which they were confident would give the big bang necessary to convince the world. This 'political bomb' enabled the Government to confidently announce that tests of Britain's hydrogen bombs would take place in the central Pacific Ocean in early 1957.

After much debate, a small uninhabited atoll called Malden Island was chosen as the site to test Britain's H-bomb. Logistics and support troops would be based on Christmas Island, 400 miles to the north; it was infrequently inhabited by about 100 natives from nearby islands who harvested copra. A disused airfield, last used by the Americans in World War 2, had to be completely rebuilt and a site prepared for at least 3,000 troops and RAF personnel. The aircraft carrier HMS Warrior would be the command ship for the naval fleet. Hawaii, 1,200 miles away, was the nearest civilisation.

The codename 'Grapple' was chosen for the forthcoming trials, its four prongs a symbol of cooperation between the three armed services and the Aldermaston bomb makers.

Preparations began at once. Army sappers from 35 Field Squadron, the Royal Engineers, on their way home from a year's posting in South Korea were suddenly diverted; the only information they were given was that their destination was "somewhere in the Pacific." The troops, kitted out in cold weather clothing in preparation for Britain's more temperate climate, found they were sweltering in 100 degrees heat as they clambered ashore at Christmas Island.

It was weeks before the supply ships arrived with tropical gear and the equipment they needed to get on with the task in hand. Meanwhile many men 'went native', walking about half naked and spending their days fishing and swimming in the warm waters. There were shortages of certain foodstuffs such as bread and milk, but their diet was supplemented by the plentiful supply of fish and coconut milk. One thing they were not short of was beer: a huge amount had been off-loaded from their troop ship in preparation for the setting up of a NAAFI. The men naturally made good use of this unexpected largesse, and often went swimming in the lagoons afterwards, with inevitable consequences. Although the waters looked calm enough, they were deceptive and the reefs just offshore hid a treacherous drop-off point into very deep water. Several men lost their lives as they were sucked into the abyss, or by being attacked by sharks.

Finally the supply ships arrived and order was restored; the men were soon hard at work building the base camp for the imminent arrival of thousands of troops from Britain. In a few months, a 7,000-foot runway for the Valiant aircraft that would drop the bomb was built; 25 miles of tarmac roads followed, and special buildings for the bomb assembly were erected. With little natural fresh water, a sea water distillation plant was also installed.

By May 1957, the scientists were ready for their first test, but international opposition was growing. The Japanese, who had more reason than most to oppose the bombs, threatened to stop the test by sending a 'suicide fleet' to the danger zone.

To avoid embarrassment, the Air Ministry entered into an elaborate subterfuge with a journalist from the *Daily Express* who agreed to fake a story implying that the tests had been delayed and that William Penney was flying to Australia on a special mission. The flight plans as well as the code name, 'Mr Elmhurst', that Penney habitually used to avoid unwanted publicity, were also leaked to convey the impression the scientist was planning more bomb tests in Australia. A body double was used to impersonate Penney at several high-profile gatherings. Whether the Japanese were fooled is not known, but there were no 'suicide protesters.'

The task force ships, led by HMS Warrior, moved into position a few miles off Malden Island and the British Government announced that a vast area of ocean covering 750,000 square miles was a no-go zone. It was a clear signal to the world that the bomb tests were imminent. The passage of several Valiant bombers, resplendent in bright white livery to deflect heat, through Hickam U.S. air force base in Hawaii was another certain indication.

With the eyes of the world now on a tiny dot in the middle of the Pacific Ocean, the government was most anxious to avoid looking foolish. But Penney under enormous pressure was forced to admit that he still couldn't know for sure whether their bomb would work, and to avoid any embarrassment, it was decided that no newspapers would be invited to witness the first test.

The device chosen was a two-stage (Tom and Harry) prototype H-bomb, designed to produce a thermonuclear yield as close as possible to a million tons of TNT, one megaton. The components were manufactured at Aldermaston and then taken by convoy to RAF Wittering in Lincolnshire, prior to being flown to Christmas Island for final assembly.

But things went far from smoothly; there were annoying problems from the start. The aircraft carrying the 'ball' of radioactive material for the bomb, enclosed in a 700 pound lead container, for some reason lost radio contact on route to Hickam airport where it was to be collected for the final leg of its journey to Christmas Island. Inexplicably there had been problems with communications all the way from Canada and the crew were unable to contact the Americans who, after giving special permission for the Hastings aircraft and its 'special' cargo to fly over its territory, insisted in being informed of progress every step of the way.

This led to fears the aircraft was lost, and the ensuing panic saw the entire US air force being put on 'red alert.' And although contact was eventually made, the USAF was taking no chances. When the Hastings finally landed at Hickam with its top secret cargo, it was met by a flotilla of fire engines and military vehicles that accompanied the plane, bells clanging madly right into the hangar.

With secrecy blown out of the window, the operation had to continue in the full glare of publicity from local radio stations and newspapers who broadcast sensational stories about the "doomsday flight." Plans were quickly re-drawn and the operation's scientific director, William (Bill) Cook, had to be smuggled humiliatingly into Christmas Island like a sack of potatoes on the weekly supply flight.

The problems that bedevilled the project continued. Strong upper headwinds meant the Hastings with its doom-laden cargo didn't have the fuel for the final leg and was grounded for three days. On Christmas Island there was a food-poisoning outbreak just as the dress rehearsal for the bomb test was getting under way. And in Britain a vital component for the bomb was lost after a motorbike courier transporting it from Aldermaston was involved in a traffic accident.

But the incident that really set teeth on edge occurred after the Hastings, with the radioactive core slung in a harness in the cargo hatch, finally arrived on Christmas Island. As the technicians gingerly removed the lead-lined casing, it was found the explosive shell around the highly unstable nucleus was cracked. Engineers discovered the temperature control in the bomb bay of the courier aircraft had malfunctioned causing a sudden drop in temperature which split the delicate casing. Cook, thought about sending for a replacement, but there was no time.

He went to talk things over with the Task Force Commander for Grapple, Air Vice Marshal Wilfred Oulton. The pair, both pipe-smoking throwbacks of a more genteel age, discussed the problem over a 'couple of large ones' in Oulton's quarters. Finally one of the technicians came up with a solution: Bostik glue. There was a stunned silence and the blood drained from Oulton's ruddy features. The unflappable Cook took a long pull on his pipe before, with a resigned shrug of his shoulders, telling the man to go ahead. Oulton, shocked at the thought of Britain's first H-bomb being held together with household glue, replenished their glasses.

At 10.44am on May 15th, 1957, the weapon, codenamed Short Granite, was released from Valiant bomber XD818 piloted by Wing Commander Kenneth Hubbard. It was dropped from a height of 45,000 feet, and exploded at about 8,000 feet, one and a half miles offshore from Malden Island. It was an impressive sight and newsreels released by the government were soon trumpeting the success of Britain's first H-bomb test. But the scientists were disappointed: the yield of just 300 kilotons, was not the megaton range they had promised. Whitehall knew the test didn't have enough clout to persuade the Americans to share their nuclear secrets; the mandarins were stung by one influential American senator who in private conversations derisively dismissed the British efforts as like trying to trade "a rabbit for a pony..."

The operation was further overshadowed by a tragic accident involving the Canberra aircraft carrying vital cloud samples from the bomb burst back to Britain. It crashed in a blizzard coming into land to refuel at Goose Bay, Newfoundland. Two pilots were killed. The Canberra was a PR.7 of No 58 squadron whose Order of Record Book recorded that the accident occurred "during a final approach in inclement weather at Goose Bay on 16th May, 1957. Pilot Officer J.S. Loomes and Flying Officer T.R. Montgomery sustained fatal injuries."

According to the ORB the Canberra had arrived over its destination at 48,000 feet after a 4hr 22 min flight. Its crew, under orders to get the samples back to the UK as quickly as possible, had had no proper sleep in the previous 26 hours and no meal for the previous 18 hours. The accident was kept secret to avoid an outcry, but Penney was mortified and sent a letter to the head of the RAF. He wrote:-

> I am writing to let you know how very much I and my senior staff regret the loss of the Canberra off Newfoundland, particularly as the flight concerned was in connection with the return of our samples from Grapple. We are all the more distressed by this loss because of the truly admirable effort which your Service has made in connection with these trials. I have to write this in confidence because I understand no connection between the accident and the trial is being released.

Air Vice Marshal Oulton, was worried more than most by this latest setback to the Grapple operation. An irrational fear, truly alarming in its implications, was growing in his mind, a fear that would later lead to some of his contemporaries to doubt his sanity.

Put simply, the problems that had beset the first Grapple explosion and those that bedevilled later ones, seems to have led to a bizarre conviction in Oulton's mind that the operation was being sabotaged by supernatural forces.

THE WITCH'S CURSE

This alarming fixation started to take hold after Oulton's second-in-command, Air Commodore Cecil 'Ginger' Weir walked into Oulton's tent one morning swinging a strange looking object which he casually explained (no doubt tongue in cheek) was a 'Witch's Curse'. Weir explained that the device, a stick with a small, yellowish skull stuck on the end, was being confidently blamed by airmen for a series of mishaps on Shackleton aircraft en route from Britain to Christmas Island.

The legend emanated from the airfield in Northern Ireland where the Shackletons were based, and an adjoining mountain which was rich in spine-tingling tales of highway robbers, murderers, sorcery and witchcraft. The airfield was Ballykelly near Londonderry, and the adjoining mountain was called Binevenagh, but nicknamed 'Ben Twitch' by nervous airmen who had to navigate around its perilous slopes often in bad weather and poor visibility. The airfield had a bad reputation: on one day alone, four aircraft were lost in various crashes after taking off from Ballykelly, adding to the superstitions already associated with the area.

During Operation Grapple the airfield was the main base for the aircraft used to supply Christmas Island. The story was that in the early days of the operation a young ground crew technician due to fly to Christmas Island was walking on Ben Twitch when he came across an unusual object, a small yellowish skull with a hardwood stick firmly stuck through the top. He idly picked it up and strolled into the village of Limavady where he went for a drink in a local public house. Swinging the stick to and fro, the technician enquired of the assembled company if anyone knew what the strange object was. There was a sharp intake of breath all round, and he was informed the object was a 'Witch's Curse', a very powerful device which should be handled with great care.

The technician, much amused, decided to take the object with him to Christmas Island to liven things up, as he had heard life out there was pretty dull. As he boarded the plane the following morning he threw the stick together with his bag into the baggage rack at the back. Oddly, there were troubles with the flight from the beginning. The aircraft was beset by technical problems and was delayed for four days. It was then struck by lightning, the radio and radar were knocked out, and two engines failed nearly causing a crash.

By the time the aircraft reached Christmas Island, the 'Witch's curse' had become the talk of the squadron. In exasperation, the Chief Technical Officer, Wing Commander Ron Boardman, confiscated the device and took it to his superior Air Commodore Weir, who was much intrigued. After a spot of banter, Boardman retired and Weir absently tapped the object on the edge of his desk as he contemplated his charts on the wall. As he did so, he heard a small and unusual noise which he eventually traced to his wristwatch, a beautiful Omega which had been a wedding present from his wife, 25 years ago. Something in the escapement had broken and the hands were whizzing round.

Weir was amazed and excitedly took the device to show a wide-eyed Oulton, and suggested it be taken on the next 'live' drop and dumped at sea, "to help the explosion". Oulton, didn't see the joke, and was having none of it: "No! Absolutely not!" he cried in alarm. "I'm not going to tempt fate." Weir was instructed to take "the thing" away and get rid of it.

This was an odd reaction from the military commander in overall charge of Britain's most devastating secret weapon. The supernatural, most people would expect, featured rarely in military circles. But many RAF pilots, especially during the war, were known to be extremely superstitious and often carried charms of various kinds with them on sorties. Oulton was no exception, and it was well known he was a firm believer in fate which stemmed from his childhood.

Born in 1911, he was a precocious child and won an open Scholarship from Abertillery School to University College Cardiff. From there he passed into the RAF College at Cranwell as a prize cadet with exceptional marks. In 1935 he became a commissioned pilot officer and two years later joined a flying boat squadron at Southampton. In September 1939 he was posted to anti-submarine patrols over the English Channel. His exceptional abilities were soon recognised and in 1943, he was given command of 58 Squadron, a Halifax bomber squadron specially converted for maritime operations. He was soon embroiled in Britain's life and death struggle to keep the seaways open for the convoys, who were taking a terrible mauling in the Atlantic from the marauding U-boat wolf packs. His first 'kill' was the German U-boat U-663 which surfaced in the rough seas of the Bay of Biscay. Oulton attacked with depth charges causing it to sink with no survivors. Eight days later, his crew spotted U-463. Oulton took his plane into a steep dive and released six depth charges that blew the sub out of the water. At the end of the same month, he attacked and crippled U-563, a submarine that had sunk 10 allied ships. Follow-up aircraft finished it off.

Oulton was awarded the DFC and the DSO and was mentioned in dispatches three times during his war service. His swash-buckling adventures attracted the attention of Winston Churchill who chose him as an aide when he made a visit to see President Roosevelt. He was soon playing host to General, later President, Eisenhower at a base in the Azores. Eisenhower was so impressed he asked how he could repay him for the hospitality. Oulton suggested some fruit for his men and was surprised when a short time later a whole plane load of oranges arrived.

After the war he became the first RAF director of the joint anti-submarine School at Londonderry, but then in his own words, "destiny beckoned". The RAF's top commanders summoned him to a secret location where he was told: "we've got a job for you. We want you to go out and drop a bomb somewhere in the central Pacific Ocean and take a picture of it with a Brownie camera."

Oulton was nonplussed...until he was told the bomb in question was a "thermo-nuclear' megaton H-bomb..."

"Good God," he muttered, overcome with emotion. It was fate: his scientist father Llewellyn Oulton had been there at the dawn of the nuclear age, as a member of Sir Ernest Rutherford's team of physicists that worked on splitting the atom. The novel and almost limitless possibilities of nuclear power had been a regular feature of discussions in the Oulton household when he was a boy. Now fate had chosen him to play a pivotal role in the release of that mystical power.

Oulton hurled all his considerable energies into the task of organising, supplying and conveying 4,000 men half way across the world. It was a wonderful adventure and Oulton relished the challenge of carrying out a vital military operation against the romantic backdrop of swaying palm trees and white sands. His was a bygone world where friends and colleagues were all part of the cosy Old Boy network, and where everyone seemed to be called "Chalky", or "Ginger." And at first it all went swimmingly until, in his mind at least, the elemental collided with the paranormal in the form of the 'Witch's Curse'. Suddenly Oulton's dream turned into a nightmare.

Mishaps, big and small, were now ascribed to its supernatural powers. One of the most startling examples came prior to the second drop of the Grapple series when the very large and unstable uranium core for the massive fail-safe atomic bomb malfunctioned in the assembly hangar at Christmas Island.

Chief scientist Bill Cook was overseeing a group of technicians who were gently screwing together two copper hemispheres surrounding the radioactive core when they became stuck. The technicians first tried to uncouple the two hemispheres to start all over again. But the assemblage was stuck fast. Two more technicians were summoned to apply more pressure. For nearly an hour, sweat dripping down their necks, the taut scientific team tried to dislodge the two hemispheres by gradually increasing the force whilst simultaneously trying not to disturb the delicate radioactive core. All to no avail; the thing was solid.

As the tension mounted, a warrant officer, pressed into trying to uncouple the spheres, suggested that the only thing left to do was to "clout it." The scientists looked at each other in dismay, but after a short while agreed that, indeed, that was the only course of action left, short of cabling back to Britain for a replacement.

Watched by the others and with a nonchalance no-one else felt, the warrant officer rummaged around in his tool box and fished out a seven-pound, copper-headed sledge hammer. An assistant was positioned with hands supporting the two hemispheres to absorb the shock. After a deep breath the warrant officer gave the flange round the middle of the radioactive core a hefty thump. After a short heart-stopping moment, the warrant officer once again tried to screw the hemisphere's together. They moved "as smooth as silk," according to Oulton who gratefully retired to the mess bar with Cook for 'a fortifying drink.' (It was a past-time they indulged in a lot).

Fortunately everything went well with the rest of the preparations. The newly-assembled bomb, code-named Orange Herald, was borne aloft in Valiant XD822 and released at the correct height and position. But then, another heart-stopper: a sudden instrument failure caused the bomber to stall and go into a high-speed spin during its escape manoeuvre. Only superb airmanship by pilot David Roberts prevented a catastrophe.

His Official Record Book entry states that the operation ran into a "critical situation" when the Valiant bomber stalled shortly after the weapon was dropped. He wrote:

The bomb was released at 10.44 and after a slight pause I initiated a steep turn to port. Simultaneously, the aircraft stalled and the bomb aimer, who was making for his seat, returned to the bomb aimer's well with some force.

Oulton ordered a news blackout. The press, who had been invited along to record events, were given no inkling of the drama overhead. The crew was not made available for interviews as had been planned, and only the scarcest of details about the drop were issued. All they were told was that there had been a successful H-bomb drop and there had been negligible fallout. Neither statement was true: the bomb was a giant A-bomb which caused considerable radioactivity because of its almost pure uranium core. Oulton was uncharacteristically glum as he attended the traditional "after-bomb" party aboard HMS Warrior that evening. He knew the difficult challenges to make a fully working hydrogen bomb had not yet been resolved.

The third, and final test in the series, took place on June 19th but this failed dismally; it was the lowest yield yet. And this test also brought with it another series of frustrating failures and calamities: A Hastings with vital supplies had to make an emergency landing after its undercarriage failed, and a Shackleton bomber was nearly lost after three of its four engines failed on the 400-mile trip from Malden to Christmas Island. Four Avenger aircraft on board HMS Warrior had to be jettisoned over the side because their engines were too radioactive for further use. One of the pilots nearly lost his life when the last Avenger crashed on take off. Oulton was often seen sitting alone outside his tent contemplating the sunset and no doubt pondering his fate.

Meanwhile back in Britain, Penney and his team were summoned to Whitehall for crisis talks. Penney bluntly told Defence Minister Duncan Sandys that further work was needed if they were going to build a 'true' H-bomb and they needed to conduct further tests to ensure it worked. An impatient Sandys said that was all very well, but time was running out. The international ban on testing might be only months away.

In August 1957 Prime Minister Harold MacMillan held an uncomfortable meeting at Aldermaston with Penney. It was acknowledged the first set of tests in the Pacific had not produced a working H-bomb design. All Britain had to show so far was a massive A-bomb masquerading as an H-bomb. But it would have to do. The weapon was rushed into service with the

RAF. Dubbed the interim weapon, it would be carried by Vulcan bombers in the event of nuclear war.

But this contingency brought its own problems because to deliver the yield required, the bombs had to be filled with huge amounts of highly unstable uranium 235 which apart from being dangerously volatile was also enormously expensive. Bomber Command, which had to take control of the bombs, was not happy. It was thought too tricky a weapon to handle because if damaged, say in transport, the core's sub-critical masses could come into contact with each other, causing a meltdown.

And of course if they caught fire the consequences would have been catastrophic. The Chiefs of Air Staff were also not happy with the safety measures installed in the bomb, which amounted to inserting thousands of ball-bearings into a rubber bag "similar to a feminine condom" and lowered into the core. This may have made the weapon safe. But if it became necessary to use it, the ball-bearings had to be drained from the core. This took at the very least 15 minutes, sometimes longer. The RAF required a weapon they could keep at four minutes alert.

There were angry exchanges between Bomber Command and Aldermaston with the RAF bigwigs accusing the scientists of "selling them a lemon." If there was an international crisis, Britain would be virtually defenceless in nuclear terms. The bad-tempered row rumbled on.

But while everyone was arguing, Penney quietly got on with the major problem of building a 'true' hydrogen bomb. The breakthrough came when he was given access to the latest US computer technology. To everyone's immense relief Penney was soon able to tell the Prime Minister that he believed he could now design a better bomb thanks to the number crunching power of Aldermaston's new electronic computer, recently arrived from America. All he needed was a few more tests in the Pacific.

So they got to work; they investigated faults and deficiencies, and their new IBM computer was helping enormously. Finally they came up with a new design a hybrid, a cross between an atomic and hydrogen bomb, similar to a design already successfully tested by the Russians.

Preparations to test the new design code-name Grapple X got under way. There was much more confidence in the success of this bomb and American observers were invited to the trial. It was hoped that they would be so impressed by Britain's development of the H-bomb that collaboration between the two countries would be restored.

The task took on a new urgency when the Soviet Union launched Sputnik 1, the first artificial earth satellite, in early October 1957. This event shocked the Americans to the core. It caused a widespread feeling of national humiliation. The launch vehicle, a large ICBM, was already in use and showed that the Soviet Union was capable of hitting targets anywhere on the earth's surface. Up to then, the United States had always felt secure in its superior technology. Now suddenly the balance of power had shifted.

The event was viewed in Britain as an immense opportunity to seek improved nuclear defence co-operation. The pressure for results was intense. A fateful decision was taken, to save both time and money. But it was enormously risky, especially for the thousands of support troops, for it was decided that Grapple X, would be detonated over Christmas Island, instead of 400 miles south at Malden island.

Oulton credited himself for this extremely risky decision, describing how it came about as he and Cook strolled along the foreshore at Christmas Island drinking the inevitable gin and tonics. Oulton recalled: "Cook said to me, 'I'm sorry to have to tell you Wilf, but we've got to do it all over again.' That was the first inkling I had of it. I said, how soon? And he said as soon as possible and I said how soon is as soon as possible and he said certainly not more than three months."

That was a tremendous shock to Oulton, who said: "We were completely exhausted, both manpower-wise and equipment-wise. And effectively to do the whole thing over again at Malden Island would have meant another 18 months, which we didn't have. And so I thought well we could perhaps do it at Christmas Island. So after 10 minutes thought I said to Bill: 'It is 30 miles from here to the south-east point of the island. I think we could do it here. All the information we had at that date said 30 miles would be OK. Cook said everything couldn't be a hundred per cent sure, but it seemed a very reasonable proposition.'"

This was a dangerous decision involving many risks, not least to the thousands of servicemen on the island who would now be placed in close proximity to enormous nuclear forces. This, naturally enough, led to fears for their safety. Penney was also worried when the decision was conveyed to him. His team was confident the new bomb would produce a big bang. It was a boosted design incorporating large quantities of lithium-6, but they had no way of knowing just how big it would be. They were in uncharted territory, and there were real fears the bomb might get out of control with unknown consequences.

In the middle of all this came news of a disaster which threatened to jeopardise the whole operation. On October 10 there was a catastrophic fire in a nuclear reactor at Windscale which was producing the uranium for the weapon. A vast quantity of radiation was released into the atmosphere. There was a threat to milk supplies in 150 farms in a 200 mile radius around the site. Newsreels showed urns of milk being emptied into drains. The whole area was put on standby for evacuation.

Prime Minister Macmillan was in a panic. Not only did he have CND breathing down his neck, but the incident threatened to derail delicately poised negotiations with America over nuclear cooperation. He summoned Penney to sort the mess out. One of his first priorities was to ensure the fire didn't prevent sufficient radioactive fuel from getting to Christmas Island.

Penney, dragged from his desk at Aldermaston, set up an inquiry which duly reported to Macmillan on October 28. Faults in "procedure and organisation" were blamed. More specifically there were accusations the cause of the catastrophe was the pressure the managers were under to produce the fissile material for the nuclear bombs. Penney was scathing in his criticism of the way the site was managed. The Prime Minister wasn't happy with the findings: "How do we deal with Penney's report?" he pondered gloomily in his diary on October 30. "It has, of course, been prepared with scrupulous honesty and even ruthlessness."

Macmillan feared if the full extent of the failings at Windscale were to be publicly revealed, US-UK nuclear collaboration might be ended by those in America who did not want to help Britain. He decided on only a partial release of Penney's report on the grounds of national security. The result was that Penney was blamed unfairly in many circles. Opponents in the closed scientific community accused him of conducting a whitewash. Penney, ever the patriot, took it on the chin and returned to Aldermaston.

ON THE BRINK

Meanwhile back in the Pacific, the forthcoming H-bomb test was spawning feverish rumours among the servicemen. One wild claim was that Christmas Island, perched as it was perilously on top of an extinct volcano was, in the event of an H-bomb explosion, in danger of tipping up and depositing the troops into the abyss. Another was the island was so low-lying that a large explosion could cause a vast tsunami to overwhelm the island

Oulton and Cook discussed the problems as they sat drinking on the patio of the mess tent with the Pacific waves lapping at their feet. The Task Force Commander was at low ebb. He confided to Cook he just wanted to get off the "infernal island" as quickly as possible. Cook was worried about the effects any delays in preparations might have on morale. He decided to make a flying visit to Aldermaston to smooth over any last minute problems. Air Commodore Denis Wilson, the RAF's most senior medical officer, had joined the discussion. He was concerned about possible health effects on the men and decided to accompany Cook. Wilson had made a speciality of the effects of radiation on the human body and wanted to check problems of possible contamination on the island after the explosion. It was up to him to establish the safe limits for the amount of radiation a person could absorb. He had always erred on the cautious side, but he told Oulton the radiation safety limits might now have to be recalibrated upwards. Oulton said they had better sort the problems out "pretty damn quick" and placed a Canberra at their disposal instead of the usual Shackleton which was very much slower.

No sooner were Cook and Wilson under way than the Christmas Island 'curse' struck again. The Canberra got lost in heavy cloud over Hawaii and because of radio trouble couldn't raise Hickam air force base. They flew blind for over an hour and as the plane circled frantically looking for a gap in the cloud cover, it was forced to shut down one of its engines to conserve fuel. With 13,000-feet high volcanic peaks looming either side, the hopelessly lost Canberra was finally forced to make a crash landing on a disused air field at Kahului on the island of Maui. As the plane bumped to a halt, so did the one remaining engine. They were out of fuel. Cook, the most important British scientist after Penney, and Wilson one of the most senior officers in the RAF, suffered the indignity of having to be rescued by a local unit of the National Guard and having to 'thumb a lift' from a passing US Navy aircraft which eventually took them to Honolulu International.

There were red faces all round when the hapless pair finally arrived back in London. Oulton blamed the 'curse' and was in a dark mood when he also made a visit to Britain to confer with defence minister Sandys. The task force commander was furious about a decision taken by Sandys to give as little warning as possible to shipping about the forthcoming test. The government was anxious, he said, to avoid the possibility of 'suicide ships' from nuclear protesters sailing into the danger area.

Oulton protested that innocent ships, those on the high seas with legitimate commerce, might well accidentally sail into the area and disrupt the whole operation if adequate warnings were not issued. He wanted a broadcast to go out at least two months in advance and was apoplectic with rage when Sandys, whom he disparagingly called "this unsmiling character", said that was too long and decreed that three weeks was enough warning. Oulton pointed out that in the vastness of the Pacific, most ships took many weeks to get from one port to another and therefore might be unable to receive the warning.

But it was to no avail and Oulton grumbling furiously returned to Christmas Island. His mood wasn't helped when he was met by reports of growing dissent on the island by troops protesting about conditions. He toured the island giving pep talks to the men, but he was worried about the ugly mood that was developing.

The new influx of scientists from Aldermaston was also unhappy. They were used to home comforts, but some of their complaints were farcical. On one occasion during vital rehearsals for the drop, Oulton was called to an urgent meeting with a group of scientists who had 'downed tools' bizarrely because of some badly made sandwiches. One senior technician, driven to distraction by the conditions in one of the forward areas where he had to live, apparently complained about the sandwiches were only good for feeding the land crabs that constantly invaded his tent. He didn't like what was on the sandwich, the packaging it came in, even the way it was cut. Oulton, doubtless biting his tongue, had no choice but to call a helicopter to bring some fresh sandwiches from the cookhouse 15 miles away before the scientists would agree to continue. They were frustrating days for Oulton who now found he spent most of his days quelling an increasing number of complaints.

Somehow they got through the difficulties and in early November the components of the newly designed weapon were delivered to Christmas Island. The final assembly took place in a shielded off hangar in a corner of the airfield. This time the two-stage thermonuclear bomb had a much more powerful atomic trigger, equivalent to 45,000 tons of TNT. It was 'layer-cake' design with a beryllium tamper which was hoped would generate sufficient energy to bring about the massive fusion reaction.

D-day was November 8. The last minute preparations were completed and it was hoped the fully primed bomb would produce an explosion of sufficient power to impress. But it was still by no means certain it would work satisfactorily. After a frustrating delay while an errant Liberian ship was shepherded out of the danger zone, the heavily-laden Valiant rose in the air and climbed to 45,000 feet. With Christmas Island so close to the target, the precise aiming of the bomb was crucial.

All the buildings had been evacuated. Aircraft not needed in the air were tethered to the runway, and tents were vented to allow the shock wave to pass through. Ground crew and other servicemen were mustered at the northern end of the island as far as possible from ground zero. The special reinforced camp for the scientists at the forward area, 20 miles from the projected ground zero, was dismantled, with only a few personnel remaining in specially built steel and earth bunkers.

Oulton was one of several officers who chose to be in the bunker for the big bang. He hunkered down behind the heavy steel doors as the countdown commenced. The lights were dimmed with the only illumination coming from a screen behind them which glowed white from a tiny hole in the steel wall. It was a classic pin-hole camera, through which Oulton and rest could watch the explosion projected on the screen. When it came it took everyone by surprise: it was huge. Many buildings were damaged, tents collapsed wholesale, and helicopters had their windows blown out.

A large number of native huts at Port Camp were damaged. The islanders were safe: they had been evacuated to ships moored miles off shore. Their homes suffered, however, which they later complained about. A small tribunal to assess the damage was convened, and minutes duly recorded. According to official records the Christmas Islanders were compensated by the British Government to the tune of £4 sterling for the damage caused.

Oulton and the scientific staff decided to leave their bunkers about 15 seconds after the explosion so they could experience the blast wave. Given the scientists were not sure just how big the explosion was going to be, this was a brave decision. Typically Oulton brushed aside these concerns and one can imagine him standing facing the blast, jutting chin, a heroic glint in his eye as the nuclear whirlwind approached. His only comment on the experience: "It was no worse than being at the bottom of a Welsh rugby scrum."

The scientists worked out the Grapple X test had achieved the largest yield yet at 1.8 megatons and this had been brought about partly by a thermonuclear reaction. It was a tremendous relief. At last Britain could claim with some justification to be a nation with the H-bomb, albeit a prototype. The Prime Minister sent a letter of congratulation to the scientific team.

Flushed with success the Government spin went further than was strictly true. While the explosion had certainly been impressive, the new bomb still used huge quantities of Uranium 235 which made the combat use of the weapon impractical. And it still wasn't the 'pure' thermonuclear bomb the politicians craved. Penney was summoned to another high-level meeting and another test was ordered. This time there were to be no half measures, nothing left to chance. The mixture had to be right; there were to be no mistakes. This could be the last chance Britain might have to join the top table. They wanted the world to sit up.

ISLAND OF THE DAMNED

The euphoria back home was not reflected on Christmas Island. The troops complained, as they always do. But after Grapple X, there was a different edge to the grumbles. The men complained about everything: they received no extra hardship money; the tents they lived in were cramped; when it rained conditions inside them were atrocious. The latrines were disgusting and they preferred to dig holes in the coral dust rather than use the official lavatories. These were fairly normal complaints, but things were somehow different.

A lot of nuclear veterans have told of an indefinable sadness that came over them in the aftermath of the explosion. Some were affected more than others, but the deep melancholy was almost tangible. And for others it developed into something darker. Mutiny was in the air. There were more fights, drunkenness was rife, orders were disobeyed, discipline was laughed at, officers were ridiculed; Christmas Island was teetering on the edge of madness and anarchy.

Low morale and disorganisation eventually led to a complete breakdown of law and order. One night the NAAFI was destroyed in a mini-riot. A drunken naval rating ran amok in a bulldozer, destroying a huge tented area. Homosexual acts (a criminal offence at the time) were common. Men were drunk all the time; one grainy newsreel which surfaced years later, shows drunken servicemen staggering around the tents, wearing floral bonnets, Hawaiian shirts and painted faces. The men were out of control.

One of the most serious incidents erupted after a blizzard of "Dear John..." letters arrived from home where sensational newspaper articles had warned the men's reproductive organs would be damaged by radiation. (A very prescient warning, as it turned out.) As the sacks of mail were delivered to the camps, sounds of grief and outrage filled the air.

In a letter home one of the men wrote: "It was awful to hear. Grown men crying! It was the last straw for them and they didn't know what to do. They were trapped on the island and now their sweethearts were abandoning them. There was a big fight later. They took it out on each other."

Many serious assaults were carried out at this time. Servicemen fought vicious battles with knives improvised from sharpened can-openers. There were reports of several gang rapes. The worst offenders were sent home via Changi prison in Singapore. The island did not have its own prison. A large steel cage, like a rubbish skip, cannibalised from a water distillation tank, was used as a temporary 'brig' for miscreants who were simply tipped in until they sobered up.

News of these events was hushed up, but a few managed to get through. Questions were asked in Parliament after a report of fighting on Christmas Island appeared in the *Daily Mirror*. But mostly the lid was kept tightly on.

Being just soldiers, no real account was taken of their concerns, but the scientists from AWRE were a different matter. These were civilians, not soldiers and therefore subject to different rules. The politicians, terrified that they might refuse to go to the island, ensured they were pandered to. The Aldermaston men were given better tented accommodation, ablutions, showers and latrines. A second-hand ice-cream making machine from a British base in Benghazi (cost $800) was sent out. A selection of gramophone records was also dispatched as well as '12 teapots and fifty knives to remedy the shortage of crockery and cutlery.' The library was to have 250 extra books and the supply of newspapers was to be increased. A new projector and the latest films were supplied.

The scientists and other AWRE staff, though better looked after than the troops, were still not immune to depression. Some found the antidote to this was to 'go native.' They grew luxuriant beards and only ever wore shorts and boots which gave them a distinctive Ben Gun castaway image. But as long as they were doing the work, they were tolerated. Nothing was allowed to hinder them because they were irreplaceable, and their work wasn't done yet.

The troops, however, could be replaced, and arrangements were rapidly being made to send the majority back home before there was any more trouble. Many men were convinced they were being sent home because of fears they may have been contaminated after Grapple X. Ken Taylor, an army cook said: "We had a fish and chip business going four days a week. At the Port Camp there were 800 people, about 200 portions per night. Fish were taken from various parts of the Pacific. We were told there was no danger of radiation, but there was at least one story of Geiger counters going berserk when placed near crayfish caught to the south of the island."

The Ministry of Defence has always denied any radioactive contamination on Christmas Island. Nevertheless there was a sudden decision taken after Grapple X to replace thousands of troops. All over Britain servicemen were being assembled to replace them. But there was a problem. Despite the best efforts of the authorities, word about the appalling conditions on the island had reached the public, and there were increasingly lurid stories appearing about the possible effects the bomb tests were having on the men. To boost morale hundreds of RAF men were flown out, some on the new Comet jets, on what became known as the "champagne flights." Stories were placed in newspapers about ordinary RAF men enjoying lavish hospitality as they were flown "first class to paradise".

Soldiers, mainly royal engineers, and hundreds of conscripts were told to report to Southampton docks where they would board a 'cruise ship' that would take them to the South Pacific. They were advised to take 'suntan lotion, swimming trunks and light footwear', as they would be spending 'many hours of leisure activity' during their 'sunshine posting.'

Even some of their wives were corralled into taking a 'trip of a lifetime.' Sadie Midford, aged 28 a mother-of-two from Canterbury was startled to receive a knock on her door from a senior officer in her husband Tony's regiment. He asked her if she would like to go out and meet Tony on Christmas Island.

She recalled: "Of course I thought he was joking. But he wasn't. He said it was all above board, but I would have to make my mind up quickly because the boat was leaving shortly. He said all it would cost was £25 for me and £12 for my eldest daughter; the baby went free. Well I dashed round to my mothers and she said, 'go, we'll get the money together.'"

Mrs Midford was told to report to Southampton on New Year's Eve where she was to board the ship for her 'sunshine cruise' to the Pacific. Before that she was told to attend a medical with her two children at the nearby hospital. The family was given a clean bill of health and a blood sample was taken from each of them.

The ship waiting for them at Southampton was the TT Dunera, a WW2 troopship that had seen better days, but it was comfortable enough for Mrs Midford who was soon joined by thirty more wives together with their 31 children. They were shown to spacious quarters on the top deck of the ship, while more than 1,000 relief soldiers for Christmas Island were crammed below decks, four to a cabin or slung across the galleys in hammocks.

Alcohol had been banned for the trip, but it was New Year's Eve and there was a large contingent of Scots; a party was soon in full swing, thanks to someone managing to smuggle a crate of whisky aboard. There were inevitable consequences the following day as the Dunera nosed into the Atlantic and headed into the storm-tossed seas around the Azores: the decks rails were lined much of the way with seasick soldiers. Luckily the weather turned benign and most of those on board soon recovered. Three weeks later the Dunera reached Curacao in the Caribbean and passed through the Panama Canal for the last leg of its journey across the Pacific to Christmas Island.

It was a propaganda coup for the War Office as photographs of the Dunera, with smiling wives and children waving from the decks were flashed home. The *Daily Mirror* enthused: "Happy, happy family day….that's the sort of day it was among the palm trees and coconuts of Christmas Island when the troopship Dunera sailed into the palm-fringed lagoon…"

Mrs Midford said: "There were a couple of ladies from the WVS waiting for us and we all had a big party. Tony, my husband, didn't recognise me at first because I'd had a new hairdo. And I hadn't seen him in over a year. The children loved it. We were only on the island two or three days and they played in the sand or swam in the lagoon the whole time. Our three-yr-old played in the water for hours."

Mrs Midford's trip of a lifetime was marred on the way back, however, when her daughter suddenly began to lose her hair. She said: "I noticed she had developed a bald spot as we sailed home on the boat. At first it was small, about the size of a sixpence, and I didn't think much about it. But over the months it gradually got bigger and bigger until it was about the size of the palm of my hand. I took her to a doctor who said he had no idea what was causing it. He asked me if I had changed her diet, things like that, but I said I hadn't. Then I told him about my trip to Christmas Island, and he didn't believe me; he said: 'Are you seriously asking me to believe that the government sent children to an H-bomb testing zone?' I said they most certainly had, but he still wouldn't believe me, and just sent me away."

This was an illuminating exchange: clearly the doctor believed it was a bad idea to send children out to a nuclear test site. So why was it done? This was a question that Mrs Midford and her husband asked themselves many times in the years to come. And it was even more urgent when their daughter contracted cancer at age 28. Mrs Midford said: "At the time I thought the trip was an example of a kindly government but now I'm not so sure. I have got so many questions: why did they take blood samples? Why did they choose only mothers with children? Were they trying to find out something they didn't tell us about? We have never been given answers to any of these questions."

Searching questions about possible ill-effects have always been asked by nuclear veterans. At the time, however, these questions didn't unduly worry Penney or his Aldermaston scientists. All they were concerned about was producing the 'big one', the weapon that would finally prove that Britain was now truly worthy to be a member of the exclusive megaton club. The new bomb, codenamed Grapple Y, would contain many new elements designed to boost yield. And this included a confection of chemicals never used before.

The exact nature of this hellish cocktail is still secret, but according to historian Lorna Arnold it was made up of 'intimate mixtures of materials, consisting of micron-sized particles of uranium-235, uranium-238 and lithium deuteride.' The chemicals thorium, beryllium, cobalt and other deadly isotopes were also thrown into the mix. It conjures up a cartoon image of a mad scientist cackling gleefully over a smoking test-tube as the final mixture for Grapple Y was being prepared.

Grapple X had provided valuable information about the fusion processes that had baffled the scientists so far. Now they believed they had the means to make a 'pure' H-bomb without the need for a huge atomic bomb as the trigger. Early 1958 was the deadline given to the scientists to perfect and test the new weapon.

By this time Oulton had been relieved of his command of Christmas Island, and replaced by Air Vice Marshal John Grandy, another former Battle of Britain ace. Whether or not Oulton's arguments with Defence Minister Sandys had anything to do with this decision is a matter for conjecture. But it could well be the High Command was more concerned about his continued obsession with the 'Witch's Curse.' Oulton was still displaying his worrying obsessions months later.

He makes a point in his memoirs of recounting how Wing Commander Ken Hubbard went out to HMS Warrior for a farewell party prior to its departure for England. According to Oulton he took with him the Witch's Curse, concealed in his jacket. As the party got into full swing, Hubbard popped the device behind a picture over the wardroom fireplace. Oulton was clearly worried if the 'curse' had had any effect on Warrior and quizzed Commodore Roger Hicks about the trip home when they met for lunch at the Services Club on Pall Mall.

Oulton recalled: "Hicks said he had never had such a bloody awful trip in his life. It had all started well enough visiting

Ratotonga and Pitcairn Island. But then came a series of calamities. His boat had been stolen in Callao! They'd had a very rough passage round the Horn. At Buenos Aires, the splendid ceremony of 'Beating the Retreat' laid on by the Royal Marines had been a disaster in a torrential rainstorm. In Rio a lot of the ship's company had had a stand-up fight with the police. Then they had come through that hurricane which had sunk the famous German sailing ship *Pamir* and caused immense damage to Warrior particularly to a lot of stuff in the ward-room on which the insurance had lapsed..." Oulton of course wasn't at all surprised by this list of calamities, although he thought it wise not to inform the Commodore of the Witch's Curse lurking behind the wardroom picture.

But he felt duty bound to speak out when the Warrior was later sold to the Argentine Navy with inevitable (in Oulton's mind) consequences. Warrior, now renamed the Independencia was beset by a series of catastrophes resulting in the Argentine Navy's Commander in Chief being court marshalled. Oulton invited the Argentine Naval Attache in London to lunch and told him about the Witch's Curse. It is not recorded what comment the official made, but Oulton reported: "He turned quite pale."

Thankfully Oulton's strange fixation had no effect on Penney who assembled his scientists at Aldermaston for the last "great push." He outlined his plan for Grapple Y and told them to smooth out any final problems with the design. At a meeting on January 10, 1958 it was announced the bomb was ready.

Penney also had a surprise for the assembled company: he told them he would be flying to Christmas Island to take personal charge of the drop. His deputy Bill Cook, who had thus far been the man on the ground made no comment. The decision didn't surprise those in the know, however. It was whispered there had been a certain amount of 'bad blood' between the pair since the failure of the first series. Cook, apparently blamed Penney for bringing "duff information" back from America; Penney blamed Cook for the string of failures and mishaps.

They put their differences aside as they prepared to showcase Grapple Y to the world, but the problems that seemed to beset the Grapple project were not over yet.

DITCHED

On the 26 February, 1958, Grapple Y, the biggest bomb Britain would ever build, the bomb destined to make the world sit up, toppled off the back of a lorry and rolled into a ditch.

The accident occurred near the small village of Wansford in Cambridgeshire as the truck, travelling in a heavily-guarded convoy, encountered a fierce blizzard that had brought much of the east coast of Britain to a standstill. Struggling up a steep incline, the convoy slithered to a halt ten miles short of RAF Wittering, Bomber Command's main V-bomber nuclear strike base. The specially modified Foden truck, its contents shielded by black tarpaulin, went into an uncontrolled slide, mounted the kerb and toppled over on its side into a ditch. The driver managed to scramble clear and was gingerly examining the contents of the truck as armed guards swarmed everywhere, closing the road and forming a protective cordon.

Emergency calls went out to Aldermaston and RAF Wittering. In the gathering gloom, a detachment of men was deployed to try to clear the snow, but two hours later the convoy was still stuck fast. A decision was taken to wait until morning before attempting to get it moving again. Meanwhile rations and blankets were sent out to the men who had been ordered to stay with the vehicles. A group of armed airmen arrived to help guard the convoy.

Some time later a clutch of scientists and technicians sent from Aldermaston approached the stricken Foden and peeled back the heavy folds of the tarpaulin covering. In the harsh glare of hastily erected arc lights, the darkly glistening metallic casing of the huge bomb was revealed. It was 24-feet in length, five in diameter and weighed 8,000 lbs. It appeared to be undamaged, which must have been a considerable relief to the scientists and the War Office, not to mention their political masters in Whitehall.

Grapple Y was more impressive than Grapple X. It was another 'layer-cake' device with an atomic trigger, but with less uranium-235 and considerably more lithium-7 deuteride. Various other modifications were also incorporated, and the scientists now believed they had the weapon that would blow away any remaining doubts about Britain's credentials for membership of the megaton club. But it was still an experimental weapon and was so unstable that a file supplied with the weapon emphasised the absolute requirement that the bomb could only be assembled under the strict supervision of scientists from AWRE. RAF Wittering, home of No. 49 Squadron was where the bomb was to be loaded aboard one of the distinctive white-painted Vickers Valiant bombers, for its 10,000-mile journey to Christmas Island.

Now the bomb was lying on its side in a snow-drift on the A1. There were more than a few heads-in-hands in Whitehall that night. William Penney must have been in despair. Oulton, if he had known about it, doubtless would have blamed the Witch's Curse. Much to the relief of the assembled scientists, there appeared to be little damage to the awesome weapon. The Operations Record Book at RAF Wittering for 26 February 1958 states:-

Owing to heavy falls of snow, a convoy from AWRE was stuck in a snow drift at Wansford Hill at 1500hr. An officer from this unit was sent to investigate. At 1700hr the vehicle was still unable to be moved. Rations and bedding were sent to the convoy from AWRE and an officer and a team of airmen were detailed to stand by throughout the night to give help if required. It was not until the following day that vehicles began using the A1. The convoy arrived at the main guard room at 1200 hr. Personnel were sent immediately for a meal. Unloading was commenced at 1400hr..."

The measured tone of the report was in stark contrast to the way James Challinor, a local garage owner, who was put on standby with his pick-up truck on the afternoon of the accident. He recalled: "I was in my workshop when there was a tremendous hammering on my door. When I went round I was confronted by a group of armed soldiers in a land-rover. They said they needed my pick-up and I followed them up to Wansford Hill. By this time the weather had really closed in and it was dark. Up ahead I could see some considerable activity. There were vehicles all over the place with lights flashing everywhere. Men were waving their arms and shouting orders; there was a hell of a flap. It was chaos."

Mr Challinor was ordered to wait some distance away, but he could clearly see a ring of armed servicemen surrounding a lorry that had pitched into a ditch. He was eventually told that his pick-up wasn't required and that he could go home. He distinctly remembered one of the soldiers cautioning him not to talk about what he had seen. It was only years later that he learned what had happened. He recalled: "I had no idea what it was all about at the time, and no-one told me anything. But if I had known then what I know now I would have gotten out of there as fast as I could, armed men or not."

Of course the device was not armed: there was no way there was going to be a mushroom cloud blooming over the Cambridgeshire countryside that snowy afternoon. But unless the British government is prepared to open up the archives, there is no way of knowing if the fissile core had already been installed. The assembly work for the bombs was usually carried out on Christmas Island, but Grapple Y was such a special bomb that it is possible that only the firing mechanism had to be installed. To give some idea of what *could* have happened, you only had to look at a terrifying event that occurred just two days later involving two American bombers at the Greenham Common air base.

At 4.25pm on February 28, 1958 a US B-47 aircraft awaiting take-off on the runway was engulfed in fireball when a wing-tip tank carrying 1,700 gallons of fuel from another B-47 flying overhead was accidentally dropped. The fuel tank landed just 65 feet behind the parked aircraft, igniting on impact and engulfing the plane. Both aircraft were from 310th Bomb Wing (part of 3909th Combat Support Group) which carried Mark V nuclear bombs with yields up to 60 kilotons. Each warhead had a plutonium core surrounded by enriched uranium and TNT high explosive. The enriched uranium is used to increase the bomb's yield.

If there was a fire both the enriched uranium and plutonium would be released in the form of a deadly oxide powder. Both aircraft were destroyed in the fire which was allowed to burn out because of the intensity of the blaze. The base commander Colonel Arthur Cresswell issued a denial that nuclear weapons were involved. That isn't surprising as the British and US governments in top secret protocols agreed in 1956 to always deny that nuclear weapons were present in any accident involving American nuclear bombers stationed in the UK. These agreements surfaced in 1976 after details of another crash involving a B-47 which exploded in a nuclear bomb storage bunker at RAF Lakenheath.

Suspicions about nuclear fallout from these accidents have lingered ever since. Environment groups like Greenpeace have evidence of leukaemia clusters associated with both areas.

Penney and his band of Aldermaston weaponeers must have feared the worst as they later examined their prized bomb in a hangar at RAF Wittering. But the safety harness around it had done its job and Grapple Y seemed to be none the worse for its mishap. It was later flown safely to Christmas Island in plenty of time for the intended firing date.

No-one, not even Penney, was sure just how big Grapple Y was likely to be: estimates ranged from 2.5 – 7 megatons. But they were taking no chances. Thousands of anti-flash hoods, gloves and white boiler suits were provided for the men on the island. Lessons had been learned from Grapple X and special attention was given to the effects of the blast wave on buildings. To avoid damage, loose items were to be secured; all glass windows, doors and partitions were to be removed and all electrical equipment not essential for the test switched off. Cupboards had to be laid on their sides. Pets were to be rounded up and put into containers; efforts were to be made to round up any stray animals. All tents were to be vented and furnishings tied down.

It was a very worrying time for all the scientists involved; Penney also had the added worry of keeping his own involvement as secret as possible. Whether he liked it or not, by this time he had become an international celebrity. He was flown round the world in his own specially converted Hastings aircraft and given VIP status wherever he went. His aircraft was always 'parked' in areas reserved for world leaders and even the Australian premier complained because he had to be 'vetted' by Penney's personal armed guard before meeting him.

Journalist Chapman Pincher was in thrall to the super scientist. He enthused in one of his dispatches: "What sort of man is this Penney who without any political touting or personal magnetism can command such power and authority? Never before in history has the British Government placed such reliance on one man's word. On Penney's assurance that his entirely untried H-bomb would work, the Government revolutionised the Forces, and invested millions in atomic works. I yield to no man in my admiration for this excellent man. I have witnessed his outstanding mind in action in the conference room, over the lunch table and during the tenseness of atomic blasts. His extraordinary position is unparalleled in the free world..."

All this hero worship only served to antagonize Penney who loathed publicity and had never been known to grant an interview. He avoided all contact with the press and even referred to Pincher as 'Chapman Stinker' in one dispatch from Australia

Getting him to Christmas Island without fanfare was a major operation. He eventually arrived on an American sea-plane (his favourite mode of transport) from Honolulu while his Hastings together with his normal entourage, were sent on a decoy trip to America.

Penney's arrival was noted with some excitement by the RAF ground crew who shepherded the seaplane, a Catalina, to its slot on the runway. For as the doors opened out popped Penney, accompanied by four very attractive models. Aircraftsman Archie Ross recalled: "They were real stunners, and to us men who hadn't seen a woman in months, a real tonic. We set up a chorus of wolf whistles as the little group made its way to the terminal. The girls gave us a wave before they disappeared. I think they were part of a film crew, but what they were doing with Penney I haven't a clue. The Catalina didn't stay long before it was off, with the four pretty girls back on board, which was more the pity."

Penney was met by Cook and other scientists and taken to a private tented complex near 'C' site, the forward area. No official minutes have been released about the visit, but his arrival was duly noted by Ralph Gray, a steward in the catering core.

He had had a pretty good idea that "something big" was about to happen when he was ordered to report to 'C' site. His orders were to "look after a few gentlemen...and keep your mouth shut." He was directed to a tented complex bristling with aerial equipment and surrounded by heavily armed guards. He was thoroughly searched and checked out before being allowed into the inner sanctum where he was introduced to the people he was to look after for the next few weeks.

The "few gentlemen" turned out to be none other than Sir William Penney, Bill Cook, Air Vice Marshall John Grandy, Air Commodore J.F. Roulston, the highest ranking Navy officer, Captain J.G. Western, and the Army's Task Group Commander Colonel R.B. Muir. Half a dozen scientists from Aldermaston were also present making it the largest gathering of top brass Gray had ever seen. After perfunctory introductions, Gray was put to work serving what appeared to be everyone's favourite drink: large gin and tonics infused with lashings of ice.

Gray delighted in the work. He was now living and working in comparatively lavish surroundings...a far cry from the primitive conditions the rest of the island had to endure. Duckboards on the floor were covered with comfortably-padded groundsheets, and the sleeping quarters contained real cast-iron beds with sparkling white linen sheets. Padded chairs and large deep armchairs were liberally spread about. An area set aside for drinks and food preparation had a large dining table and a modern well-stocked fridge. And the young steward could hardly believe his eyes when he discovered there was even a washing machine...an unheard of luxury on the island.

Gray, just 21 at the time, set about his duties with enthusiasm. He washed and ironed clothes, polished boots and cooked and served dinner every night. And he was always on hand to replenish the crystal glasses as the "few gentlemen" fortified themselves while they talked and planned well into the night. Of course Gray understood little of what the great men were talking about, but he did gradually become aware of a deep sense of unease that pervaded much of the table talk. From what he could gather Penney and Cook had only a vague idea of what to expect from the bomb and argued furiously as they pored over blueprints and calculations.

Penny and Cook were not getting on at the time. They had always formed a perfect partnership at Aldermaston and together had worked wonders to progress the development of Britain's H-bomb. But now they appeared to be increasingly irritated with each other. The pressures were obviously mounting.

Cook was one of the ablest men in his field and the making of the hydrogen bomb showed him at his most typical and effective. He had worked in defence science all his career, was in close touch with defence policy, and had no moral qualms about the need for the weapon.

He was brought in to Aldermaston in 1954 as Sir William Penney's deputy essentially to make sure Britain had a workable bomb in the shortest possible time. The theoretical side was, of course, primarily the work of Penney, but Cook played a vital part in harnessing theory to application. Cook had been in charge of the 1957 series when the first, unwieldy bomb was exploded: then in 1958, he was recalled to finish off the work and to take charge at Christmas Island again.

He might have viewed the arrival of Penney as a slur on his abilities and reacted accordingly. But nothing prevented him from working all hours of the day, or night. There is no doubt he missed his old drinking buddy, Wilf Oulton, and was often seen sitting alone next to the sea pondering a problem (accompanied by a whisky and soda) far into the night.

Despite their outward calm, both Cook and Penney were very worried men and Gray could sense the rising tension. "I got the distinct impression they didn't have a clue what was going to happen," he said. "They weren't happy with their calculations and fretted continuously."

As D-day approached, Penney and his team toiled in a large heavily-guarded corrugated iron "workshop" out of sight of prying eyes. Archie Ross used to watch the comings and goings. He said: "Every time some important part arrived, they would screen off the area surrounding the workshop with large pieces of canvas. I was never quite sure what they were hiding from us, but they were obsessed with secrecy." Ross had been on Christmas Island since mid-1957 and had witnessed Grapple X. But there was something different about the preparations for this latest drop. "The activity was more intense," he said. "There was definitely tension in the air."

INTO THE JAWS OF DEATH
April 28, 1958.

The men didn't need much prodding from their bunks; everyone knew there was going to be a bomb drop and the excitement was palpable. In the half-light of daybreak, they could see that weather conditions were far from perfect. It was raining heavily at Main Camp and the countdown was delayed. The gloomy weather was recorded in the Operations Record Book for No. 76 Squadron, the Canberra aircraft used to collect samples from the mushroom clouds.

After noting the heavy rain and 'almost complete cloud cover' the book records:

There was considerable speculation as to whether the weapon would be set off that day as the squadron aircrews sat around straining to hear the extremely inadequate Tannoy across the dispersal tarmac.

Despite the delay, and with little fuss and a minimum of noise, trucks began ferrying thousands of men from the Main Camp to allocated "viewing" positions in palm groves and on beaches near the Port area. This was also a precaution against a radiation leak in the event of a crash landing at the airfield which was near to the Main Camp. Unusually, a dozen or more landing craft were moored on the beaches and the word spread they were there for a quick getaway should the bomber crash on takeoff.

The rain gradually cleared and the men were ordered to their viewing positions. The word spread: "It's go!" The men faced the sea, their myriad cigarette ends glowing darkly red like fading fireflies. There were nervous chuckles and a few bad jokes, but an almost supernatural stillness descended as the first roar of the Valiant engines signaled the start of the operation.

Meanwhile Ralph Gray was scratching his head over the fact his 'few gentlemen' seemed to have vanished in the night. "I walked over to their tents, but they were all empty. Even the guards had gone. They had all packed up in the night and departed without telling me. And I knew they were not coming back because all their clothing and personal belongings had disappeared with them. All that was left was the smell of tobacco smoke and some half empty gin glasses. I walked across to the other tents and spoke to an officer who told me they had gone somewhere safe…very safe. He told me not to ask questions and advised me to make for a small corrugated iron Nissan hut near the beach."

Gray wasn't to know, but Penney and most of his entourage had boarded two Dakota aircraft that ground crew had prepared for take-off. Just before the scheduled time for the bomb drop, the aircraft took off and headed south toward Malden Island, 400 miles away. The flight is recorded in the Operations Record Book. The log reports that eight people were aboard, although they were not mentioned by name. But at least one aircraftsman noted the portly figure of William Penney boarding the lead Dakota.

The countdown was delayed by one and a half hours, and Valiant XD825 was finally swung into position just as the sun broke through. Its whiteness dazzled onlookers as it reached the centre of the runway. With a tremendous roar the engines revved changing soon to a high-pitched scream as the plane picked up speed.

At Port Camp hundreds of men were ordered on to the landing craft moored in the shallows. Scores were crammed into each vessel and there was standing room only. There was much nervous laughter as the ungainly craft bobbed about in the swell, the men hardly able to move.

Archie Ross recalled: "It was ludicrous really because if the Valiant did crash on takeoff, God alone knows what we would have done. The landing craft were just not suitable for putting to sea. They would have been swamped as soon as they reached the big rollers breaking a hundred yards from the shore."

There was an audible sigh of relief from onlookers all over the island as XD825, piloted by Squadron Leader Bob Bates with its 8,000 pound load, rose smoothly into the air and headed into the blue. It was followed by the other Valiant, the grandstand aircraft that would take up position a mile behind to film the bomb drop. Finally the five Canberras of 76 Squadron took off in quick succession. Three circled the proposed dropping zone. These were to act as spotters, sniffing out the highest concentrations of radiation. Two others flew a hundred miles downwind ready to track the onward migration of the cloud as it drifted over the Pacific ocean.

Canberra WH980, with Flt Lt Eric Denson at the controls, was the last to go. His aircraft like the rest was smothered with a sticky, cream substance that had the consistency of molasses. This 'protective varnish' had been invented by the atomic weapons research boffins back at Harwell, and was designed to absorb radioactive fallout leaving the interior of the aircraft relatively clean. At least that was the theory. Denson took

WH980 straight up to 40,000 feet and waited. Then into his headset a harsh metallic voice announced, "Bomb gone..."

On the ground, speakers mounted on tall poles, announced in their tinny, alien voices, the countdown. The metronome voice marked off the seconds like footsteps on the gallows.

As Grapple Y was released from the bomb shackle and began its fall, it automatically turned on the telemetry recording instruments that were focused on the point in space where the bomb was planned to explode, some 8,000 feet above the ocean. Its release from the shackle also switched on the clockwork timing mechanism which would set off the firing sequence. Extensions to the fins on the tail of the bomb snapped into place and began to damp down its oscillations to a graceful arc through the morning sunlight.

The firing sequence began a series of events lasting only a few millionths of a second. At 42 seconds, the uranium-rich atomic core exploded followed almost immediately by the high explosive supercharge, squeezing the beryllium tamper. This in turn crushed the lithium deuteride fuel with enormous force, reducing it to a ball of super-dense liquid metal as hot as the centre of the sun. The core now went into an uncontrolled chain reaction. This implosion phase had taken some 70 millionths of a second. The explosion phase followed at 300 millionths of second.

FIRE!

A light so bright and white it could only have come from the very heart of creation momentarily turned the island and every man and creature upon it into stone. Then, with a whiplash snap, the light was gone to be replaced by a steadily rising heat as though someone was slowly opening the door to a gigantic furnace. The men lined up in quaking masses slowly turned to each other, an unspoken question on their lips: "Where's the bang?" But there was no sound at all...No birdsong, no wave crashing. It was as though the universe was holding its breath.

Thousands of indigenous frigate birds nesting near the southern tip of the island where the bomb exploded were the first casualties. They were turned instantly into blazing flying feather balls or incinerated on their nests. Next, large shoals of dead and dying fish floated to the surface as huge areas of the ocean boiled. Lush green vegetation withered instantly as though irrigated with boiling acid, and palm trees lashed furiously about before snapping like dry twigs.

The eerie silence that followed the blast remained unbroken for a minute, but it seemed like hours. Most of the men were on their feet now, thinking it was all over. Suddenly the loudest bang anyone had ever heard rent the air like the crack of doom. The noise sent everyone crashing to the ground and the men could only watch helplessly in goggle-eyed awe as on the horizon a dark shadow, rippling like billions of tiny fish, formed and raced toward them with terrifying speed.

The realisation hit home that the blast wave was about to overwhelm them. Panic set in. Men threw themselves about in desperation. Some began a futile run for shelter. Too late, the blast wave like a giant hand, slapped down..."

Ken McGinley, a young Royal Engineer who had arrived on the island along with a thousand other troops on the Dunera a month earlier, was sitting on the beach when he heard a roar "like a thousand stampeding horses" as the blast wave approached: "We had had a talk from an officer on what we could expect, but nothing compared me for this. This was the daddy of all bombs. There was something incredible sinister about this shimmering line of energy skimming over the ocean with amazing speed. I dived to the ground and as it hit I felt an impact and a crack like lightning had hit close by. The huge fireball forming above me seemed to stretch from horizon to horizon. I knew straight away we were far closer than we should have been for a bomb that size. It was truly awesome; a great rolling, roiling, boiling mass of fire. Then a spout seemed to rise from the ground and the familiar mushroom cloud began to form."

Archie Ross: "To be honest, I considered myself a bit of a cool dude. I remember being mildly surprised when the impact of the blast wave hit and my goggles were slapped against my face. Some people near me were panicking but I felt sort of detached. But then things began to happen that made me realise just how small and insignificant I was when compared with the forces of nature. I still remember, as though it was yesterday, the stem of the mushroom cloud reaching down to the sea and the waves parting like that famous scene from the film the Ten Commandments when Moses causes the Red Sea to part. I remember seeing the water rushing up the spout, followed by all the mud and sand from the seabed, all being sucked up into the cloud like a giant vacuum cleaner. I remember the cloud spreading and becoming a hellish green on the underside..."

Ralph Gray: "In my corrugated hut I was close, very close. The bomb seemed to go off right over my head. Through a slit hole I saw the blast approaching and it was as though the whole island was being shaken. As I watched palm trees were suddenly flattened; a large oil bowser was tossed around like a leaf; a huge refrigerator that had recently been delivered and was too heavy to move was shunted neatly into the space allotted to it. It was a terrifying experience."

Forty thousand feet in the air Eric Denson was suspended between heaven and hell. Above him the clear, blue sky, clean and serene. Below the dark, boiling mushroom cloud rose to meet him like fumaroles from the bowels of hell.

Instructions from his squadron leader 20 miles upwind filled his earphones. Sophisticated monitoring equipment in the Canberra targeted areas of maximum radiation burn. Denson assimilated the information, adjusted his controls, took one last deep breath and flew his aircraft arrow straight into the maw of the monster. As he entered the cloud he intoned over and over again Tennyson's tribute to foolhardy courage in the Charge of the Light Brigade: "Into the jaws of death, into the mouth of hell..."

Denson fought with the controls as WH980 was tossed around like a leaf. The controls were loose and floppy, it was like trying to steer a car on an icy lake in a blizzard. He made several passes through the mushroom cloud. When the aircraft emerged after the final run it was alive with radioactivity. And when it landed and taxied to a halt at the far end of the runway near the decontamination pits, the Canberra sent every radiation counter crazy. His log book showed he was in the air for 1 hr 55 mins

Kevin Murphy, one of the ground crew, recalled: "We were told WH980 was the hottest aircraft ever to return from a cloud sniffing mission. We were on the far side of the runway, but we could see there was a hell of a flap on about it. Men in protective suits were running around, but no-one went too near. They sprayed hoses on to the aircraft, but that was as close as they got..."

Flt Lt Glen Stewart, the navigator of a Shackleton aircraft on patrol 60 miles from ground zero watched as the sky around the explosion boiled with clouds and smoke. He noted that the blast set off a chain of violent thunderstorms that marched in a line toward Christmas Island, and his aircraft ran into torrential rain on its return. He said: "The rain entered the unpressurised cockpit like a sieve, turning the only detector, a small rudimentary device on the captain's lapel, immediately the wrong colour. I believe another Shackleton was caught in the same predicament."

An RAF observer in one of the cloud sampling "sniffer" planes, also testified the aircraft was lashed by a belt of heavy 'black rain' which he saw cascading down the sides of the mushroom cloud. Flt Lt Joe Pasquini recorded his aircraft was suddenly "pelted" with rain and all the radiation monitoring equipment lit up "like a Christmas tree." The downpour lasted for about 30 seconds and he estimated the rain belt to be three nautical miles wide.

He recalled: "We were flying near the stem of the mushroom cloud when I saw quite clearly a huge belt of black rain. The heat from the fireball had obviously vapourised the surface of the ocean which sent up huge quantities of steam into the stem of the cloud. As it rose, it cooled and came back down to earth as this dirty rain." Pasquini watched in awe as the cascading waterfall of rain scythed across the island in a sizzling curtain of radioactive droplets.

The phenomenon was observed by a senior RAF officer on the island, Squadron Leader Kenneth Charney. He was in the reinforced steel and concrete bunker at 'C' site about 17 miles from ground zero. After a nerve-jangling few moments as the blast wave made the steel structure creak and groan, he and a group of scientists ventured outside to examine their instruments. As they scrambled about the scorched terrain they were hit by a sudden belt of rain that disappeared almost as soon as it arrived. Charney knew instinctively that this was 'bad' rain and like so many others he was to pay a terrible price in the future. The swirling curtain of rain moved up the island like a tsunami gathering strength from the crackling air, and by the time it reached Port camp, it had morphed into a full-blown tropical storm.

Unaware of the dangers servicemen, used to only saltwater bathing because there was no natural freshwater on the island, stripped off their clothes and ran naked and whooping into the downpour. They opened their mouths to suck the moisture into their parched bodies and only the arrival of a posse of scientists, garbed in protective 'moon-suits', alerted them to the danger. But no warning was issued to stop thousands of men from later swimming in the lagoon at Port camp, where most of the heavy rain fell.

Caught out in the open RAF fire crewman Jim Wallace welcomed the storm. But he soon changed his mind. For this was like no tropical storm he had ever experienced. "The droplets were unnaturally large," he said. "And then I realised they were black. This was a dirty rain that I'd never seen before. I knew then that something had gone wrong with this bomb."

Archie Ross also remembered: "After the blast the clouds started building in the sky and I noticed they were a peculiar shade of deep green and turquoise. And then it started to rain, very sudden, very heavy and very wet."

Thousands of men received a radioactive shower that day. But nearly everyone on the island was contaminated in one way or another from either drinking water distilled from the sea, or from the lagoons where they swam.

Out at sea the ships were last to receive a radioactive bath. HMS Narvik, the scientific and supply ship, which was 30 miles from ground zero, was anchored just offshore from Port London. Bernard Geoghan, an officer on board described how the cloud "developed and developed and developed."

"It was absolutely enormous," he said. "Eventually it came right over the top of the ship and passed the ship. Then it started raining…it absolutely bucketed down; a real tropical drenching. We were all soaked to the skin. Most of us were wearing the cotton zoot suit and perhaps a pair of tropical shorts. We were all very apprehensive. Here was this rain coming smack out of the nuclear cloud right over our heads. Inevitably everyone was pretty petrified about it. Very soon after that a broadcast came from the bridge assuring us that there was no contamination registered on the ship, which we did not believe for one minute. It was a while before we were allowed to disperse."

Most of the islanders had been evacuated to the Narvik. Mrs Sui Kiritome, reporting to an official inquiry some years later, told how the islanders had been roused at 3am ready for evacuation: "We were told the test would take place early in the morning around 5 or 6am and that we should be at the wharf ready for evacuation from the island. We were transported to the ship on landing crafts."

Mrs Kiritome's husband acted as interpreter for the British officers. A roll call was taken and the people were grouped on the basis of their home islands (most of the people were migrant workers from nearby islands). People made their way to landing crafts as their names were called. Before leaving their homes, the islanders were told to remove items hanging from walls as well as ensuring that pets and other animals were put out of harm's way. Once on board they were escorted to the holds were a movie show of Disney cartoons had been set up.

Large bags of sweets were handed round by two WVS ladies, Billie and Mary Burgess

As the countdown began, Mr Kiritome told the people to put their hands to their ears to muffle the sound of the blast. There were a few screams as the shock wave hit and the screen went blank. But everyone soon recovered. Later the islanders were allowed to troop up on deck --- and found everyone else wearing white cotton overalls, covering their heads, faces and bodies. Some of them were studying the effects of the bomb with binoculars.

"We didn't have any protective clothing. We went on deck wearing our normal clothes," said Mrs Kiritome. "We were watching the black cloud and smoke from the blast drifting toward us. When it came overhead, I felt something like a light shower falling on me. I thought it was rain. My husband stood under a lifeboat so he was protected from the shower. I felt wetness on my head, face and skin."

After several hours the islanders were taken back to their homes. Mr and Mrs Kiritome found all the windows and doors blown in and a concrete wall cracked. Their pet frigate bird was running round the house, blind. A few days later Mrs Kiritome was alarmed to discover that something had happened to her hair. Every time she brushed it large strands came loose. To make matters worse she developed burns to her face and parts of her shoulder.

A New Zealand navy ship HMNZ Pukaki was stationed 80 miles east of ground zero. She was an observation and weather reporting vessel which had been present at most of the Grapple tests. As she took her final position for the blast there was a flurry of excitement: the radar operators reported a small but firm radar contact about 12 miles away. The ship immediately started to close on the unknown contact at 12 knots.

There was high tension on board and all the men were put on maximum alert. Then as the ship closed to about five miles, the radar contact disappeared. The word was the intruder was a submarine and the sonar team began searching the depths. The ship reached the contact area, but there was no sign of an intruder. An urgent message was sent to Christmas Island and within an hour two Shackleton aircraft arrived on the scene and continued the search. Nothing was found.

It all added to the extreme anxiety that the crew were now feeling. After more than an hour's delay they were all ordered up on deck and issued with protective 'anti-flash' gear. They were told to sit down with their backs to the blast. Even at a distance of 80 miles the flash was intense. They felt the heat at the same time. One of the crew described it like sunbathing on a cloudy day and the clouds suddenly opening to let the sun through. The heat could be felt through white overalls. Then they heard a double crack of explosion, like a double barrelled shotgun blast.

But more than anything else the crew were amazed at the size of the fireball that formed on the horizon, and the towering mushroom cloud that began to grow was awe-inspiring. Within minutes everyone on board was looking up at the swirling mass of cloud boiling over their heads.

Crew member Gerry Wright recalled in his diary: "Silence. Everyone just watched in amazement at the power of energy that had been released before them. Only the cries of blinded frigate birds broke the silence. They would soon die as uncounted casualties of modern science."

The danger of fallout from the giant cloud, now stretching a hundred miles from horizon to horizon, was not lost on Pukaki's captain, Bernie Elliott. In the ship's log, he noted the size of the cloud and the fact that it had stretched over Pukaki "and far beyond" despite the ship being upwind, adding: "But such was our faith in the scientists ashore that no-one was heard to say, 'I hope it doesn't rain.'"

Meanwhile back at the airfield, the decontamination unit worked on WH980 all day. One of the crew recalled the desperate attempts to bring the radiation count down. In a sworn statement before he died in 2003, Ken Sutton, an Australian aircraftsman, said: "It was the hottest aircraft we had ever handled. No-one was even allowed near it; we just hosed it down from a distance. But the following morning I was taken by two men in white overalls, scientists I believe, who had stop watches. They instructed me to climb into the Canberra to retrieve some calibration equipment they wanted. I was told I had just two minutes to get in…and then get out. I asked, 'Why only two minutes?' They just looked at me and one said, 'Any longer than two minutes and you might as well not bother.' In overalls and face mask, I climbed into the aircraft and worked faster than I had ever worked in my life. I had the strangest feeling because everything looked so normal, yet I knew it was the most dangerous, lethal place I had ever been in. I got out as fast as I could, handed the instruments to the scientists and dived for the showers. I spent 30 minutes in there scrubbing down."

WH980 spent another day 'cooling down'. Kevin Murphy

reckoned it would be several more days before it would be released. But to his surprise the following day, Eric Denson showed up at the airfield once again, driven in a Jeep. He gave Murphy a wave of acknowledgement as he made straight for the aircraft. Murphy was amazed to see the Canberra being cleared for takeoff. "They never took off so soon after coming out of the clouds. The planes were just too dangerous. It would usually take several days, at least a week, for them to be scrubbed clean. I wondered what the hell was going on…"

The aircraft, with Denson at the controls, took off once again. Murphy scratched his head as it flew into the blue. It was in the air for 1 hr 15 mins, according to Denson's log book which also revealed the nature of the mission: a routine radar calibration and formation exercise. Murphy saw it return and taxi back to the decontamination unit. He saw Denson's lean, wiry frame climb out of the cockpit…and he never saw him again.

"He was abruptly sent home," said Murphy. "No-one told us why."

No reason has ever been given for this second flight which went against all normal procedures. But everything about this bomb was unusual.

Pukaki, in the gloomy half-light caused by the cloud continued on routine weather balloon runs throughout the day and into the night. On Tuesday morning April 29, it was ordered back to Christmas Island. But instead of taking the usual route via the west side of the island, the ship received orders to take the easterly route which would take the vessel through ground zero.

As it passed tests were carried out to monitor radioactivity in the seawater. The water was tested after being drawn up through the ship's water inlet valves in the keel, 12 feet below the waterline. At first all was well with a zero radiation reading, but suddenly a huge spike appeared on the graph recording radiation levels.

The on-duty Petty Officer sounded the alarm as the graph rocketed to well above danger levels. There was panic as other officers joined the scramble to view the instrument. Finally the captain came down to restore order. It was suggested there had been an error in the vertical axis, but that didn't convince anyone.

As soon as the Pukaki sailed into Port London, she was boarded by two stern-looking men in plain clothes; word got around they were from naval intelligence. They examined all the ship's paperwork over the previous 48 hours and left with most if it secured in a briefcase.

They also interrogated the radio officers about the 'disappearing contact' on the morning of the bomb test. When one of the officers speculated the contact might have been a Russian sub, one of the officials was overheard to say: "Who said they were Russian?" (An unconfirmed report later said that a Royal Navy sub HMS Aurorchs had been present for the Grapple Y drop and in fact had been ordered to surface soon after the blast. It was speculated the sub was used as a spot check method of testing the island's defensive radar equipment. The allegation came from a former crew member who insisted on anonymity. No official records exist of the incident, although it has been established that Aurorchs was in the general area at the time.)

The curious sense of gloom and depression noticeable after Grapple X was in evidence again after the Y explosion. A general malaise pervaded. Men didn't go fishing; no beach games were played and there were no picnics on the beach. The birds had all gone and even the sea seemed sombre and empty. It was as though the very air was dead.

Huge quantities of alcohol were consumed, and word got round that the officers wanted the men to drink as much alcohol as possible because it warded off the effects of radiation! Joe Pasquini, one of the Canberra pilots said: "There was certainly a feeling that beer could stop you getting a dose of radiation. I had heard the same thing from American pilots who had flown through mushroom clouds. Either way it was a good excuse to get plastered." (This rumour may have originated in tests carried out on foodstuffs after an American A-bomb test in Nevada codenamed Teapot. It was discovered that while other foodstuffs had been heavily contaminated, crates of beer had measured little radioactivity.)

To try to boost morale, the officers organised a 'squadron regatta', a race between rival landing craft around the harbour. But the event was marred by the appearance of large numbers of seriously injured manta rays and sunfish, gentle creatures prone to basking on the surface of the ocean. The wings on the manta rays, which could stretch to 30 feet, were severely burnt, while the large sunfish were badly seared on their upper sides. The creatures were clearly in great distress, but there was nothing anyone could do to help them.

Later that afternoon, as was customary, a party of naval officers went ashore for an island tour. They borrowed a Land

Rover and headed for the south east point where the bomb had been detonated. Through coconut plantations, many bearing the scars of the blast, the small party headed through low scrub which gradually yielded to a scorched moonscape. The bare land, still smoking in places, was littered with dead birds and mounds of boiled land crabs.

At a low concrete bunker in one of the forward areas, the little group came across hundreds of oil drums strung together at varying distances from the shoreline. These were Penney's trademark apparatus for measuring the strength of the blast wave. The drums were filled with varying amounts of water; it was a technique which Penney had perfected at the American tests in Bikini.

With the completion of the test, it was time for Pukaki to return to New Zealand and a farewell party was held attended by senior officers and scientists from the Task Force. For those who went ashore, it was a drunken, boisterous night enlivened by a commotion at the 'wet bar' in Port London when scores of servicemen ran amok. A full-scale brawl broke out during which a two-ton lorry was revved up and sent hurtling into the canteen, scattering men in all directions.

Pukaki crew members were hastily rounded up and returned to their ship. The vessel steamed away from Christmas Island the following morning leaving the smoking debris of the night's depredations far behind. They, of course, from their vantage point of 80 miles from ground zero, were spared the worst effects of the bomb. The damage caused to their systems by the radiation released would not become apparent for many years.

But for those on the island and closer to the action, the effects started to manifest themselves within days. It started with a trickle, but soon long queues were forming in the sick bays with men covered in rashes and large blisters. Some had woken in their tents coughing up blood, while others suffered temporary blindness and nausea. These were classic signs of radiation sickness, but if records were kept, they were never made public. And for a very good reason: the military were all too aware of the uproar caused by an earlier American test at Bikini atoll, the piece of paradise in the Marshal Islands named as the US Pacific proving grounds.

On March 1st, 1954 a huge H-bomb, codenamed Castle Bravo, was exploded on a small uninhabited atoll. The scientists had calculated the bomb would be in the region of five megatons. But someone got their sums wrong and the resulting explosion was at least three times that. The atoll was vaporised leaving a crater 300-feet deep. Trees burst into flames 30 miles away and islanders taken to 'safety' were showered with 'snowflakes' of radioactive coral. They soon started bringing in natives with hair falling out and skin peeling off. Three hours after the explosion the Japanese fishing boat Lucky Dragon was hit. More than 20 crewmen were contaminated. One died after reaching port. It was an International sensation, and the Americans were finally forced to admit there was heavy fallout on neighbouring islands.

The US tried to blame the weather. But official records came to light that showed ships were ordered further out to sea, suggesting fore-knowledge of what was going to happen. And nothing was done to warn the islanders or 28 servicemen stationed at an observation post downwind of the explosion. Thousands of square miles were contaminated and dose limits for those caught in the fallout were said to be 100 times higher than normal levels.

Measurements taken on Christmas Island after Grapple Y were even higher, but this would stay secret for at least 50 years. Meanwhile Britain's military planners ordered that any hint that the island was contaminated was to be avoided at all costs. So when men reported sick they were told their injuries were caused by coral dust or allergies. When they applied for their medical records years later, many found they had disappeared or been destroyed. Later manifestations of more serious illnesses were dismissed as "coincidence".

Bob Bates, the pilot of the aircraft that dropped the bomb subsequently died of leukaemia, as did Squadron Leader Kenneth Charney. They were just two out of scores of servicemen who later contracted blood cancers after witnessing the bomb test. Records show that hundreds of men later suffered cancers, bone disease and a variety of illnesses that can all be linked to radiation exposure. The authorities were not too concerned about these because most emerged through the passage of time and could be explained away.

But the early victims were a different matter; they could not so easily be ignored and had to be hidden at all costs. Flt Lt Denson was sent packing as soon as it became clear he had 'exceeded the recommended safe dose' for radiation exposure. He was told not to talk to any of the other men, but to return to his home base at Bassingbourn at the earliest possible moment.

Joe Pasquini remembers seeing Denson in the decontamination centre. He said: "Eric was a quiet sort of guy, but he was always sociable and at his ease. When I saw him he was being violently sick in the washroom. I pretended not to see him in case I embarrassed him. He was obviously not a well man." Pasquini resolved to have a drink with him later, but he never saw him again. "He just took off with hardly a word to anyone," he said. "We were a pretty close-knit little unit, and it was unusual. But we knew not to ask questions. I'm sorry now that I never spoke to him."

Denson took off alone in a borrowed Canberra. His route took him through Nandi airport in Fiji where he felt so ill he decided to spend the night in a hotel. He ended up staying in Fiji for two nights. Denson, in typical "stiff upper-lip" fashion, never spoke much about it. No official record exists of this short sojourn, but Denson's illness was a clear sign that all had not gone well with Grapple Y. Officially, however, things couldn't have gone better. Grandy's jubilant telegram to London stated: "The RAF delivered the weapon to the right place, it exploded at the correct height and the measurements taken were gratifying."

One thing he didn't mention was that the weather deteriorated rapidly after the blast. Even official historian Lorna Arnold admitted the weather was so bad that "had there been any further delay the operation could not have taken place during the rest of that week. As it was, cloud conditions reduced the number and quality of the photographs obtained."

Official accounts give no hint of what really happened after Grapple Y. They talk only of it being "a clean bomb" that precluded water or dust being drawn up from the surface which may have given possible radioactive fallout

Nothing could have been further from the truth.

THE COVER UPS

In June 1958, Mrs Kathleen Jones, a Red Cross blood donor who worked in a London bank, got a priority summons to attend the Masonic hospital where her blood, a rare type, was urgently needed. She was told it was a matter of life and death. Mrs Jones dropped everything and rushed to the hospital. Not knowing the area she arrived hot and flustered ten minutes late. The doctor told her not to worry as she was the sixth person they'd summoned to give the patient blood. She was shown to a waiting room which was near a small private ward. She was intrigued to see the ward was guarded by two military policemen, and asked the doctor who the occupant of the ward was.

Her curiosity was piqued further when the doctor refused to answer; he hooked her up to the drip without saying a word. As soon as the doctor left she asked one of the nurses what it was all about. The nurse whispered it was because the patient was a young soldier who had been sent home from Christmas Island suffering from blood cancer. Mrs Jones was shocked: "There was quite a fuss about it, but everyone had been told not to say anything. It was all very hush-hush and mysterious. I gave my blood and went back to work, but I couldn't get it out of my mind."

Later, while on her way home, she decided to return to the hospital to find out what had happened to the soldier. The young nurse she had spoken to earlier was coming out of the door. Her eyes were red and she had obviously been crying. She didn't need to tell Mrs Jones that the young soldier was dead. "How old was he?" She asked. Just 20 was the reply. But all the staff had been warned not to say a word. Mrs Jones never forgot the incident. In an interview she told of her "total conviction" that the authorities were covering up the young soldier's illness because he had been on Christmas Island.

He wasn't the only one: William Brian Morris, a 20-yr-old soldier in the Royal Engineers, was another who died within six months of returning home from Christmas Island. In scenes eerily reminiscent he, too, was heavily guarded as he lay on his death bed. Even his close family was not allowed to visit leading to distressing scenes outside the hospital ward.

Private Morris's inquest was told he died from leukaemia and that he had an amount of radioactive Strontium 90 in his body. His father told the inquest that his son had been in perfect health up to the time of witnessing the Grapple test. He began to feel ill soon after returning home. Against the wishes of their son, who remained loyal to his country right up to the end, his parents demanded an inquiry. Researchers at Harwell examined the deceased soldier's right femur and found 15 strontium units in the bone structure. And the inquest was told there was a definite connection between leukaemia and radiation.

On the face of it this seemed a clear-cut case of a servicemen dying because he was irradiated by a nuclear bomb. Not according to the coroner, a certain doctor O.G. Williams, director of Swansea Hospital where Private Morris died. He astounded the inquest by declaring that in his opinion there was absolutely no connection between the soldier's death and the atomic bomb. A verdict of death by natural causes was subsequently recorded.

This was just one of many puzzling decisions handed down by coroners on nuclear veterans in the 1950s and 60s. Veterans are convinced some coroners took it upon themselves to hand down 'safe' verdicts. Coroners were doubtless aware that any verdict blaming the bomb tests would have been hugely controversial and it is possible many simply did not want the aggravation.

But a charge often made is that the coroners could have been following secret government guidelines for dealing with cases involving nuclear veterans. (If this sounds far-fetched, you only have to consider the case of a atomic veteran Ken McGinley, of whom more later. He managed to get his health records from the department of Health after a long wrangle. Clearly marked on one document were the words, "politically sensitive case.")

Professor Joseph Rotblat, who had been awarded a Nobel Peace Prize, was one of a number of eminent scientists who was convinced there was skullduggery at work. He said in a 1985 interview: "The fact that servicemen were dying because of their participation in nuclear bomb tests, wasn't a surprise to anyone, except, of course, the governments carrying out those tests. We had a very similar situation with the survivors of Hiroshima. Of course they wanted to cover these things up; that is what governments do."

Even former premier Harold Wilson was sceptical when assured that the death of one of his constituents had nothing to do with his witnessing bomb tests. Wilson had expressed a keen interest in the case of Sapper Samuel Duggan who died five years after returning from Christmas Island. In 1965, he had been in correspondence with Private Duggan's widow and had been persuaded there was a link with his death. He wrote to the Ministry of Defense about his concerns, and received the following bland assurance from his defence minister Fred Mulley:-

"From the copy of Mr Duggan's death certificate, which we have seen, I understand that he died of a rare form of cancer. There is no evidence that this form of cancer would be induced by exposure to ionising radiation, and the film badge which Sapper Duggan wore, in common with all those liable to be exposed to radiation, gives no record of exposure. I think we can take it, therefore, that Sapper Duggan did not die as a result of his service on Christmas Island."

In common with many people before and since, Wilson was unhappy with this explanation. He knew the Ministry of Defence was notorious for obfuscation and would always be 'economical with the truth', even with prime ministers. He wrote to Sapper Duggan's widow: "Although the Minister says that the rare form of cancer from which your husband died was not caused by his service on Christmas Island, I do intend to make some further inquiries about cases of leukaemia and similar diseases developing after service on the island. Unfortunately I have not yet had an opportunity to do so."

Unfortunately it is not known whether Wilson made any "further inquiries" or indeed the nature of them. The letter was the last Mrs Duggan heard of the matter. Inquiries in 1984 to the then Lord Wilson asking about private Duggan received no response.

Many veterans allege they have proof that initial reports on their sicknesses were not included in their medical records. In the aftermath of explosions, ill health tended to be ignored or even hushed up. And even those whose health was so serious that it could not be ignored, often faced a frightening and bewildering ordeal.

Raymond Drake was an RAF fire officer on Christmas Island when Grapple Y was exploded. Mr Drake was in one of the forward viewing positions when he and the rest of his small detachment were blown clean off their feet. "The bomb was massive," he said in a statement. "The whole island seemed to shake. I thought the scientists had made a mistake and that the place was just going to blow up. We thought we were all going to die..."

Mr Drake survived the blast, but a few days later he began to experience intense chest pains. He also coughed up blood and felt so weak he could hardly stand. It was decided to send him home for treatment.

It was soon obvious to Mr Drake that he was getting special treatment. On his arrival at Gatwick airport he was surprised to see a small convoy of military vehicles and what looked like a specially modified police ambulance. He was even more surprised when he realised the little convoy was waiting for him.

As soon as the doors opened on his aircraft several medics came aboard and strapped Mr Drake to a stretcher. Without a word being said, he was stretchered into the ambulance which took off at high speed, all sirens blaring. "It terrified the life out of me," he said. "I thought I must be dying and that they had not told me."

The convoy took him to the RAF Teaching Hospital in Middlesex where he was ushered into a side ward. "I was surrounded by doctors who examined me as though I was some sort of laboratory animal. The examination was rather cursory, as I recall. I had no idea what they were looking for. After only a short time, I was again loaded on to a stretcher and shoved back into the ambulance. We then sped off again, with all the lights flashing. This time the destination was a special isolation hospital at RAF Wroughton in Wiltshire. No-one told me a thing about what was going on. I was ordered not to ask any questions. I couldn't even contact my family. It was all very bewildering."

During the next three weeks Mr Drake was put through a series of rigorous medical tests. Samples of blood and skin tissue were taken daily. Mr Drake said: "They were obviously looking for something, but would never tell me what that was. After five weeks in hospital I was discharged." The doctors put his condition down to emotional stress and nervous tension caused by the size and huge force of the blast. Mr Drake's chest pains never went away and he soon developed cancer.

Mr Drake's experience indicates there was in force at the time of the bomb tests a well prepared contingency plan for dealing with men who might be affected. It was a meticulous plan, carried out in secrecy. It was obviously in the best interests of politicians and military planners that the public were not made aware of strange illnesses and deaths among atomic personnel. The Government needed public opinion on its side if it wanted to continue its testing program. It also suggests the military were fully expecting casualties from the atomic bomb tests. The smooth and efficient way Mr Drake was 'processed' suggests it had been used on more than one occasion.

One man in a unique position to verify the official cover-up in action was squadron leader Ken Charney, one of the most senior officers at Grapple Y, who, in July 1958, was ordered from Christmas Island to a high-powered meeting at Aldermaston.

The Meeting was attended by Air Vice Marshal Grandy, Roy Pilgrim, scientific director for Grapple, Air Commodore W.R. Stamm, in charge of the famous Princess Mary RAF hospital at Halton, Aylesbury, and a galaxy of other Top Brass. According to a document marked "Secret" dated July 15, 1958, this was to discuss, "Radiological safety precautions at Christmas Island" and was called to thrash out worries about the health of servicemen in the aftermath of Grapple Y. Doctors had recommended that all the men should be given blood tests before the next series of tests, codenamed Grapple Z, scheduled for later in the year. It was an idea that didn't go down well with the assembled company.

Charney, assigned to take the minutes of the meeting noted the objections by Group Captain Muir of the Air Ministry who thought the idea of blood examinations for servicemen was "unsound." He was supported by another RAF bigwig, Air Commodore Stamm, who wanted "reasons" for the blood counts.

A Dr J. Lynch from the Atomic Weapons Research Establishment insisted that people with counts above or below normal or those with any blood abnormality must be barred from taking part in any future tests. Air Commodore Stamm objected that if a man developed leukaemia, "it might be difficult to refute the allegation that this was due to radiation received at Christmas Island."

The standoff was resolved by both parties agreeing that only men in the forward areas would be given blood counts. A decision on the rest of the servicemen would be taken at a later date. This bad-tempered exchange is clear evidence of growing concerns, among the medical fraternity at least, about the after effects of Grapple Y.

At the same time MPs had got wind of things going wrong at Christmas Island and were asking questions in parliament about servicemen contracting leukaemia. The Rev Li Williams MP, who represented a large Welsh constituency, pointedly asked Defence Minister Duncan Sandys in a parliamentary question in the summer of 1958: "What is the number of serving personnel who have been involved in the Christmas Island nuclear explosions and who have since died of leukaemia?"

Sandys replied that two had died, but he was quick to add: "There is no evidence of a medical connection between the circumstances."

But the fact that servicemen were dying from leukaemia so soon after the Grapple Y explosion was enough to raise eyebrows. And there was of course no telling how many men had contracted blood cancers and had yet to exhibit signs. MPs and others were unconvinced at the insistence by the Ministry of Defence that there was no connection between these extremely rare diseases and the Christmas Island tests. But with no hard evidence to back up their suspicions, the issue faded away.

Charney of course knew there was a connection. In later life he often said the island was "alive with fallout" after the Grapple Y shot. And he knew he had been contaminated. He also knew an uncertain fate awaited him even as he sat taking the minutes at Aldermaston three months after the blast.

NO WAY TO TREAT A HERO

Kenneth Langley Charney, born in 1920, was raised in Argentina, the son of Harry Charney, a manager with the Anglo-Mexican Petroleum Co. They were a well-to-do family and young Charney led a racy lifestyle in Beunos Aires. A love of fast cars and his good looks ensured he was never without female company. As luck would have it Charney's father had close associations with one of the first commercial airlines in the area. The precocious youngster replaced his beloved cars for something far more exciting: aircraft. Aged just 16, and with tutors including French pilots Jean Mermoz and Paul Vachet, Charney was soon flying planes on the mail run down to Patagonia.

The Charney family were living in the same hotel as Antoine de Saint Exupery, another pilot who would later become famous as fighter ace and author. At the outbreak of World War 2, Charney, Exupery and many other Argentine volunteers went to England to join the RAF.

Charney's flying skills were soon appreciated by the instructors at Cranwell. He was fast-tracked and he earned his wings in April 1941. One of his contemporaries was the famous French flyer Pierre Closterman and the pair wreaked havoc with the Luftwaffe over France. Both received the DFC and Bar, Charney earning his citation for his courage and skill in the Battle of Malta. He was given the soubriquet the 'Black Knight of Malta' when he shot down seven enemy fighters.

Later, flying over Falaise in 1943, he was the first to spot the German 7th Army trying to escape. He called on the radio: "Send out whole Air Force!" The result was a massacre that helped cripple Hitler's war machine. Churchill sent him a personal note of congratulation and Charney received his Bar. He lost many of his former colleagues during the battles of France and Malta which affected him deeply. He was taken off combat duties soon after Falaise and was sent to 53 Operational Training Unit.

But it didn't suit him and he got a transfer to 602 'City of Glasgow' Squadron as a flight commander. He was joined by the French fighter ace Pierre Clostermann and flew escort missions with Flying Fortresses over Germany. In one afternoon he shot down two Messerschmitts over Normandy. In 1945 he was posted to 132 Squadron, a specialist unit used to attack the V1 and V2 sites.

After the war he became part of Louis Mountbatten's staff in the Far East as a liaison officer. He was later put in charge of a new airfield in Palembang, Sumatra, on the site of a former POW camp, and scene of many atrocities by the Japanese. He was transferred to Ceylon (now Sri Lanka) and from there to Sylt in Germany where he was an instructor.

His stint on Christmas Island in 1958 earned him a posting back to England where he was put in charge of the RAF Cadet School in London. He retired as Group Captain in 1970 and became an instructor in the Saudi Air Force for three years. During his career he had flown 36 types of planes and had 2,300 hours in jets and fighters. He lived in Spain and then settled in Andorra; the climate suited his by now frail health.

Charney was a modest hero and was reluctant to talk about his war experiences. He left that to his Andorran friends who were in awe of his bravery. Whenever anyone broached the subject his stock reply was, "there were far braver men than me."

He met June, his future wife, in a café in the little village of L'Aldosa three thousand feet up in the Pyrenees in the La Massana parish of Andorra. She was sitting in a corner silently sipping a coffee with a lively group of people. Born in South Africa, June had decided to live in England following the break-up of her marriage, and was on an adventure holiday in Europe when she decided to stay awhile in Andorra.

She recalled: "Ken was a good 10 years older than me, but I was attracted to him straightaway. I heard all these stories about him being a war hero and all that, but I found him to be very shy and not at all boastful. In many ways he seemed lost to me, and one day he told me why. His brow sort of darkened and he told me he had been to a place that no-one should have been sent to. I thought he was talking about somewhere in the war years. But he said, 'no...that's not it.'

"He told me he had been sent to a tiny dot in the middle of the Pacific Ocean called Christmas Island for a number of years. Ken was the personal assistant to the officer commanding on the island and was involved in all these bombs going off. I distinctly remember him saying the whole place was 'red hot.' He said between the bombs there wasn't much to do except swim in the lagoons and drink. He used to take a lot of photographs. And he was fascinated with the birds. He became very friendly with the reverend on the island. They played a lot of chess. When the bombs started going off, I don't think he was overly concerned. He wasn't enamoured to be there, but it was his job.

"Ken used to swim a lot and of course there was an awful lot of coral there. And one day after an enormous bomb went off he cut himself on the coral, all down his side, and of course all that rotten water went in there. He said it was just after the 'big one', a bomb that shook the whole island. He said it was quite amazing. He laughed when he said the bigwigs must have known something because they all skedaddled before the explosion.

"Ken was in one of the forward positions, in a bunker. The only way he could see was through a sort of mirror. He said nothing in the war terrified him as much as this one; he really thought he was going to die. The bunker shook like mad. When he got cut by the coral, he landed in hospital, but it all turned nasty. He knew that water was very contaminated and often worried about it. But Ken had such a zest for life that he just laughed it off. He said we all had to die, and in the meantime he planned to carry on living life to the full."

This he proceeded to do, although even then his health was already failing. "He told me he would never go to the doctors. He was always afraid of what they might find. He said that even while he was jet-setting between England and the continent he felt the sword of Damocles hanging over him." Not long after he married June, Charney began to lose weight and his hair thinned alarmingly. "We both knew he was very sick, but we never discussed it and I am so sorry that we never did. All he would say is that he was doomed after swimming in the lagoon.

"About three or four years before he died he was bedridden for much of the time. It was so degrading for a man like him; I used to cry alone looking at some old photographs that showed him as he was in the RAF. I didn't realise it then, but this was the onset of leukaemia. I'm not a medical person, but all the signs were there. He knew what was wrong with him, but he was too frightened to face it. We tried to brush it aside and even went to South Africa for Christmas; we went out for three months and we took an apartment. He loved it so much he wanted to buy a place. But, of course, he was too ill. He said to me one day, about a month before he died, that he hadn't got long and that I should start thinking about my future. We both cried like babies and he cursed what he called that 'dot' in the middle of the Pacific.

Ken Charney, died on June 3, 1982, aged 62. An inept local doctor certified the cause of death as heart failure. No other cause was given. Apart from his pension, Charney had little to show for his 30 years service in the RAF. What savings he had went on paying a few bills and tying up his affairs. He had few personal possessions except for one intriguing item: a small leather-bound suitcase that he always kept carefully under his bed.

June said: "Ken always said the content of the case was dynamite and that I should never open it. I thought he was joking, of course, and I thought I had better open it to see if there was anything important. I found a couple of Dunhill pipes and some RAF insignias and a brooch. There was also a mass of official looking paperwork, but I was in deep mourning and didn't take any notice of them. I contacted Ken's old squadron and asked them if they would like the badges for their museum. I also told them about the paperwork. Out of the blue two women appeared on my doorstep. I was surprised because I'd only sent the letter a couple of days previously.

"They asked me if they could look into Ken's case to see if there might be "anything of interest". I saw no reason not to let them, and they rummaged around for a while. One of them started asking me about Ken, and she was delighted when I said they could have his insignia's and brooch for the museum. The other just read all the papers. They stayed for quite a while and we parted on very good terms. They took all Ken's things with them, including the papers. The badges ended up in his old squadron's museum, but I have no idea what happened to the papers."

Mrs Charney moved back to London and thought no more about Christmas Island until she saw an item in a newspaper about nuclear veterans fighting for compensation. By that time she was short of money and was only on an ordinary widow's pension. She wasn't entitled to the more generous RAF pension because she married her husband after his RAF service ended.

She decided to apply for a war pension because of her husband's participation in the Christmas Island tests. But she was turned down. "They authorities were not interested in Ken, or me," said Mrs Charney. "I told them all about his service during the war, but they said it wasn't relevant. I appealed against their decision about the war pension, but again they turned me down flat. It seemed very harsh."

Mrs Charney eventually wrote a letter to *The Times* which was published; a short while later she received a phone call from one of her husband's old colleagues who was now a Harley Street consultant. He asked Mrs Charney to send all her husband's medical notes to him. From those he was able to establish that Charney had died from leukaemia. After lengthy consideration, Mrs Charney was finally awarded a pension. "It's not much, but it helps," she said. "But this was no way for England to treat a hero."

THE LONG DEATH

Ken Charney was just one of many nuclear veterans hit by illness and early death in the aftermath of their participation in nuclear bomb tests.

All over the country men were dying from radiogenic sicknesses as they drifted back from Australia and the Pacific. They went home to their towns and villages and were conveniently forgotten by the armed forces who were only too glad to see them disappear into obscurity.

The medics never consciously made the connection. Doctors professed bewilderment and the NHS refused to discuss the possibility.

The men's families knew, of course. Deep down, they knew. They could see it in the eyes of their loved ones. But when they complained, or tried to get a pension, or tried to bring it to the attention of the wider world, they were ignored, sometimes even vilified.

The Government scoffed at their claims ruling they received no more radiation than they would in a chest X-ray. They forgot to mention that X-rays only expose tissue to radiation very briefly.

A miniscule particle of plutonium that may have been picked up from contaminated soil or water and lodged in the body constantly radiates into the surrounding tissue.

Atomic veterans suffer 'a long death.' Like some nightmarish parasite it eats away at them from the inside until all that is left is an empty husk. You can't taste it or smell it, but it is there. You cannot put it on the news and show its devastating effects.

It rises like a seeping gas and suffocates like a slowly rising tide of effluent. And the 'long death' takes no account of rank or position.

These forgotten warriors of the cold war know that their deaths will never be perceived as heroic, even though their battlefield was every bit as dangerous as their colleagues fighting in more conventional wars.

Most know they have a date with death that will never be celebrated in the annals of war. And most have endured it knowing all the time that they have been betrayed by their government.

Some decided not to wait for the creeping death and took their own lives. Others found life was not worth living after their brush with The Bomb.

Glen Stewart, the Shackleton pilot who graphically described in a TV documentary how the explosion set off a chain of thunderstorms over Christmas Island did not die of disease; the bomb found another way to kill him. His body was discovered by a man walking his dog at West Sands Beach, St Andrews, Fife, near the town's famous Old Course golf course. A hose was attached to the exhaust pipe.

Relatives are convinced Stewart was hounded to an early grave by senior Establishment figures after he was involved in a hair-raising near miss at Heathrow Airport.

As a senior pilot with British Airways, his Jumbo was approaching the airport following a long flight from Bahrain. It had been a nightmare trip with several cabin crew members and his co-pilot going down with food poisoning. Visibility was poor and out of the murk, the runway lights rose to meet Stewart's 747. Suddenly the autopilot indicated the aircraft had deviated from the approach.

Stewart realised the lights were not runway lights at all, but road lights belonging to a carriageway running alongside the airport. He was just a hundred feet from landing on the A4, but with consummate skill Stewart took over the controls from the auto pilot and lifted the Jumbo clear. The giant aircraft missed a hotel by just 12 feet, setting off all the alarms in the car park. It was an escape that made headlines, but for all the wrong reasons as far as Captain Stewart was concerned.

A civil aviation board of inquiry blamed him and took his precious pilots licence away. Also, in an unprecedented move, the government decided to prosecute. A jury, despite clear evidence to the contrary, found him guilty of negligence. He was fined £2,000, and never flew again.

It was a crushing blow from which he never recovered. The decision to prosecute, he always maintained, had been taken by people who had started their careers in the RAF and were now in the upper echelons of the Civil Aviation Authority. Giving the TV interview about his experiences at Christmas Island was perceived as a betrayal of his country; it also broke 'omerta', the code of silence ingrained in most senior RAF officers. Stewart always believed 'they' had taken their revenge

Flt Lt Eric Denson, the man who flew through the mushroom cloud created by Grapple Y, came to a tormented and ignoble end in a woodland clearing, his wrists slashed with a knife.

He never recovered from the massive radiation dose he received as he grappled with the controls of his Canberra aircraft. Denson struggled for 18 years to rid himself of an overwhelming feeling that his mind was being attacked by a "dark cloud" before he could take it no longer.

The RAF and the Ministry of Defence ignored his torment and refused to give his widow a war pension. There was no traditional 'fly past' at his funeral. They tried to bury Denson's reputation along with his body, but they reckoned without his formidable wife, Shirley.

SHIRLEY'S STORY

At about the same time as the newly-knighted Sir William Penney was tucking into his Sole Monte Bello and basking in his new-found fame as father of the British A-bomb, young Shirley Gubbins, had her eye on a very special man.

Just 18 years old, blonde with a trim figure honed by frequent exercise and horse riding, Shirley was enjoying the attentions of a small army of suitors.

She had accompanied her brother Brian, a young Royal Air Force flying cadet, to one of the lavish balls regularly held at Cranwell, the famous pilot training school on the Lincolnshire coast. It was Shirley's first real 'outing' as a young debutant, and her father, a well-to-do paediatrician, acted as chauffeur, chaperone and general factotum to his youthful offspring.

Shirley's mother, a buyer for a major department store, had made sure her beautiful daughter had a ball gown fit for the occasion. Flawless white, strapless with satin bodice and wearing her grandmother's matching pearl earrings and necklace, Shirley dazzled as she swept into the ballroom on her brother's arm.

Almost immediately she was surrounded by a gaggle of would-be suitors, and she enjoyed every minute of it. "What girl wouldn't enjoy all that lovely attention?" She recalled. "All those handsome young men, in full dress uniform, what more could a girl want? The band was playing, the champagne was flowing, and I was being swept off my feet by a succession of young men who wanted to dance with me. It was wonderful and I'd never felt so happy."

As she was swirled around the dance floor, Shirley couldn't help feeling sorry for a large group of rather plain-looking women who sat glumly to one side, toes tapping, but with no man to dance with. She had heard one of the young officers referring rather unkindly to the sad little bunch as "grimmies", service slang for wallflowers....girls who never received any attention from the smart young officer cadets.

Except, that is, for one. He was tall, dark and possessed of the chiseled features of a man who could look after himself. With great courtesy and without a hint of condescension, he invited each of the grimmies in turn to dance with him. Shirley found herself rather hoping he would ask her to dance.

"I don't know what it was about him, there were better looking men than him vying for my favours, but he seemed to have some special quality," said Shirley. "Then all of a sudden

I knew what it was: he looked slightly dangerous, which always appeals to a young girl."

In between dances, Shirley asked her brother who the mysterious cadet was, and was even more intrigued when the reply, "that's killer Denson", came back. Her brother explained that his name was Eric Denson and he was called "killer" because he was captain of boxing at Cranwell and possessed a killer right hook. Apparently Denson always punched above his weight, and in inter-service boxing tournaments had never been beaten. In fact no-one had ever gone the distance with him because of that famous killer punch.

Shirley was not remotely interested in the finer points of pugilism, but she did wonder what it was about Denson that made him take the time to dance with the grimmies. Her brother said he always did that. Apparently Denson hated to see anyone left out and made a special point of dancing with them at every ball.

Shirley was impressed. Then she was annoyed at herself for thinking of him at all. She tried to dismiss the enigmatic Denson from her mind. Later, however, her brother introduced them. Denson it turned out came from Burnley, Lancashire which was not far from the market town of Chorley where Shirley lived with her parents in some style in a manor house.

The ball marked the end of term at Cranwell and Denson was travelling back to Lancashire the following day to spend some time with his parents. On an impulse, Shirley offered him a lift home. Denson accepted, subject to the agreement of her father who, knowing Cranwell 'do's' tended to go on all night, had retired to one of the dormitories. As the night wore on, the young couple found themselves sharing almost every dance. Shirley made a point of finding out everything she could of her new beau.

Denson came from humble origins, but had won a scholarship to the prestigious Colne and Nelson grammar school where he excelled. He was one of that rare breed who could combine a first-class brain with outstanding achievement on the sports field. He was captain of both the athletic and boxing teams, and his tutors thought he could achieve anything he put his mind to. And when he brought in a series of top-grade 'A' levels, they said he could have his pick of universities, even Oxford or Cambridge.

But young Eric had other ideas. Ever since he was a small boy he wanted to be a pilot in the RAF. As a schoolboy during World War II, he would often lie on his back in the fields surrounding his home town and watch the fighter squadrons returning to their Yorkshire bases after skirmishes with the Luftwaffe. He dreamed of being up there with them, high in the sky defending his country against the evil invader. More than anything in the world, Eric Denson wanted to be one of 'the few.'

It was therefore no surprise when he shunned the overtures of the more prestigious universities and applied instead to go to Cranwell.

He was accepted immediately and his unique talents ensured he was fast-tracked for pilot officer training. Shirley recalled: "According to his colleagues, Eric was a natural; he took to flying like a duck to water and was marked down very early on to get to the top. He was only 20 when I met him, but he was mature way beyond his years."

After the ball, which went on until dawn, Shirley's father drove the small party back to Lancashire. Shirley slept all the way in Eric's lap.

She recalled: "Eric came to my home and I made us all bacon and eggs. By this time it seemed we'd known each other for ever, and we sat talking for hours. I had never met anyone like him; he had this sort of old world charm that I found very attractive. He talked for hours about the Battle of Britain and how close we had been to defeat. It was all very patriotic stuff, but that's the way we talked in those days. We were immensely proud of our country. I felt safe in his hands, and I knew that Britain had every reason to be proud of men like him. He was quite literally willing to lay his life down for his country, he loved it that much."

Shirley lived in a large, rambling seven-bedroom house surrounded by fields and woodland. There were stables, and Shirley had her own pony. There was a swimming pool, a rarity in those days. By contrast, Eric lived in a little two-up and two-down in one of the poorer districts of Burnley. But it made no difference to Shirley, who recalled: "Eric had very special qualities; he was the stuff of heroes. I had several boyfriends, but no-one compared to him. I couldn't stop thinking about him, and was sad when he had to go back to Cranwell."

The romance blossomed in letters and phone calls in the months that followed. By the time of the next Cranwell ball Shirley, always very single minded, had made up her mind. "The funny thing is that I always told daddy I wouldn't marry a pilot because they were always being sent off somewhere. But with Eric it didn't seem to matter. I decided he was the only man for me, and I was determined to get him. I know that sounds shameless, but I have always been a great believer in the old adage that all's fair in love and war."

The couple soon became inseparable. He visited her at home every weekend. Shirley said: "We were madly in love, but we never made love. We both felt it wouldn't be right until we were married. Eric said he would never betray my father's trust. Daddy knew this and respected Eric enormously for it."

In early 1954 Eric received his much-coveted "wings" and he passed out with honors as a fully-fledged pilot at a colourful ceremony at Cranwell. Six months later Shirley and Eric were married in a traditional ceremony, complete with honour guard, in an English country church near Shirley's home.

But there was no conventional honeymoon. Eric, as one of Cranwell's rising stars was already involved in some very secret work which necessitated staying on site at the base. Eric would never talk about his work; all Shirley knew was that he had been inducted into the Canberra squadrons, which included patrolling the edges of the iron curtain countries.

The mid-1950s was a period of intense fear and paranoia as the world watched the two superpowers squaring up to each other. America and the Soviet Union seemed to be hell-bent on destroying the planet as they vied with each other to produce bigger and ever-more fearsome weapons of mass destruction.

America was laying waste to huge tracts of the South Pacific Ocean as it detonated ever more fearsome thermonuclear weapons. The Soviet Union was doing much the same thing in the vast wastes of Siberia and the Arctic Circle. Britain was desperately trying to hang on to their coat-tails by testing its own nuclear devices in the Australian outback.

Into this feverish maelstrom were thrown pilots like Eric Denson who were being trained to fly the planes that would deliver Britain's nuclear response should the Soviets launch an attack. They had to be on standby 24 hours a day and the aircraft of choice was the Canberra which was capable of flying higher and at faster speeds than almost any other aircraft in service at the time.

Eric Denson took to flying the Canberra as though born to it. He was soon leading training squadrons and he excelled at penetrating the defensive radar screens of other forces. Low-level and night operations were given special priority.

On one occasion Denson caused a minor diplomatic incident when he made a low-level run that took the US air force base at Lakenheath completely by surprise. To rub salt into the wound, he cheekily flew back over the base on his return...all without being detected.

The Canberra squadrons remained Britain's first line of attack until 1957 when the huge new Valiant bombers came into operation. But the military still had plans for the Canberras...and for Eric Denson.

On the ground, Shirley got on with life as best she could. She recalled: "We were constantly on the move. We never had our own home and had to rent wherever we went. But we made the best of things. Eric was always busy and he was away an awful lot. The Cold War was intensifying and he seemed to be permanently in the air. I can still remember there was real fear at the time that the world was going to come to an end. By that time we had all seen the dreadful consequences of the Hiroshima and Nagasaki bombings. We were in the front line, and the threat of destruction was all pervasive. Eric was performing a vital part in defending our country. We were willing to put up with any inconvenience and no sacrifice seemed too great. I was very much in love with my husband and very proud about what he was doing. I worried about him all the time and I used to make a point of watching for his squadron returning to base. Eric always tried to fly over our cottage at the end of the runway, just to reassure me."

The couple was based back at Cranwell in 1957 when Denson suddenly received an urgent message. Shirley said: "There was a flap on over something and Eric was required for urgent duties. Before I knew it we were off again, this time to the big base at Basingbourne in Kent. I had to give up the little job I had managed to get at the local university and I even had to give away a gorgeous little red setter puppy Eric had bought me. But life was like that and we just accepted it. We packed our things and off we went. I was never told what all the fuss was about. All Eric would say was that he had to train for a special operation. He looked extremely worried for quite some time.

"Then one day he arrived back at our little flat and I sensed immediately there was something wrong. I was in the kitchen cooking dinner, but Eric didn't give me a little cuddle at the cooker like he always did. I went into the living room and Eric was just standing there with his back to the door. To my utter surprise I could see tears in his eyes. I knew it was serious, then. I had never seen Eric cry in my life. It just wasn't the sort of thing he did. He was only 25 at the time, but old beyond his years. I rushed up and put my arms around him and I remember saying, 'Darling, whatever is the matter...?'"

It was some time before Eric could reply. Finally he led her gently to the sofa and informed her he had to go away on a top secret mission, and he would be away for at least six months.

Shirley was distraught: "I could hardly take it in. Six months was a lifetime for me to be without my husband. I asked him what it was all about and he said he couldn't tell me because it was top secret. I told him I would go with him, but he said I couldn't because he was being sent to a remote base in the Pacific Ocean. He said he would be involved in some very special training before he left, but he couldn't tell me anything about it. He looked very worried as he told me, and I just knew he wasn't telling me everything. It was as though he had a premonition that something terrible was going to happen. I had never known him to be so vulnerable. I couldn't help feeling that it was all so unfair. After all Eric was a married man with a small child. But we were both very loyal to the RAF and our country, and in the end reconciled ourselves to the task in hand."

In early 1958, Denson departed for Australia where Britain had a permanent base deep in the outback called Woomera. Shirley received several letters, which suddenly ceased in March. By secret mail, she was told her husband had been sent to Christmas Island, a lonely coral atoll slap in the middle of the Pacific.

The penny finally dropped that her husband was involved in the hydrogen bomb tests then taking place. Shirley had just about reconciled herself to not seeing her husband for some time when out of the blue a signal arrived by special courier from Eric's commanding officer at Bassingbourn.

"To my intense joy, I was told Eric was being sent home immediately for what was called "operational reasons. I was assured my husband had not done anything wrong, but that he had just 'exceeded his limit.' In my happiness, I never considered what that meant. I remember someone telling me that Eric had received a bit too much radiation, but not for one minute did I consider he had been harmed in any way. I had too much faith in the RAF to worry about anything like that.

"In any event, all I could think about was getting him home. I rushed to tell mummy and daddy and we planned a big welcome home party. I never considered the possibility that the man who came back to me would not be the man I had waved goodbye to. But that is what happened.

"The dear, sensitive man who had kissed me so tenderly was gone. Later, flashes of him would come back, like finding old pictures in a photo album, but they became increasingly rare as time went by. It was as though he was being slowly sucked into a vortex and I was powerless to pull him out. Something terrible had happened to my darling man.

"The change in him was apparent within a few hours of his arriving back from Christmas Island. I had been beside myself with excitement as I waited for him to walk up the pathway.

"He rang me the day before to say, 'I'm back...' That's all he said, but that didn't worry me. In fact that was typical of him, because he wasn't a very demonstrative person. At last the taxi came and out stepped Eric.

"I burst out of the door and threw myself into his arms. I was five months pregnant at the time, but I went down the pathway like an Olympic sprinter. I kissed him all over his face, and he smiled. For a while we just stood and looked at each other. My beautiful dear man was back at last.

"Mummy and daddy, who I was staying with at the time, looked on from the door, smiling. Then Suzanne, our two-yr-old daughter, came running down the path. My heart nearly burst with pride when she shouted 'daddy'; I had shown her pictures of her daddy every day since he left. I was determined she wouldn't forget him, and I had succeeded. We were a family again, and it felt so good.

"We ushered Eric into the house and later the whole family had tea on the lawn. It was so wonderful. Suzanne tumbled with her pet rabbit in the grass and we all laughed. Then we just sat for a while and watched the most perfect of English sunsets as it spread a golden light across the meadow at the bottom of the garden. The world seemed at peace.

"Eric seemed to be in a contemplative mood and a companionable silence descended upon us. I took the opportunity to give my man the once over. I had already observed he had lost weight; not much, but enough to notice. I had never known him to lose weight, or gain any for that matter. I didn't like the colour of his skin, either. He looked pasty and pallid, an unhealthy tinge to his complexion; you wouldn't know he'd been in the tropics. And I didn't like the look of the dark smudges under his eyes. He looked as though he hadn't slept for days.

"When I thought about it, he didn't look healthy at all. I gripped his hand tightly, and asked him if he was feeling well. He gave my hand a reassuring squeeze and said he was feeling fine. But I could sense there was something different about him. Mummy and daddy must have sensed something too, because they soon made their excuses and left us alone.

"After a while I asked Eric if he wanted us to go to bed, but he might not have heard. He just stared into the distance and spoke about the heat, dust and sand of Australia. Then he said suddenly, 'Have you any idea, what the aborigines would give for the peace and coolness of an English garden? You can't put a price on such beauty, you know.'

"It was a lovely thing to say, but I must admit I was a bit taken aback. I had never known Eric to wax lyrical before. I had heard him talk about flight paths, wind speeds, maps and fuel consumption. But never about English gardens. He was a deeply reserved man and never really said anything unless it had a practical outcome.

"Now I suddenly found myself confronted by a stranger, a man who seemed to want to talk about everything under the sun. There was no coherent theme to his discourse. It just seemed he wanted to talk about everything and anything. He talked about God. *God!* I'd never heard him talk about God in his life. The nature of Evil! Where did *that* come from?

"Just as suddenly we were in the Australian deserts and towns. And then he was 40,000 feet above it all, describing the endless expanse of the continent as he flew over it God-like and omnipotent.

"Then we were back in England and back to his childhood, a childhood incidentally that I'd never heard of before. Most bizarrely he started philosophising about the nature of the universe and mans place in it...this was a totally different Eric Denson than I was used to.

"I was flattered and extremely interested, of course and I tried my level best to follow his drift. But I just couldn't keep up with him. After a while I began to feel alarmed. He was talking non-stop, gabbling almost. 'Where's my Eric?' I asked myself. I finally persuaded him to come to bed and we went together hand in hand.

"We made love of course, but later he just carried on talking and talking. He was like a record that had become stuck. It seemed as though Eric was on some sort of mission to tell me everything he had ever known, knew, read or learned in his lifetime."

In the end I just couldn't take any more. It was about five in the morning when I finally called a halt. I have always needed my sleep...and I was five months pregnant. 'Eric, darling, please!' I cried at last. I took his head in my hands and told him I simply must have my sleep. I told him I had to be up with Suzanne in a few hours time. But he might never have heard me. He just carried on talking and was still talking as I drifted off to sleep.

"My dreams were troubled and, exhausted as I was, I awoke a few hours later to find Eric drenched in sweat. He was fast asleep, but it was a troubled sleep. He was twitching and groaning as though he was having a nightmare. Instinct told me something was very wrong. I switched on the bedside light and I noticed a rash on his chest.

"It was an angry red colour, stippled with tiny white blisters, and stretched from his neck to just above his waistline. I had never seen anything like it. I bathed it gently in cool water and Eric woke. I asked him how he had gotten the rash, but he was non-committal. He said it was nothing. But that didn't satisfy me. I remember thinking he had picked up some tropical disease and the next morning I asked daddy to take a look.

"He made an examination but said he hadn't a clue what it was. It was beyond his experience. Of course we realised much later that it was probably a radiation burn, but at the time it was a mystery.

"Eric never discussed with me what had happened on Christmas Island. The only time I heard him talk about it was a few days later with my father. They were sitting together and daddy suddenly said, 'What was it like, son?' I remember Eric thinking about it for a while before making a decision.

"He said he had almost lost control of his aircraft as it went into the mushroom cloud. His plane was tossed about by the most incredible forces. He said the only way he could deal with his fear was by reciting the line from the Charge of the Light Brigade, 'Into the jaws of death, into the mouth of hell, rode the six hundred...' over and over again.

"He also told daddy he had been very sick when he landed at Fiji to refuel on the way home. He had never mentioned this to me, and I asked him about it later. But he absolutely refused to discuss it. He said he would get into the most serious trouble if he talked about it in any way.

"He seemed very scared about what had happened to him and I think that he knew deep down he had been seriously affected by his experience. I never did find out what Eric had been told about his mission or the possible dangers. But I knew he would have been extensively briefed and I recalled how upset he had been when he came home to tell me he was being sent away.

"As the weeks went by, Eric's odd behavior continued. Both sets of parents noticed the change in him and were openly voicing their concerns. They suggested he got treatment for his 'rash' as well as for other ailments ranging from sudden allergic reactions, to chronic breathing problems. But Eric absolutely refused to visit the RAF doctor at the base. He said you had to be in A1 condition if you wanted to stay in the service and the first hint that all was not well could easily lead to a discharge...or worse still, as far as Eric was concerned, a one-way ticket to a boring desk job.

"But after some considerable persuasion he was prevailed upon to book into a private clinic. Eric had an operation for sinusitis at the clinic, but it was his deteriorating mental condition that was causing most concern.

"He was becoming more and more frenetic and hyperactive. His brain was racing all the time, like a piece of machinery that didn't have a stop button. It was an awful time and our marriage began to suffer. We never discussed anything anymore.

"Before he was sent away, we always talked about everything and were always planning the future, having dreams together, what we hoped for the children, things like that. From wanting to talk about everything under the sun when he came back, he now didn't want to discuss anything, and try as I might I couldn't get close to him.

"He often seemed like a shadow, someone who was with me all the time, but elusive and insubstantial. It was as though he was trying to run away from something and at the same time desperately searching for something. He was drawing deeper and deeper into himself and I simply couldn't reach him.

"Eric started to do things that were completely out of character, like 'forgetting' to give me my housekeeping money. I friend of mine remarked that I was letting myself go. I was only in my twenties, but she said I was beginning to look much older. I said everything was all right, but one day she said to me, 'Shirley, look at your feet...' I looked and she was right. It was a freezing cold day, but all I was wearing was a pair of cheap, plastic sandals and my feet were blue with cold.

"The problem was I simply did not have the money to buy myself a new pair. I simply couldn't make ends meet on what Eric was giving me. I don't think he was being mean to me deliberately. I really do believe, he just forgot...but of course that didn't help me. Looking back there were so many indications of the changes in him.

"At the annual Cranwell ball, something that was so special to me, he was completely out of character. He was no longer the perfect gentleman I had fallen in love with. He drank heavily and rather ignored me. We had two children and we couldn't be late home. But when it was time to go, he told me to go on ahead.

"He didn't come in until the early hours and to make matters worse was sick on the bathroom floor. This was so out of character. I know these things taken individually were no big deal. But taken together it added up to a very serious change in Eric's personality.

"I soldiered on hoping that one day the old Eric would come back to me, and did my best to lead as normal a life as possible. But I was beginning to realise just how distant and out of touch we had become. He was changing before my eyes. He became aloof, when once he had been approachable; he was cold, when once he had been warm.

"He barely liked to be touched when once he had been so tactile. I was so upset and worried, but Eric didn't care. I wanted him back and yearned for the days, before he went to Christmas Island when we always kissed and cuddled in bed. It was the natural thing for us to do. I longed for that wonderful closeness. I tried to cuddle him again, but he had become unbelievably cold and frigid.

"When he didn't want to be touched he used to draw an imaginary line down the centre of the bed with his finger and say to me, 'Don't cross the line. Don't touch me.' I know most women would be reaching for the rolling pin at such behavior, but I was just absolutely devastated.

"What upset me most was that this change in Eric had happened so abruptly. I may have been able to live with it if it had taken place over a long period of time; I may have been able to understand it. But this was as sudden as Jekyll and Hyde. It seemed as though one day I had a gentle, warm man and the next I had this cold, aloof creature.

"It crossed my mind, of course, that he had another woman. I looked through his pockets for all the tell-tale signs. But I found no notes, no lipstick marks. No trace of strange perfumes on his clothes. What, then? What was causing this terrifying change in his behaviour? It was happening right in front of my eyes and was getting progressively worse. I felt so helpless because there was absolutely nothing I could do about it.

"The man that came home to me every night was still the

same tall, broad-shouldered, handsome individual I had fallen in love with. But his body might just as well have been inhabited by another person; a cruel, mean individual who didn't know how to love or be loved.

"I remembered what a golden couple were once were and I shed bitter tears of regret. I yearned for his laughter, his quiet sense of humour, his kindness. Most of all I yearned for his kindness. These thoughts sustained me through many a dark night as our truncated, lopsided marriage stumbled toward the chasm.

"If only he could have talked to me; tried to explain what demons I knew possessed him. Eric refused to even acknowledge that anything was wrong with him. But every now and then I would see something in his eyes, like the despairing look of a hunted creature, and my heart would go out to him.

"I so desperately wanted to help him, but I didn't know how to. All I could do was to assume a passive role and hope that one day he would come back to me. I loved him too much to divorce him.

"Ironically the new Eric, the hard man persona, had unexpected benefits in his career. He had always been tough, but there was a new hard-edge to him which commanded respect. Men learned not to mess with him.

"You only had to look into his eyes to know he was dangerous. He developed an air of authority and he was a natural leader in formation flying. His superiors promoted him to squadron leader, one of the youngest the RAF had.

"After a while I came to terms with the new Eric, and I believed that was the way natural leaders behaved. And there were compensations. With Eric's promotion came a smart, detached cottage set in a few acres near Cranwell.

"The social life was good for me, and although Eric remained distant and aloof, his 'condition' didn't seem to get any worse. To be frank I no longer had the time to worry about the way things were. I now had three children to look after, and although Eric had changed so much, I still loved him and was going to see my marriage through to the end.

Besides, I had plenty of support from the other wives on the camp and we got on very well together. We supported each other. I joined the tennis club and I even went pony riding again, which gave me immense pleasure. It should have been perfect really, but, of course, deep down it wasn't. We never spoke much, but his 'condition' whatever it was, was always there in the background.

"Things deteriorated when we were moved to the RAF Watton in Norfolk where Eric was assigned to top-secret work involving low-level Canberra flights.

"The work involved night flying under radar and was apparently immensely dangerous. There was this huge radar dish at the back of our home which hummed and buzzed all the time. It was transmitting 24 hours a day. Eric used to say it made his teeth chatter.

"I don't know if this had anything to do with it, but not long after his condition worsened considerably. The strain of his work began to tell in a big way and his mental condition, which had stabilised, returned with a vengeance.

"He became paranoid and was suddenly convinced I was having affairs with every Tom, Dick and Harry on the base. He watched my every move and it was a nightmare when we attended a dance or a function. He thought everyone I spoke to was having an affair with me. When not seething with jealousy he was hit with the darkest of dark depressions.

"He withdrew deeper and deeper into himself, to a place I could never reach. He got into the habit of coming home from work and going straight to the bedroom. He never said a word, never complained of feeling unwell. He would just draw the curtains and lay on the bed. Try as I might I could never get through to him. He was in such misery, it was heartbreaking.

"On the few occasions I got him to talk he said he couldn't understand what was happening to him. He said he felt as though his brain was in a dark cloud. The cloud kept closing in on him and no matter how hard he tried, he couldn't push it away.

"I went to see a doctor friend of ours who advised Eric to see a psychiatrist. To my surprise, Eric agreed, provided the visit was kept totally private. I went with him to the consultation in Norfolk. The psychiatrist was a lovely man who assured us that everything was going to be all right.

"Eric had many consultations over a period of about six months and although I didn't really notice any change for the better, I felt happy for the first time in years. I really thought the treatment would work and Eric would be cured. But my optimism was short-lived. At the final consultation, the psychiatrist called us both into his consulting rooms.

"I remember every detail of what he said. 'Squadron Leader Denson,' he said. 'I don't think I have felt so helpless in all my life. I can tell you now. You are not a psychopath, you are not paranoid, you are not a manic depressive and you are not schizophrenic. The truth of the matter is I do not know what is wrong with you. All I do know is that you are suffering very, very deeply. I can see you are in agony. But I cannot do a thing to help you. It is totally beyond my experience...'

"Every word fell like a hammer blow. Every word destroyed my hopes and dreams for a 'normal' life. I was devastated. I cried for two days and nights while Eric showed hardly any emotion.

"While I wept, Eric turned his wrath on his fellow officers. He wore a permanent stern expression on his face which struck terror into his subordinates. It wasn't long before Eric's superiors caught on to the fact there was something seriously wrong with him.

"From some of the other wives I learned that discreet inquiries were made about him. It wasn't long before they discovered Eric had had psychiatric treatment. Things happened pretty fast after that. Eric was ordered to take further psychiatric treatment and was immediately posted to RAF Leeming in Lincolnshire. After years flying one of the RAF's most sophisticated aircraft Eric found himself doing what he had always dreaded: flying a desk.

"The psychiatric treatment didn't work and Eric spiralled out of control...as I discovered one morning when I was awoken by a noise in the kitchen of the cottage we were renting.

"I have always been a heavy sleeper, and it took a lot to wake me. But something jerked me awake in the middle of the night. Cutting through the silence was a sound that literally made my hair stand on end. It was a sort of rasping, scraping noise that for some unaccountable reason reminded me of the swishing of a scythe.

"Heart palpitating I stumbled to the top of the stairs; the sound appeared to be coming from the kitchen. Slowly I descended the stairs, every nerve in my body jumping. I looked into the kitchen, and my heart stopped.

"Eric was sitting at the kitchen table, bathed in a shaft of moonlight. He was stark naked, and a trickle of blood ran in a little rivulet down his chest. In his hand, glinting wickedly was a large woodcutter's axe we kept in the garden shed. He was slowly sharpening the axe with a file. The rasp, rasp, rasp of the file was the noise that had awakened me.

"I stood in the doorway, but Eric never looked up, so engrossed was he with the sinister task he had given himself. I stood there for a long time trying to make sense of what was going on. In the end I stammered, 'Eric, darling what on earth are you doing?'

"Eric slowly raised his head; it seemed to take an age before his eyes met mine. Even then I could tell by the blank stare that he hadn't focused on me. He gazed at me for a long time before I finally detected a flicker of recognition.

"At last he spoke. In a matter-of-fact tone, chilling in its normality, he said: 'What am I doing? I woke up and I had the idea that I might quite like to kill you. Then I might kill myself...'

"The horror of what he was doing suddenly left me and was replaced by rage. I rushed over to him and slapped him as hard as I could across the face. As his head jerked backwards, I wrenched the axe from his grasp and threw it into a corner.

"Eric's eyes cleared and he looked at me with surprise. I wanted to hit him again, but he put his head into his hands and began to sob. I let him cry while I struggled to remain calm. Finally he went to the bedroom and slept for 12 hours.

"We never talked of the incident again, but Eric was deteriorating. He began to self-harm. At first it was just small nicks across his wrists and arms. It was enough to draw blood, but not deep enough to sever an artery. When I asked him about it, he merely said he liked to watch the blood flowing. He said it helped keep back the 'dark cloud.'

"By this time I was so used to his miseries, I confess I took it in my stride, even insisting that he always wore long-sleeved shirts to hide the evidence of his disturbing obsession. But as his mental condition worsened, he was no longer able to mask it from his superiors.

"After many interviews with his commanding officers and several visits to doctors, Eric was prevailed upon to leave his beloved RAF. But as feared, it only served to hasten his descent into darkness.

"He got a job as a commercial pilot. He was getting paid more than what he had been getting from the RAF, so our circumstances improved. We moved into a pretty cottage near Oxford and tried to settle down.

"It was illusory, of course. The demons were always there, but I had become adept at ignoring them. He became more reckless in his everyday life. He began to drink an awful lot. He was still self-harming, cutting his arms usually, and always wore long-sleeved shirts so no-one at the airline would notice. I did worry about his ability to fly an aircraft, but he dismissed my concerns. As usual I shoved it all to the back of my mind.

But there were some things I couldn't ignore.

"One day I arrived home and noticed an odd smell of burning as I came through the front door. I shouted out, 'What's that awful smell?' But the house was eerily silent. I was suddenly afraid. 'Eric, dear, where are you?' I cried. But there was still no reply.

"I sniffed the air; it really was a foul odour. I checked in the kitchen, but there was nothing on the stove, and no sign of Eric. I went into the living room and looked in the garden. Still no sign. I followed my nose to the foot of the stairs. The vile smell seemed to be coming from the bedroom.

"I ran up the stairs and threw open the bedroom door. Eric was lying on the bed, naked. He turned his head to look at me, but there was no recognition in his eyes. And then quite deliberately he took a lit cigarette and stubbed it out on his chest. To this day I can still hear the sizzle of burning flesh as my husband slowly extinguished the cigarette on his chest which was literally covered with blisters from charred and blackened stubs.

"I ran from the house and just walked for hours. When I returned I told Eric I couldn't take anymore and that I was leaving with the children. We had four by that time. Eric took it surprisingly well.

"By this time he had composed himself and looked as though nothing unusual or untoward had occurred. He told me he understood how I felt, and that there was no need for me to leave. He would go and with that packed a bag and left.

"I cried for hours, but I knew I had reached the end of my tether. It was several weeks before I heard from him again. One of his colleagues rang to say he had booked himself into a psychiatric clinic. He said Eric hadn't been sectioned, but was responding well to treatment.

"I was relieved that he was ok; despite everything I still loved him. As soon as I could I went to visit him. It was a nice place, with fresh flowers in reception and an air of tranquility. A doctor told me Eric was doing well, but like his predecessors, he didn't have a clue what was wrong with him.

"Eric was very calm and we walked in the pretty little garden at the back of the sanatorium. We kept the conversation light; we wanted no shadows. But we both knew the dark cloud that enveloped his brain was still there. After a few days I took him home.

"Death finally took my darling Eric on July 8, 1976. His body was found in Bagley Wood about six miles from our home in Kennington.

"He had bled to death after slashing his wrists as he sat under an oak tree. He left a blood-stained note saying he couldn't take anymore. It was a sad, lonely little death and I shed bitter tears that I hadn't been there to comfort him in his final hours.

"The RAF sent a representative to his funeral, but there was no fly-past, the honour normally afforded to men of his rank. Eric was quietly ignored by the service he had dedicated his life to. It was a humiliation I never forgot."

DID YOU KNOW HE WET THE BED?

Shirley Denson's showdown with the Ministry of Defence took place at the Pensions Appeals Tribunal's headquarters in Procession House, 55, Ludgate Hill, near London's Royal Courts of Justice. Her appeal was set to be heard before a tribunal of three people, a barrister, a medical officer and a retired brigadier who would decide whether Mrs Denson was entitled to a war widow's pension. It was 25 years since her husband died.

Mrs Denson was shown by an usher into a small ante-room near the main body of the court where she would wait for her case to be called.

"She is a tall, striking-looking woman with iron-grey hair and a very straight back. With her smart, expensively-cut navy blue suit and crisp white blouse, Mrs Denson could easily be mistaken for a barrister awaiting a client. A leather briefcase and a copy of that day's *Times* newspaper completed the ultra-cool, very business-like impression she wanted to create. In truth, her clothes had been bought in a charity shop, her briefcase was borrowed from her daughter, and her stomach was doing somersaults.

After a while there was a commotion at the door as the Ministry of Defence team arrived. It consisted of three men, noisy, boisterous, brimful of confidence and all very smartly dressed. Each had an armful of very important looking papers. Mrs Denson's heart sank when she realised these were the people she would have to face at the tribunal.

One of the men, obviously the leader by virtue of his seniority and deference shown by the others, detached himself from the little group and strode across to her. He was very friendly; jolly even. "Ah, Mrs Denson, how very nice to meet you," he enthused. "I've heard a lot about you. Good luck with today."

Mrs Denson felt more at ease. Perhaps it wouldn't be such an ordeal after all. When they were called, she was invited to sit on a single chair directly in front of a long, mahogany conference table where the tribunal sat. The Ministry people, obviously used to the routine, quickly occupied a couple of tables to the side.

They had a considerable number of bulky files and boxes spread before them, and they whispered importantly to each other as they waited for the hearing to begin. Mrs Denson eyed them with some trepidation. Her file of evidence lying forlornly in front of the panel looked positively puny by comparison.

Shirley Denson had been widowed in 1976 and with four young children to bring up, life, to say the least, had been a struggle. Three of her children were in poor health and she had been forced to live in charity accommodation provided for the families of ex-servicemen. It was only recently that she had been advised to apply for a war pension because of the unusual circumstances of her husband Eric's demise and death. Although it hadn't occur to her at the time, Mrs Denson now believed there was a link with her husband's Christmas Island experience and his death.

She thought the least the Government owed her was a decent pension, and was indignant when the Ministry of Defence rejected her application out of hand insisting her husband's death had not been 'service related.' Mrs Denson had appealed. The tribunal was now sitting to hear the evidence and decide who was right.

The chairwoman, a middle-aged barrister, started the proceedings by explaining that although the tribunal had all the powers of a legal court, every effort was made to make it as informal as possible.

The man from the ministry stood up, bowed and in a chummy 'we know what it's all about voice' averred that that suited his team fine. The chairwoman ignored him. Turning her full attention to Mrs Denson she enquired if she was comfortable and would she like something, a glass of water perhaps? Mrs Denson felt that perhaps the panel was on her side.

The chairwoman switched her attention to Mrs Denson's bundle of evidence. She explained the tribunal had already studied the dossier and were fully conversant with its contents. "If you have no objection, Mrs Denson, we'd like to ask the men from the ministry what they have to say about it…"

Mrs Denson said she didn't mind.

The man from the ministry rose. Without preamble he said: "Mrs Denson. Are you aware that your late husband suffered from childhood nocturnal enuresis, which is bed-wetting to you and me?"

Shirley Denson gasped. She had expected them to challenge her appeal on the grounds her late husband's depressive illness had nothing to do with his duties at Christmas Island. But this? This was beneath contempt.

She took a long look at her inquisitor and noted he held in his hands a bundle of medical notes, doubtless containing evidence of her late husband's childhood bed-wetting.

Mrs Denson breathed deeply, but before she could say anything, the chairwoman interposed sharply. With a withering glance at the man from the ministry, she said: "Whatever your reasons, I strongly advise you not to go down *that* road. Do I make myself understood?"

The man nodded and shuffled his papers awkwardly. He had a lot of papers: two box files, in fact. He selected another bundle, but before he could speak he was stopped in his tracks by the formidable chairwoman: "I have one question to ask of you. Is it true that Squadron Leader Denson was *ordered* to fly through the mushroom cloud to collect samples of radioactive material at Christmas Island on April 28th, 1958?"

The man from the ministry looked at his papers. He looked at the panel. He looked at his feet and cleared his throat. Finally he said: "Yes, Ma'am."

"Thank you," the chairwoman said dismissively. "I don't think we need trouble you further." The man sat down, looking decidedly sheepish.

Despite the intervention, Mrs Denson was not about to allow the ministry people to get away with even suggesting her husband had psychological problems before joining the RAF, which was clearly why they had delved so far into his past. With the panel's permission she told them about her husband.

Eric Denson had applied to be a flight cadet with the Royal Air Force in 1952, and was subsequently invited to a rigorous selection procedure, a four-week course. He was passed as being suitable and was accepted as a flight cadet. He completed two years of intensive training. He was placed under constant scrutiny. Those showing any psychological flaws or weakness were ruthlessly weeded out. Only a small number of entrants were accepted, her husband being one of them. He 'passed out' with his wings as a fully-fledged pilot officer in the spring of 1954. Mrs Denson strongly emphasised the point that her husband when accepted into the RAF was 100 per cent fit, both physically and mentally.

Mrs Denson turned to the matter of her husband's involvement in the bomb tests. She told how he was sent out to Christmas Island under conditions of top secrecy and was expected to spend at least a year there. Then there was his abrupt return home after only a few months, and how he had changed. She told them of the strange rash on his chest, breathing problems, allergies, mood swings and restlessness. And he appeared to have undergone a dramatic personality change.

Her husband's mental state deteriorated as the years went by. But not once did Mrs Denson link it with his involvement with the bomb tests. It was only some years after he died that she came across some authoritative research from America which suggested strongly that people exposed to radiation could undergo profound psychological changes. Mrs Denson reminded the panel that she had included this research in her statement of claim.

The chairwoman looked puzzled and conferred with her colleagues. Finally she said they were unable to find this research and could Mrs Denson show them where it was included?

Mrs Denson went through the paperwork with a rising sense of panic: it didn't appear to be there. As a matter of routine, all Mrs Denson's evidence had been sent to the Pensions Agency headquarters in Blackpool where it had been typed and prepared for scrutiny by the tribunal. But the vital evidence didn't appear to be there.

She looked helplessly at the chairwoman who eventually called for a 15-minute recess. Mrs Denson went through her documents again, but with no success. The chairwoman said she had no choice but to adjourn the hearing to a later date, to give Mrs Denson an opportunity to find the missing material.

Then she did a strange thing. Leaning forward, she looked Mrs Denson straight in the eye and told her: "When you receive notification about the date of your next hearing you must insist on the same tribunal members as are sitting here today...and no-one else." The chairwoman repeated this, "...so no-one could be in any doubt."

Mrs Denson was mystified. A clear message had been imparted to her, but she was uncertain what it meant. She went home, her mind in turmoil. Was the chairwoman suggesting that she and the other tribunal members were the only ones that could be trusted? And if so, why?

She had been warned several times of suspicions that pension tribunals were routinely "rigged", especially in matters relating to Britain's nuclear tests. She'd never really believed them, but now she wasn't sure. Luckily she was able to get a copy of the missing research and immediately informed the Appeal Court.

Three weeks later, she received a letter from no less a person than the President of the Appeal Court offering a date for the new hearing. Astonishingly he announced that he, personally, would sit as chairman.

Mrs Denson, mindful of the warning she had been given, wrote back rejecting the president's offer and insisting that the tribunal members who had sat previously on her case, be reconvened. By return of post she received a curt reply informing her that her request could take several months because the three people she wanted were, "very busy people." Mrs Denson informed the president she was quite prepared to wait.

A month later, Mrs Denson received a letter from the Pensions Agency. To her utter astonishment she was informed she had been awarded a full war widow's pension --- and it had been back-dated from the time she had first made her application. A phone call to the agency confirmed the award. The appeal hearing had apparently gone ahead in her absence and had come down in her favour.

At first Mrs Denson was delighted. But one thing concerned her: the reason given for the award stated that Squadron Leader Denson's death had been marked down as "attributable to service." This was far too vague for Mrs Denson's liking. She wrote back asking for the wording to be changed to, "attributable to radiation exposure in service." By return post, Mrs Denson was told the wording could not be changed. The tone of the letter left no doubt that as far as the Agency was concerned, the matter was closed.

If the "powers that be" thought that would be an end to the matter, they seriously underestimated Shirley Denson. All her life she had been a patriot. She believed absolutely in the British sense of justice and fair play. She had loved her husband and had always been immensely proud of him As far as she was concerned he was in the same mould as 'the few', the brave pilots who had defended Britain in World War II. Now she felt he had been betrayed by the country he gave his life for. She made a pledge there and then not to rest until the truth was told.

REVELATIONS

It was 30 years before the burgeoning scandal of the victims of British nuclear bomb testing burst on the public consciousness.

It started with a simple letter to a local newspaper in 1983 from Ken McGinley a former private in the royal engineers who had spent a year on Christmas Island in 1958. McGinley had vivid memories of Grapple Y, but at that time he had no idea of its significance; to him it was just another bomb test.

For a long time he had suffered flashbacks of the time he woke up in his tent to find himself covered in large blisters. Later his stomach ruptured and he coughed up blood for days. He reported to the sick bay and was told he had an ulcer. He was just 20 years old.

McGinley was later discharged from the army and returned home to Johnstone, west of Glasgow. He hailed from a staunchly Catholic working class family and was soon absorbed back into the close-knit community where he grew up. Alice, his childhood sweetheart with whom he had corresponded throughout his tenure on Christmas Island was waiting for him.

They married and the couple looked forward to starting a family. Unfortunately it was not to be. After tests Mr McGinley was told he was impotent. When he asked 'why?' a doctor examined his notes and told him cryptically: "You'll rue the day you ever stepped foot on Christmas Island..." He would not elaborate, and the McGinley's were too upset for questions.

It was a bitter blow, but the couple settled down to a more or less normal life. McGinley obtained various jobs, mainly as an administrator and book-keeper and the couple saved enough money to open a small guesthouse. It was a good life, living in their little B&B in the picturesque town of Dunoon nestling on the banks of the Clyde, a couple of miles from Holy Loch. At the time Holy Loch was home to a large United States nuclear submarine base. The business prospered, with a large proportion of the guests being US Navy personnel.

The McGinley's got on well with the Americans, and they were frequently asked to attend dances and other functions at the naval base. They became honorary members of the Sergeants Club, the social hub of the base where the dollar was the currency and US law prevailed.

Ken and Alice, like most Scots, remained close to their family roots and made frequent trips back across the Clyde to Johnstone to catch up with relatives and friends. It was on one of these trips that Ken met the mother of an old school pal who had joined the Army at the same time as him. He was shocked to learn his friend had died.

Cancer had taken him at the age of just 32. She told him her son had also been sent to Christmas Island to witness the bomb tests and came back very sick; he never recovered, she said. The woman went on to tell him there were four or five other young 'Johnstone boys' who had returned from Christmas Island with incurable cancers.

McGinley was consumed by curiosity and decided to track the families down. He was shocked by what he discovered: there were at least eight other local lads all sent to Christmas Island at about the same time. Three had died, while the others were suffering chronic illnesses.

Thoroughly intrigued, McGinley contacted the letters page of *Daily Record* newspaper asking anyone who had been to Christmas Island at the time of the bomb tests to contact him. A sharp-eyed news editor recognised a potential scoop and dispatched a reporter to interview him.

The subsequent story, spread over two pages of the newspaper, caused a sensation. Scores of men from Scotland contacted the newspaper complaining of cancers and other illnesses. They had all been out to the Pacific and witnessed nuclear bomb testing.

The story was picked up by newspapers and TV stations in the rest of the UK, and it was soon apparent that a hornet's nest had been kicked over. The wires and the ether buzzed with hundreds, then thousands of complaints from every corner of the UK.

Over and over again the story was told: the men recalled how they had been lined up with nothing but shorts, sandals and coconut palms for protection, while gigantic bombs were exploded scarce miles away. They talked of an intense light in which they could see the bones of their fingers through clenched fists; they told of an unbearable heat, huge blast waves and towering mushroom clouds.

And then, of course, there were the health consequences. The sheer numbers of ex-servicemen now complaining of illness was translated into a wave of protest which swept the country finally, washing up in Whitehall and Downing Street. The Thatcher Government had to do something to stem the flow.

Ministry of Defence mandarins stalled for time and commissioned the National Radiological Protection Board, a quasi-official nuclear watchdog agency, to look into the men's claims. Sir Richard Doll, an eminent epidemiologist, was chosen to head the study team. The research would take two years, he said, adding that everyone should just calm down and wait for the results.

McGinley wasn't about to wait two years or even a single day. He was a man in a hurry, and with a mission. By now, the quiet book-keeper had morphed into a full-blown, anti-nuclear campaigner, becoming something of an international celebrity into the bargain.

He was a media 'natural', quick-witted and always ready with a newsworthy quote. McGinley found he was in demand from TV stations, newspapers and other media outlets from all over the world. Greenpeace, the international environment group, recognised his propaganda value and whisked him off on a whistle-stop tour of the United States.

These were heady and exciting days for McGinley, and he embraced his destiny with all the fervour of the true convert.

In the New Mexico desert, at the site of the world's first atomic bomb blast, he defied a phalanx of armed soldiers guarding the Trinity site at Alamogordo as he railed against nuclear imperialism. On the Yucca Flats and in the Utah desert, (accompanied by an ever-growing media pack) he spoke with the 'Down-winders', a vociferous community of farming folk who believed they were cursed by radiation from the hundreds of atomic bomb tests the US carried out a few miles from their homes.

He later met with Loretta King, the outspoken widow of the peace campaigner Martin Luther King, and even had a meeting with John Wayne's widow Pilar who was convinced the great screen cowboy had died as a result of making the movie, The Conqueror, on location in Nevada, downwind from the bomb tests in 1956.

McGinley rounded off his triumphal six-week tour with a peace rally near the Lincoln Memorial and a personal meeting in Washington with Senator Edward Kennedy, and other members of the famous political dynasty.

Returning home he threw himself into a whirlwind round of meetings with MPs, doctors, peace campaigners and various anti-nuclear groups as he pushed the profile of his army of nuclear veterans ever higher up the political agenda. As the pressure mounted, the opposition Labour Party seized the initiative and launched a spirited attack on the Government in the House of Commons. A Private Members Bill brought by a

North East MP called Bob Clay, gained support from both Tory and Labour members and looked set to hand a famous victory to McGinley and his veterans.

But the hand of the all-powerful Ministry of Defence reached into the political bear pit and activated a caucus of Tory MPs with historical links to the armed forces. Amid a cacophony of protest from the Labour benches, several MPs took turns to pour scorn on the proposed Bill.

They said all the evidence showed that no serviceman had been harmed at the bomb tests. They conjured every conceivable excuse. Each point was talked about in minute detail in a classic filibuster manoeuvre; the debate descended into farce. Despite outraged protests the Speaker announced he had no option but to call 'time out' and the Bill failed.

McGinley and a contingent of nuclear veterans watched the proceedings from their vantage point in the public gallery. As the House rose for the night, McGinley stared down at the MPs who had so cynically scuttled the veterans' chance of justice. One of the MPs, an Eton educated son of a former Army General, met McGinley's eyes. The two gazed at each other across the chasm, and for the first time McGinley realised the extent of the uphill fight he faced.

McGinley, his faith in the democratic process shredded, determined to carry on the fight with renewed vigour. He resumed his travels the length and breadth of the country attending inquests, public meetings, inquiries and pension tribunals.

At home he burned the midnight oil compiling and tabulating medical and service records of the three thousand-plus nuclear veterans that had now joined his protest campaign. His book-keeping skills were brought to good use for this work, and he kept detailed records of every member.

Even a cursory examination of these records revealed evidence that the rates of cancers among test participants were far higher than was normal. Several illustrious scientists including Alice Stewart from Birmingham University who discovered the dangers of X-rays on unborn children agreed and piled on the pressure for official action.

While the scientists and the politicians argued, disturbing new allegations added to the feverish atmosphere. Newly-discovered government documents suggested nuclear servicemen were deliberately used as 'guinea pigs' to see what the effects the bombs would have on them. These claims opened up a whole new territory for McGinley and his veterans to exploit.

NUCLEAR GUINEA PIGS

Were servicemen deliberately exposed to radiation for the purposes of scientific experimentation? It is a question that has been bitterly argued about for decades. It all started with the release in 1983 of a 'Top Secret' document from the government's Defence Research Policy Committee, dated May 20, 1953, which contained the statement:-

The army must discover the detailed effects of various types of explosion on equipment, stores and men with and without various types of protection.

This oft-quoted document was clear proof, according to McGinley and his supporters that servicemen had been used as human guinea pigs during the atomic tests.

The government disagreed, arguing that dummies in various uniforms had been used to test the effects and it was wrong to suggest that men had been used as laboratory animals.

At first the government line held sway as historian Lorna Arnold and others with privileged access to government archives provided supporting evidence in the form of photographs which showed that dummies had been placed strategically on the firing ranges.

Armed with this information, the Ministry of Defence went on the attack. Supporters in parliament spoke of their 'utter conviction' that the twenty thousand servicemen at the bomb tests were not exposed to any danger whatsoever.

Statement after statement declared no British troops received a measurable radiation dose; British troops were not affected by blast or heat; British troops were stationed so far away from the blasts that they stood more chance of getting a radiation dose sitting at home in England than on the bomb sites in the Pacific. They made witnessing a nuclear bomb test sound like a routine training exercise.

Curiously, the other nuclear weapon nations took a different view. They openly admitted that men were, indeed, deliberately exposed to see how troops would react in battlefield conditions during a nuclear war. They saw it as a patriotic duty for their men to be shown in the frontline of a nuclear attack.

Photographs and newsreels were released of soldiers marching through fallout, and even charging through ground zero within seconds of the explosions. American GIs were pictured unfurling the Stars and Stripes in nuclear bomb craters, and Soviet Special Forces were depicted parachuting from aircraft flying through the mushroom clouds. The Chinese used the novel approach of dispatching 100 sword-brandishing horsemen in a cavalry charge toward the towering explosions.

The British government remained in denial even though more declassified documents emerged from the Public Records office at Kew Gardens declaring that servicemen were indeed used to study the effects of blast and fallout.

One particular document set out in graphic detail how at least 250 servicemen were ordered into positions, some just two miles from an atomic explosion.

The report refers to a series of tests, codenamed Buffalo, at Maralinga in 1956. Headed "Indoctrination of Service Personnel," it tells of a plan to use servicemen in an experiment to 'discover the effects of atomic weapons.' Detailed planning arrangements are discussed, including the problems of transporting the 'indoctrinees' to the bomb sites and how they would be deployed once they got there.

Lectures and general instruction were to be given the men, and there were to be conducted tours of the range areas prior to the explosions. When the big moment came, the men were taken to between two and four miles from the blast and 'exposed to flash, heat and blast effects.' What protection the luckless indoctrinees were to be given during this stage of the operation is not made clear.

Later the servicemen were required to pass through a health control unit and don protective clothing to enter the contaminated areas. On their return the men passed through decontamination centres and finally underwent monitoring by doctors.

After their 'indoctrination' the men were to be dispersed back to their units. No official records have yet been released to indicate what happened to these men. A few of the survivors, however, emerged in the mid-1980s to tell their stories.

Under oath, Colonel Peter Anthony Lowe of the Royal Horse Artillery, told an Australian royal commission how he had been stationed in Munster, West Germany, when he got a phone call from his commanding officer.

His statement read: "The phone call came out of the blue and he asked me if I would like to go on a trip to Australia for three weeks. I said that of course I would. Within a few days I had discovered from talking with fellow officers that there were atomic trials in the offing and observers were required."

Colonel Lowe was sent to the proving grounds at Maralinga and watched an explosion from a hillside about five miles from ground zero. Later he went into the target area wearing gas masks, boots and protective clothing. He recalled he did not suffer undue trauma from his first encounter with an atomic explosion.

The second was different: "I observed the second blast stationed in a closed down tank. This was very scary indeed. I do not know exactly how far the tank was from ground zero, but the blast moved the tank about ten feet sideways. I was watching through a periscope and it went opaque straight away because of the sand blasting effect which ruined the optics. For this exercise I was wearing ordinary military gear with no film badge. After a decent interval I was told to evacuate the tank and return by truck to the camp."

Colonel Lowe suffered serious health consequences which he blamed on his atomic experiences. He developed duodenal ulcers soon after returning home and then he contracted cancer which required his stomach to be removed.

The Australian Royal Commission threw up many similar examples. It heard how servicemen were deliberately exposed to radiation by being ordered to 'crawl, lie, walk and run' in radioactive dust after each nuclear test. The purpose of this was not explained to the hundreds of men involved. Admittedly, much of this evidence was anecdotal, but the sheer number of veterans who came forward to tell similar stories was compelling.

Other experiments were more clinical in their use of servicemen as human guinea pigs during the bomb tests. One of these included the deliberate blinding of 'volunteers' during an A-bomb test in 1956. A secret document, written by a Captain C.D.B Bridges of the Royal Army Medical Corps, discusses the 'visual incapacity in human beings following exposure to a nuclear explosion.'

Bridges reports that rabbits could be blinded by a nuclear explosion 42 miles away and that scientists had calculated that human beings would receive burns to their eyes at comparable distances. Bridges goes on to report exactly what happened to three of these servicemen:-

Case 1: In daylight, he viewed the latter part of the flash from a distance of six miles from an atomic weapon. The left eye viewed through the optical system of a camera, the right eye viewed it directly through the open window. There was immediate dazzle, blurring and haziness. Extreme photophobia developed later.

Case 2: The left eye was covered and the patient viewed the flash with his right eye from a distance of five miles. He was blinded for 15 seconds, and had only a hazy view of his instruments after 25 seconds. This lasted for 8-10 minutes. Seven months later a paracentral scotoma was found in the upper temporal quadrant of the right visual field.

Case 3: The patient viewed the explosion with both eyes from a distance of 10 miles. Subjective visual difficulties lasted for five minutes. Five days later a paracentral scotoma was found in the left eye. A blanched area was found nasel to the fovea, adjacent to the branch of the inferior temporal artery leading to the paramacular area. The artery appeared blocked, and was bloodless distal to the lesion. The area was surrounded by oedema, although this disappeared after about one month.'

What all this means, of course, is that the unfortunate victims of this experiment suffered varying degrees of blindness after being ordered to gaze upon a nuclear fireball. It is interesting to note the use of the word 'patient' in the context of the experiment and also the fact that medical examinations were carried out upon them many months after the event. It would be harder to imagine a clearer definition of the term 'human guinea pig.'

The Royal Navy was also playing its part in finding out the effects of radiation on men and equipment. And as befits the 'senior service', it did it in a big way.

In early 1956, HMS Diana, a Daring class destroyer slipped its moorings and set sail for the Indian ocean. She was bound for the Monte Bello islands off the Australian coast where Britain's first atomic bomb was exploded four years earlier

She was to take part in two atomic experiments and her mission was top secret and potentially deadly. Diana was fated to be the first manned warship to deliberately steam through the radioactive cloud created by an atomic bomb.

Her 278 officers and crew had been fully briefed about the purpose of the mission. Before departing, her crew underwent special training in radiological warfare. They had been issued with protective clothing and for weeks they had trained in tight security in a huge warehouse near Devonport dockyard.

The training consisted of putting the men through a series of obstacle courses that had been 'mined' with quantities of radioactive isotopes. Each man was issued with a Geiger counter, and he was required to detect and mark 'hot spots'. All the time clouds of steam and smoke were blown across the course to simulate battlefield conditions.

While all this was going on, HMS Diana was also being well prepared for the rigours that lay ahead. She had been fitted with powerful pump and sprinkler systems, and she bristled with air filters and scientific measuring equipment.

Diana arrived at the Monte Bello islands on May 2nd, 1956 and took up position five miles from Trimouille Island, the main one in the group, where the tower-mounted bomb was to be exploded. There followed a series of exercises to ensure the men were ready and the ships equipment was in working order.

One administrative record reveals it was decided not to issue film badges, used for detecting radiation exposure, to the ship's company. This was a curious decision given the ship was soon to be enveloped in a radioactive cloud. It was even more puzzling when the same records showed that little was done to protect the crew from contamination.

A scientist, who boarded the ship on May 3rd reported: "Originally it was intended to have the ship shut down all the time during the fall-out, but present information on the length of time they may be in the fall-out zone makes it impossible to do this. In order to open up, certain personnel have to leave the Citadel, go out into the open and return to cover."

The scientist thought this operation could be carried out quite safely using protective clothing. But he warned: "Complete protection of the personnel in the engine room is more difficult to arrange since it is difficult to assess the hazard involved." It is clear from this that scientists fully expected radiation to enter parts of the ship, making the decision not to issue film badges even more incomprehensible.

When the bomb was detonated, the entire ship's complement was on deck to see the fireworks. About 30 of them were mere boys, cadets, aged just 15.

John Kay was an 18-yr-old national service seaman, on board at the time. He recalled: "I was badly frightened, but not surprisingly these boy sailors were more terrified than anyone when the bomb went off. I was thrown onto my face by the force of the blast. The whole ship rocked and I knew we must be very close to the explosion. Men were groaning all around me and the young kids were crying as we scrambled round the deck. My first thought was that something had gone wrong.

"Suddenly the battle stations were called and we a great sense of relief we scrambled down the hatches which were then tightly battened down. We stayed below for hours as the ship zigzagged to stay in the fallout. It was very hot and claustrophobic. I remember officers constantly checking instruments for radiation. At one point there was a high-pitched alarm indicating the instrument readings were too high. It was very unnerving."

According to other accounts, men in the engine room, even those wearing protective gear, had to be evacuated, because of high radiation counts. As the men quavered below, scientists in 'moon suits' moved from compartment to compartment checking radiation levels. Several areas were evacuated. Above, a deadly radioactive rain poured down onto the decks as Diana doggedly tracked the mushroom cloud.

The second phase of the experiment began when Diana emerged from the mushroom cloud. Wash-down parties were ordered on to the decks where a thick layer of contaminated coral dust had accumulated. Mr Kay, who had been 'volunteered', was one of the first out of the hatches.

He said: "We were dressed in black capes with hoods attached. I remember it was very overcast and there was an eerie purple and yellow glow in the sky. Our first job was to remove some canvas coverings from the deck. We worked in silence and it was very scary to see the other men moving about in this weird light looking like big black bats. There was dust everywhere and the sprinklers were going full blast. At one stage my hood came off and I was immediately ordered to the decontamination unit. One of the scientists put a Geiger counter to my head and it started to buzz like crazy. I spent three hours in the showers after that."

After several hours swabbing the decks, Diana finally returned to her mooring to await a repeat of the whole operation, this time with an even bigger bomb, in a month's time. After that Diana was ordered to steam home, but was refused docking facilities at Fremantle near Perth because the Australians didn't want the 'ship of doom' on their doorstep.

To make matters worse many men began reporting sick. This was not uncommon on long voyages, but the sheer numbers was soon causing concern.

Former crewman Doug Atkinson was an orderly in the sick bay. He recalled: "At first there was just a trickle of men complaining of boils and sores, not that unusual. Then more and more began to be brought down. The sick bays were soon full. Lots of men now had terrible sores and were passing blood. The medics were rushed off their feet and the officers were worried. They tried to keep spirits up, but a lot of men began to blame the bomb tests."

As rumours about radiation poisoning swept the destroyer, Diana, like a mediaeval plague ship, made full speed for home. Unfortunately, the Gods seem to have deserted Diana. When she reached Aden she found herself marooned for weeks because of the Suez crisis.

In recent years strenuous efforts have been made to trace the 278 crew members on Board Diana at the time. But very few have been found despite extensive publicity in naval magazines and other publications. Most of those found reported sicknesses.

Doug Atkinson suffered spinal disintegration and was confined to a wheelchair. He had a whole body scan at Exeter University to measure radiation in his body. Instead of an average reading of 137, his scan showed a reading of five thousand-plus. Doctors were amazed. He was told that according to the readings he should have glowed in the dark.

Diana's navigating officer, Lt Commander M.W. Butler died of cancer in 1975. His widow Sheila, of Liskeard, Cornwall, said: "It was a horrible death. My husband was taken from me at the age of 49. But he would never say anything against the Navy. He felt it unseemly for an officer. But he did admit to me once that there had been very little safety precautions to protect the men."

Margaret Rogers, a Diana widow who had remarried, said her sailor husband John Furlong, died of cancer in 1981. Mrs Rogers of Lanarkstown, Glasgow, said: "John always said he had been affected by the tests, but no-one really believed him. Only when all the publicity came out in 1983, did people finally believe him. Of course it was too late then."

The Diana incident has never been disputed. Government ministers who have commented on it tended to dismiss it as a one-off experiment on a fully battened down warship with all possible safety precautions in place to protect the men. But three years before Diana steamed into her nuclear fate, another experiment involving a Royal Naval ship and radioactive dust took place just 50 miles off the British coast.

In August 1953, the frigate HMS Starling prepared to leave Portsmouth harbour for what was understood to be a routine dummy anchorage exercise. Everything appeared normal to the crew as they went about their duties. They had carried out similar exercises on many occasions and they had no reason to suspect that anything was different. No new equipment had been taken on board and the officers had not indicated that anything was out of the ordinary.

But about an hour before Starling was due to cast off, a large grey van pulled up alongside the frigate and several men in thick overalls carried aboard a large sealed container. This excited little curiosity from the crew who believed the container was carrying more supplies. Considerable interest was aroused, however, when a large black limousine carrying a group of civilians drew up alongside. The men, dressed in Trilbies and Macintoshes, quietly boarded the Starling which then headed into the Atlantic.

The ship's grapevine soon identified the mysterious civilians who were berthed with the captain and were rarely seen. It was the famous scientist Sir William Penney and his entourage. What was he doing aboard Starling? Had he brought an atom bomb on board? The men were agog with excitement.

The ship eventually anchored about 50 miles off the North West coast of Scotland. It was a bright, sunny day and most of the crew where on deck. Able seaman Harold Brown and several others were taken to one side and told by an officer they had been assigned some special duties. They were told the ship was about to be bombarded with 'a spot' of radioactive dust and they would be required to wash the decks after the experiment was over.

Recalling the incident, Mr Brown said: "It was said very matter-of-factly and we were assured there was absolutely no danger involved. Being young I wasn't at all worried. I do remember feeling peeved because of the extra duties, but like the rest of the men I was trained not to question orders."

Soon the men were ordered below deck and the hatches were sealed. As they waited, the heavy rumbling sound of an aircraft flying low was heard. About 30 minutes later, Mr Brown and the other 'volunteers' were taken up on deck.

They were given no special clothing to wear and Mr Brown got a soaking from the ship's sprinkler system which was going full blast. The first thing he noticed was that the decks were covered with a peculiar red-brown dust flecked with grey. Mops and brushes were pushed into their hands and the men got to work swabbing the decks.

Mr Brown said: "This red-brown dust was everywhere and we had to use heavy cotton-wool swabs to remove it from the rails and brass fittings. We were on deck for at least two hours trying to get rid of it all."

When that was over, the second phase of the experiment took place. The sealed container that had been carried aboard earlier was brought up to the deck. Inside was a mass of dust similar in texture to what had already been washed off the decks. As the men gathered curiously round, large cans of battleship grey paint known as 'pussers' was carefully mixed into the radioactive dust.

Mr Brown and his mates were ordered to paint the sides of the ship and the lifeboats with the contaminated mix. Most of the men were brought up on deck for this phase of the operation.

When Starling returned to Portsmouth she did not dock at her usual berth; she was taken to a special dock, well away from the main berths, and covered with canvas. Sprinklers and hoses were played on her for days. Oddly the ship's log for the period was missing when researchers visited the Public Records Office at Kew to try to verify Mr Brown's story. The Navy wouldn't acknowledge the experiment took place.

It goes without saying that the idea of the Navy carrying out a large scale radiation experiment just off the British coast would have caused widespread public alarm. Using young sailors to splash radioactive paint all over the decks shows a criminal disregard for their safety.

Mr Brown was discharged from the Navy on medical grounds two years later. In 1984, he was a very sick man and knew he didn't have much longer to live. He contacted the Ministry of Defence to ask for a pension so his wife could be looked after once he had gone. It was suggested he had made the whole matter up and was turned down flat. He died in agony some time after that. His widow Susan penned an eloquent eulogy which speaks for itself:-

"My husband was AB Harold Brown DJX566143 RN, and very proud of it. He joined the Navy as a boy of 16. He travelled the seven seas, was attached to the Royal Indian Navy for a while and was in various campaigns including Cyprus. He has three medals for serving his country; he also has a false leg and almost six feet of plastic arteries. He suffered intravascular muscle spasms, had several strokes, skin that erupted for no reason and two heart attacks. Both his eyes had cataracts; he had spondylosis of the spine, and also had to wear a hearing aid. But in July 1953 he was a hale and hearty healthy man, not impotent as he was at 40, with a zest and vim for life. That experiment he was involved with destroyed him completely. But do they care? I think everyone knows the answer."

HUMAN EXPERIMENTS

Radiation experiments on troops carried out in controlled conditions is one thing. But the secret world of nuclear weapons has an even more awful second agenda; evidence of long-standing sinister secrets buried deep in official archives that will never be opened to public consumption. Horrifying eyewitness testimonies, impossible to dismiss, tell of obscene experiments on crippled human beings plucked from asylums and psychiatric wards, and placed alongside animal test subjects near ground zero for the purposes of scientific experimentation.

Stories began to emerge of atrocities in the Australian outback in the early 1980s during British nuclear tests. Four test participants alleged that mentally handicapped people were deliberately brought close to atomic explosions for a series of experiments.

One of the Australian servicemen stated under oath: "The handicapped people were brought to One Tree, where one of the bombs was to be detonated in Maralinga, for the first of the Buffalo series of tests. One lot came into the rail sidings at Watson, another lot were brought in by air. They were kept in a special area off the main road. You couldn't see them, but you could hear them: the unearthly babble that mental patients make. After the test you couldn't hear them anymore."

The claims made in a Royal Commission hearing couldn't be substantiated at the time, but compelling confirmation came 16 years later, in June 2001, when a pilot confessed to an academic that he flew severely disabled people from institutions in Britain to the Australian desert.

According to the pilot the patients were deliberately exposed to radioactive fall-out at Maralinga in the 1950s. They did not return home and are assumed to have died. The pilot related his story to Dr Robert Jackson, a respected Australian academic at Edith Cowan University in Perth. The conversation took place after Dr Jackson gave a presentation to staff during which he mentioned the allegations about radiation experiments. The man told him: "That was true. I was one of the pilots, and we didn't fly them out again."

Dr Jackson closely questioned the man, who had become a disabled care worker, and had no doubt he was telling the truth. He said: "I was quite convinced. The man said there was no doubt the people were used as guinea pigs. They had multiple disabilities, both physical and mental. His story is quite credible when you consider the prevailing view at the time about mentally handicapped people. A lot of people believed they were a sub-human and deserved to be euthanized."

Dr Jackson said he had also heard another shocking account of handicapped people being used for experiments at the Monte Bello islands when the two A-bombs were detonated in 1956.

At least two men with Downs' syndrome were allegedly taken ashore with scientists and placed in a bunker near ground zero. The academic admitted he had no corroborative evidence to support these claims, but at least one independent eyewitness, under oath, recounted a disturbing incident he was involved with at the two tests, code-named Mosaic.

Bernard Perkins was a radio operator on the scientific vessel Narvik when the second device, equivalent to eight Hiroshima bombs, was detonated. It sent a radioactive cloud over the mainland.

Perkins was busy all day sending dispatches from air crew who flew through the mushroom cloud to collect samples. Later the ship moved closer inshore ready to pick up scientists who had been left in bunkers on the islands.

Rumours swept the ship that the fireball from the explosion finished very close to one of the bunkers. Another rumour was that there were several "retards" with the scientists.

Mr Perkins recalled in a statement: "I saw with my own eyes the scientists being brought back to the ship. I stood on the upper deck watching it with another man whose name I cannot now remember. A motor boat came toward us. There were two men with protective clothing on, and five or six others all of whom had blankets wrapped around them looking as though they were in shock. They were brought to the ship's side and came up the gangplank and had to be helped aboard. Nobody saw them again. I believe they were taken from the ship at night. To the best of my recollection they were wearing sandals, khaki shirts, stockings and shorts with no headgear."

Were these the "retards", the handicapped people, Dr Jackson had been told about? Fantastic as it may seem, similar allegations began to emerge from America.

Bob Carter was an ex-serviceman who took part in an exercise which included the explosion of a 74 kiloton atomic bomb in the Nevada desert in 1957. He described how, when moving into the ground zero area as part of manoeuvres after the explosion, he saw human test subjects handcuffed behind fenced enclosures. When he told his superiors, Carter claims he was given an unpleasant drug treatment and after a prolonged period in an isolated ward was then brought before a military panel and told to repeat his 'bizarre' story. By then Carter had learned to remain silent.

Other disturbing stories were soon to follow. A news organization in Santa Fe reported interviews with three former servicemen who were present during a 1955 series of tests known as Teapot. These men were members of the 232nd Signal Support Company and had positioned themselves far forward of other troops and occupied a slit trench near ground zero. Their job was to position and bury field telephone lines to establish how battlefield communications would function in a nuclear war. The three men camped overnight but were woken at about 2am by a truck which passed their position and stopped a hundred yards ahead.

A 19-yr-old G.I. called Jim O'Connor said that he watched as people, in civilian clothing, were placed in above ground (not dug-out), Korean War-style trenches. Later the remainder of the 232nd joined O'Connor in his trench, which was 3,500 yards from ground zero, to experience the explosion which had the destructive power of three Hiroshima bombs.

But two hours before the detonation one of the main cables to the main camp at Desert Rock malfunctioned and O'Connor and two others went out to investigate. One of the men went forward to the bomb tower and returned looking shaken. He told his buddies he'd seen a 'bunch of weirdoes' close to the tower-mounted bomb, tethered alongside dogs and sheep. Close by was an unconnected plastic covered terminal box and a remote-control camera positioned about 60 yards away, its lens pointing toward the bunker's centre.

O'Connor never really thought about the story until after the detonation when he was required to brave the radioactive dust storm to make his way to a field telephone 1,000 yards ahead. As he rounded a sandbank wall which sheltered a trench and a bench, he made a terrifying discovery. He is quoted as saying: "A guy had crawled behind the bunker, his face full of blood from his nose and mouth."

The corporal claimed that wires were attached to the man. He recalled: "I smelled burning flesh. I knew the smell all too well. In Korea, the South Koreans disposed of their dead by burning them in barrels. As in the case of Bob Carter, O'Connor soon learned not to talk about what he had seen after he was taken to a base where he was shown an endless stream of propaganda films; ten straight days of how the bomb hurts "them -- not us."

He said: "The movies started with quick flashes of Mickey Mouse, Tojo, Donald Duck, Hitler, someone's mother, then Hiroshima..."But when he asked about the writhing man he had seen near ground zero, he was ignored. Surprisingly candid, or deliberately vague, the chief spokesman of the US Defence Nuclear Agency told the newspaper: "We can neither confirm nor deny Mr O'Connor's allegations."

Stories like this abounded among the 250,000 American servicemen who took part in nuclear weapon tests. And although they were often dismissed as "paranoid ramblings", the US government didn't seem to have any qualms about using their civilian population for the dubious purposes of scientific experimentation.

In 1987 a U.S. Congressman discovered official documents which described grotesque experiments on civilians. In an address to Congress, Representative Edward Markey said his evidence proved that hundreds of Americans were used as nuclear guinea pigs during 30 years of 'Nazi-like' experiments. He said a total of 695 civilians were deliberately contaminated to discover the effects of nuclear radiation.

The experiments, which took place from the late 1940s to the early 1970s, included feeding people milk from irradiated cows and contaminated fish from rivers near discharges from nuclear plants. Hospital patients were deliberately fed radioactive materials, and nuclear waste was placed on patients' hands to see what effect it had on them. In another bizarre experiment 131 prisoners had their testes repeatedly x-rayed to determine the effects on human fertility.

Mr Markey told Congress: "These experiments and others shock the conscience of the nation. They raise one major, horrifying question: did the intense desire to know the consequences of radioactive exposure after the dawn of the atomic age lead American scientists to mimic the kind of demented human experiments conducted by the Nazis?"

In 1994 President Clinton assembled a committee of experts in medicine, ethics and law, to investigate just how far the US Government had been prepared to carry out radiation experiments on human beings. The committee found there occurred thousands of examples, as well as hundreds of cases of deliberate releases of radiation.

America's record of the use of human beings as radiation test subjects has clear parallels with Britain. The Dr Strangelove-type activities show how readily both governments were prepared to use both servicemen and the civilians in their quest for nuclear knowledge.

Karl Morgan, the founder of Health Physics, the discipline which approaches questions of radioactive dose and effects has revealed how both governments shared information on the effects of radiation on the body.

He said they consulted on a daily basis with members of both military and medical establishments. "As the cold war heated up the pressures to keep your mouth shut increased," he said. "A lot of people in the scientific establishment were told that it was unpatriotic and somewhat treasonous to publicly indicate that large numbers of people may be put at risk as a result of these activities."

British scientists unashamedly embraced this philosophy. A raft of declassified documents relating to large-scale experiments on humans was uncovered at the Public Records Office.

One of them referred to an incident in 1953 when scientists at the Windscale nuclear plant in Cumbria deliberately released thyroid cancer-inducing radioactive iodine 131 into the atmosphere with the specific objective of measuring the uptake of the deadly material in the surrounding population.

Under pressure the plant's chief medical officer, Dr Geoffrey Schofield admitted in a statement to the West Cumbrian Health Authority: "It is true that the radioactive release in 1953 was not an accident. It was a deliberate discharge as part of the operations during early nuclear reprocessing under the military program at a time when Britain was preparing its first atomic bombs. There was a need for secrecy as a matter of national security and information about the discharge has only recently been released."

Since this admission the Ministry of Defence has tried to downgrade its significance and importance. Experts connected with the nuclear industry have gone on record to state that the emission was so small as to make it negligible. These placatory statements were made in the face of further discoveries that children and animals near the plant had been poisoned with iodine in the weeks following the "controlled emission."

But these assurances were exposed as yet another cold war lie when a document referring to the incident came to light. In plain and unambiguous language, the scientist responsible for the deliberate discharge admitted: "With regard to the discharges from Windscale, the intention has been to discharge *substantial* amounts of radioactivity as part of a deliberate scientific experiment, and the aims of the experiment would have been defeated if the level of actual discharge had been kept to a minimum." (emphasis added).

Other documents revealed examples of more clandestine activities on human beings including an admission that dozens of people drank, inhaled or were injected with radioactive isotopes as part of a series of secret experiments carried out by the nuclear industry in the 1960s.

The tests, exposing humans to radioactive caesium, iodine, strontium and uranium, were carried out on so-called "volunteers." One proposal even envisaged injecting plutonium into elderly people to help assess contamination risks.

A report marked "confidential" said 10 volunteers from Harwell in Oxfordshire drank a liquid containing caesium-132 and caesium-134 in November 1962. Two volunteers from Windscale also ingested strontium 90 to investigate "uptake by the gut". A further 18 volunteers at Harwell in 1964 breathed in a vapour of methyl iodide-132 to test its retention in the thyroid gland. If anyone became ill as a result, the memo said, they would be able to sue for damages, though the risk was dismissed as "negligible".

Yet another memo discussed the "ethical problems" of feeding radioactively contaminated whelks from near Sellafield (formerly Windscale) to children. A memo from 1962 referred to grotesque US experiments in which elderly and sick hospital patients were injected with plutonium. The memo, from scientists at Harwell, suggested carrying out similar experiments in the UK, mentioning old people as potential candidates.

One bizarre document disclosed that in 1972, 21 Punjabi women in Coventry, many of whom did not speak English, were secretly involved in tests using radioactive iodine. The women had gone to their doctor with ailments that ranged from arthritic knees to migraine. They ended up as part of a nutrition experiment which involved eating radioactive chapattis delivered to their door.

This immoral use of civilians in nuclear experiments exposes an alarming willingness by the authorities to use human beings in questionable activities under the guise of cold war expediency.

The existence of these experiments was a closely guarded secret for decades as governments and their scientific stooges scrambled to keep up with the latest advances in nuclear know-how. And there is evidence that in order to keep a lid on these nefarious activities, governments and commercial interests would stop at nothing, even murder.

DIRTY TRICKS

In 1974 union activist Karen Silkwood, aged 28, was investigating serious health risks in the nuclear fuels production plant in Oklahoma where she worked. At the time she was in the process of exposing a cover-up at the company after her home was mysteriously contaminated with plutonium.

Later, while taking incriminating documents to an investigative reporter, Silkwood was killed when her car drove into a ditch.

The circumstances became the subject of enormous speculation after a sleep-inducing drug was found in her body, along with traces of plutonium. There was also evidence of mysterious dents in the rear of her car suggesting she may have been deliberately shunted off the road.

Since then, her story has achieved worldwide fame as the subject of many books, magazine and newspaper articles, and even a major motion picture. The story spawned a spate of allegations from nuclear activists who believed they were being spied upon and even 'terminated' by the evil forces of the pro-nuclear lobby.

As the conspiracy theories swept like wildfire across the political landscape, it wasn't long before it ignited Britain's very own Silkwood legend in the unlikely form of grandmother and rose-grower Hilda Murrell.

Mrs Murrell was found dead near her home just before she was due to give evidence at a public inquiry into the Sizewell B nuclear reactor where she was scheduled to present her paper "An Ordinary Citizen's View of Radioactive Waste Management".

But before she could do so, her home in Shrewsbury was burgled and she was abducted in her own car which many witnesses reported seeing being driven erratically through the town and surrounding countryside. The vehicle was abandoned in a country lane five miles outside Shrewsbury but it was three days before her body was discovered. She had been beaten and stabbed and dumped in a wood where she died of hypothermia.

Mrs Murrell was the aunt of Royal Navy Commander Robert Green, a former naval intelligence officer who was wrongly accused of leaking intelligence to Scottish MP Tam Dalyell. This was to the effect that the sub that sank the Argentine vessel the Belgrano during the 1982 Falklands War was carrying torpedoes with nuclear warheads.

Just before Murrell died, Dalyell was asking detailed questions about the Belgrano's movements before it was sunk. Dalyell later shocked Parliament when he alleged in Parliament that British Intelligence had been involved in Mrs Murrell's murder.

Many years later DNA evidence linked her death to a burglar who fuelled more conspiracy theories when he insisted that he did not act alone. Many still believe Mrs Murrell's death was caused by mysterious government agents

This suggestion of shadowy government agencies engaged in all manner of skullduggery is common currency in the anti-nuclear movement. Even Ken McGinley, who always treated the wilder allegations with scepticism believes he was targeted.

Both he and his wife insist their home has been spied on by mysterious men in cars, but more seriously he believes his tyres were deliberately slashed after he left his car at Glasgow airport before flying to London for a meeting.

McGinley recalled how the nearside tyre blew on the motorway as he returned to his home a few days later: "Luckily, I was only doing about 50 mph and managed to guide the car onto the hard shoulder. The tyre was shredded, but I noticed the other tyre had been cut in a most precise way: around the rim, close to the hub. I took the wheel to a garage and they found there was only about a millimetre of rubber protecting the tyre. The garage man said it had been done deliberately."

McGinley admitted he was rattled, but tried to shrug off the incident, but there were other incidents that disturbed him greatly such as the sudden death of Dr John Reissland, a scientist who was initially put in charge of the study by the National Radiological Protection Board to look into health problems among nuclear veterans.

Dr Reissland had apparently gone to the attic of his home after hearing a noise. As he clambered into the loft space there was a loud bang followed by a fire which killed him. At the time McGinley had been working closely with Dr Reissland providing facts and figures for the study, and a bond of trust had formed between them. Dr Reissland, according to McGinley, was sympathetic to the veterans' cause, and told him on more than one occasion that numbers of blood cancer deaths and cancer incidents were "very significant."

After his shocking death, the coroner recorded an accidental verdict, but the anti-nuclear lobby had their suspicions. McGinley's merely commented that it was a "convenient death" for the government. But there were other occurrences which gave him cause for somber reflection.

Not long after Dr Reissland's death, he was accosted by two intelligence officers, one British, the other America, as he sat minding his own business on the ferry to Dunoon. He recognized the first man as a Ministry of Defence security officer, the second man he thought he may have seen at the American sub base in Rosyth.

McGinley recalled: "The British guy sat down next to me and asked how I was doing. To be honest I never liked the man and I hoped he would go away, but before I could say anything we were joined by an American, from the Rosyth base who I knew was with naval intelligence.

"I had seen them at the base's social club, but had never spoken to them. They sat either side of me; they were both big men and I felt intimidated. The American eventually asked me how the campaign was going. I was flabbergasted. I couldn't understand what possible interest this American could have in my campaign, and I told him so. There was a bit of small talk and eventually the two got up and walked away. The incident unsettled me a bit, but I pushed it to the back of my mind."

A few days later he was sitting at home when got a phone call from a man with an American accent who introduced himself as "Bill". According to McGinley: "He said he knew that I took in US men from the sub base and wanted to know if I would have the courtesy to meet him in town because he wanted to speak to me about a private matter.

"I was mystified and suspicious, but said I would go nevertheless. He arranged to meet me at this little hotel, which was in Queen Street, and this guy was sitting in a small lounge at the back of the hotel. He obviously knew me because he stood up the moment I entered. He was only a small guy, and I asked him what it was all about.

"By way of answer he asked me if I had received a letter he said he sent me. I told him I received lots of letters; what was it about? Bill looked around to make sure we were not overheard said he had supplied details of a radioactive leak that occurred on board a U.S. submarine some years ago. He said since then a lot of men had gotten sick, but it had also affected their children. He said he had been reading about the things I had been involved with. He said he meant that in a respectful manner. He wanted to talk to me about it, the reason being...and then he started to cry...

"I just stood there embarrassed. I got him a glass of water.

As he composed himself, I told him I had received no letter about American submarines. But I did tell him about the mysterious encounter on the ferry. Bill said that didn't surprise him as he convinced his mail was routinely monitored and 'they' probably just wanted to have a look at me.

"Bill finally blurted out what he had really come to say: 'We've just had a baby, my wife and me...and there are things wrong with him. My wife is very, very upset and we just wondered, because of the things you've been involved with, whether you had any paperwork on that. He went on to say he had been warned by his superiors about spreading rumours. He was told he could get into serious trouble.

"I just looked at him and said: 'Several of my members have had babies born with all sorts of deformities. They think it was because they were exposed to radiation, and yes, I do have some literature on that. Medical papers and so on. Is that the sort of thing you are talking about?'

"Bill nodded, and I asked him if he had been exposed to radiation. He said he had, aboard his sub. He refused to go into details but said it happened a number of years ago in the Pacific, and that some of his shipmate's wives had also given birth to deformed children. There were quite a few. I asked him what was wrong with his child. He said he had no fingers.

"I told the young sailor I would see what paperwork I had and forward it on to him at the base. Bill told me not to do that. Apart from the fact it might be opened, he was being sent home next week. Could I send it there? I said of course, and he gave me an address. I eventually sent him a pile of stuff, but that was the last I heard of him."

McGinley was, naturally, troubled by all this. He wasn't surprised that he might be "a target for surveillance" because he was, after all, a well-known anti-nuclear activist who ran a hotel whose clients were US servicemen from a nuclear sub base.

In fact he would have found it more surprising if they didn't keep a cautious eye on him. He had already been informed that his phone was tapped. A relative who worked for the Post Office had warned him on the quiet. He was also told his mail was routinely intercepted.

By this time, and not unnaturally, McGinley was struggling not to join in with the general paranoia that existed over all matters nuclear at the time. But it all came flooding back several months later when "Bill's" story about a serious radiation leak aboard a US submarine was confirmed. Just as the American said a large number of submariners had been contaminated and several of their wives gave birth to children with deformities.

Mrs Jackie Jones, the Scots wife of an American submariner reported her son, Clyde, had been born with only half his left arm. But she alleged he was just one of 14 children born at the huge US navy base in Puerto Rico.

According to Mrs Jones, who was separated from her husband, there had been a US board of inquiry but the proceedings had been secret. The families involved had all been told to keep their mouths shut, but later the authorities admitted there had been a leak and that children had been affected.

But just as this information was being digested, there was a report of a radioactive leak on board a British nuclear submarine, HMS Resolution, based at Faslane near Hellenborough.

According to various accounts there had been a huge cover-up after reports alleging that crew member's wives had given birth to handicapped children. Scottish Health Minister John Mackay became involved and picked up reports about problems with Resolution crew members.

The Ministry of Defence denied there had been any problems with HMS Resolution although it admitted that hairline cracks had been found in the hull of during a refit in 1970. A statement by the Ministry of Defence said that during the 14-month-long refit, the nuclear core in her reactor was replaced, although it wasn't linked to the cracks in the hull.

It soon emerged, however, that after the multi-million pound work on the pressurised water-cooled reactor was completed the sub, which had set out on an Atlantic patrol, was forced to return to Faslane. The spokesman would not speculate on reports that the submarine first surfaced off an isolated coastline south of Oban, Argyle, and several crew members were landed before Resolution submerged.

Reports swept the base that there had been a catastrophic leak of radiation from the reactor and that members of the sub's starboard crew had been contaminated and were being treated at a special hospital on the mainland.

The MoD once again rejected this notion, repeating there had been no radioactive leak. But a year later four malformed children were born to the wives of Resolution crew members. They were born within a few months of each other and they all suffered with hare lip and cleft palate. And what's more they were all born to the wives of the starboard crew members. The

MoD only belatedly admitted that four children of Resolution crew had indeed been born deformed after several MPs asked questions in Parliament.

An MoD spokesman grudgingly conceded: "It is known that during that time (1972-73) there were four cases of children fathered by crewmen aboard HMS Resolution being born with cleft palates and hare-lips." He added, somewhat lamely: "However there is no evidence to indicate that these four cases were anything other than a very sad coincidence."

The statement caused an outcry from nuclear protesters who picketed the entrance to the Faslane base. In an attempt to take the heat out of the situation, the Royal Navy gave permission for one of Resolution's crew members to be interviewed. Chief Petty Officer Danny Davis said his son Stephen, then aged 11, was born brain damaged and with a hair lip and cleft palate. But he insisted: "We all believe that what happened to our children had nothing to do with radiation."

But his ex-wife Pat didn't see it that way and decided to go public about what she knew of the incident. She gave an interview to a TV company, and soon found herself plunged into a nightmare; her home was burgled and the word 'death' was scrawled on the cover of the notebooks in which she was compiling her evidence.

Her harrowing story was revealed in an interview: "In the early 1970s I was living with my husband in married quarters. We had one child then, our eldest son Mark. One day Danny came back from sea with bandages all over his arms. I asked him what happened, but all he would say was that he had been damaged by a spot of steam in the engine room. He didn't seem to want to talk about it, so I didn't pursue the matter.

"But then rumours began on the base. On the grapevine I heard there had been a leak on board Danny's sub, the Resolution, and that several men had been injured. I asked Danny about it, but he just shrugged it off. He told me not to listen to gossip and not to ask questions.

"I put it out of my mind, until we went to a party for Navy people on the base. Everything was going smoothly until this sailor suddenly broke down. He spoke about an incident on board Resolution which caused complete panic. The reactor had broken down and there had been a radioactive leak. This man was badly affected and just sat on the floor and wept.

"It was a very strange incident. Then I heard the man's wife later gave birth to a child with a hair lip and cleft palate. You can imagine how I felt when our son Stephen was born with the same defects about six months later. I heard of other deformed babies born at the base. In the two years after Stephen was born, three more crew member's babies were born with the same defects."

Mrs Davis made an official request to the Ministry of Defence for an inquiry after she was told of the suicide death of one of the mothers, but was turned down on the grounds her claims were inaccurate. There had been no radiation leak and she was told to not ask questions.

She and her husband moved down to Middlesex but divorced soon after. He returned to Scotland while Mrs Davis stayed in Middlesex. Free of Navy constraints, Mrs Davis began to make more inquiries about what had happened on board Resolution.

She had decided to write a book about it and tried to contact her old friends at the base. She also contacted Yorkshire Television who asked her to take part in a programme they were preparing on radiation workers at nuclear bases. Mrs Davis recorded a short interview and appealed for an inquiry into leaks aboard nuclear submarines.

Soon after, she received threatening phone calls. One came at midnight. The anonymous caller said that if she didn't cease her inquiries she would be killed.

In the weeks that followed she was pestered by numerous calls both at home and at work. After one call she broke down and had to be taken home by colleagues. Mrs Davis said: "A man rang me to say my whole family would be killed if I didn't keep my big trap shut. He said he knew where my eldest son went to school and that he also knew that Stephen was away at the time. I was obviously being spied on because he described a visit I made the day before to a dry cleaner. I reported all this to the police, but they didn't seem to be interested."

One night she was awoken by a knocking on her door, and two men, who claimed to be police officers, brushed their way in. One slapped her across the face while the other clamped a gloved hand across her mouth. They then proceeded to ransack her flat.

She recalled: "I was absolutely terrified. They were so brutal. I had the marks of the glove hand across my mouth for hours afterwards. I begged them to tell me what they wanted. I even told them where my purse was. I just wanted them to leave. But every time I spoke I got belted."

The two men left as abruptly as they had arrived leaving her bruised and terrified. She contacted the police who insisted she got a hospital check-up. But because the intruders had apparently left empty-handed, they didn't pursue the matter. It was only much later when Mrs Davis resumed work on her book that she found several chapters missing, as well as addresses, notes and ex-directory telephone numbers. She didn't bother telling the police.

Whether Mrs Davis was the victim of brutal burglars or shadowy government agents bent on deterring her from making further inquiries has never been resolved. But there was an interesting postscript: soon after her story was aired, a priest at a seaman's mission in Barrow-on-Humber, Humberside, revealed that three sailors from HMS Resolution had died of cancer within months of each other.

Fr Michael Cooke said the ashes of the three men, the oldest of whom was just 45, were consigned to the sea in separate ceremonies by a seaman's mission chaplain. Fr Cooke said he had received the information from 'an anonymous and private' source. He said he was not prepared to name the individuals involved because their families had expressly forbidden it. "My hands are tied," he said. "I cannot break a confidence, but the whole thing has left me extremely uncomfortable. There is no doubt in my mind that there should be an investigation."

The Navy once again refused to hold an inquiry. A spokesman would only say: "We need more details about the men and their families before we can mount an investigation."

Of course no investigations were ever carried out and further revelations were submerged as deeply as HMS Resolution -- which was sent on Arctic patrol hundreds of feet beneath the polar icecap, conveniently incommunicado for the next six months.

In the midst of all this, McGinley and his wife were facing their own problems: the collapse of their business. The slide began the week after McGinley's meeting with the mysterious 'Bill.'

One of the B&B's oldest residents, a senior submariner, suddenly decided that Pitcairlie House, the name of McGinley's hotel, had lost its charms. He gave only a vague explanation for his decision; something to do with wanting a change

McGinley, mindful of everything that had happened, was suspicious. This soon turned to certainty when over the next nonth or so, one by one the rest of his residents all drifted away. None gave an explanation that made any sense at all and McGinley was now convinced it was all tied up with the events surrounding the radioactive leak aboard the US sub. With winter sweeping in fast, the McGinley's faced financial ruin.

KEN AND ALICE

Ken McGinley stamped on the accelerator and the car leapt forward like a greyhound out of the trap. The heavy lorry ahead of him hogging the lane loomed larger and larger and he pressed the pedal harder. His windscreen wipers struggled against the driving rain and the steering wheel felt loose in his hands.

Why not? He asked himself. Let's end it now. There's no point in going on... His front bumper was almost touching the rear of the lorry and his windscreen was filled with water and the blackness of the load. Time was suspended and his foot hovered perilously over the accelerator pedal: one touch...one final touch and...with a jerk of his head he realised what he was doing and just in time pulled sharply over to the side of the road.

The harsh blare of the horn in the car following filled his head as he came to a halt. Sweat poured in rivers down his neck and paroxysms shook his body...

There had been health problems since returning from Christmas Island, the worst of which was coughing up copious amounts of blood as he lay in his bunk. His joints ached, there were muscle spasms; the blisters on his face and neck which he thought had healed, kept coming back.

His problems were not all physical: he was beset by nightmares and irrational fears. Not that the army medic who examined him in his barracks cared; he showed little interest in McGinley and shoved a couple of aspirins in his hand before roughly dismissing him.

Two days later McGinley collapsed and was rushed to a military hospital. He was eventually diagnosed with a serious duodenal ulcer. That put paid to his Army days; he was discharged on medical grounds and given a ticket for home.

His sweetheart Alice was waiting for him as he got off the train at Glasgow central. At first she didn't recognise the pale, gaunt figure that stumbled shakily on to the platform.

She recalled: "My God, what have they done to him? It was the first thing that passed through my mind. He looked so different from the man who waved goodbye to me almost a year ago. Kenny had lost an awful lot of weight and his once glossy black hair was lank and lifeless. The man I knew always walked with a swagger, bouncing about on his heels, full of life. Now he looked as though he was at death's door. I knew he had been ill, but it seemed to have aged him. And when I got up close I noticed he had marks on his face like blisters that hadn't been there before.

"I looked at him tentatively, not sure what to say. I had had my hair done specially and I wore a new coat I'd bought that day. He looked me up and down and then broke out into a huge smile. It was the Ken I remembered. "You look more beautiful than ever," he said, and took me in his arms.

"I met Ken McGinley in a cafe in Johnstone. He was a good looking guy with an Elvis quiff. There were loads of girls interested in him. I was only 15 and he was four years older, but we just seemed to hit it off. I was still at school of course and Kenny used to wait for me outside the school gates. He'd walk me home, holding my hand; we were both just a couple of kids.

"On a sudden whim Kenny joined the army and seemed to grow up overnight. He was sent away on training and when he came back he was a man. It wasn't long before he was posted abroad to Germany; we wrote to each other a lot. When things started to get serious he called down to see my mum and dad.

"They wanted to see what sort of guy he was. He was a strong catholic. I was a protestant. But neither family seemed to mind. We started going out steady, and sort of knew that we would probably get married one day, but we weren't rushing things.

"Kenny was very good company, always polite, but cheeky with it. He took me out whenever he was on leave; we'd go to the pictures or have a coffee in town. It was a nice, quiet little romance that suited us both; all we wanted to do was to settle down and have a little family just like any ordinary couple.

"But out of the blue he got a call: he was being sent overseas to a place called Christmas Island. I'd never heard of it, and neither had Kenny. We didn't know what to think. We looked it up in the library and there was just this tiny place in the middle of the ocean.

"Kenny was very excited; he was looking forward to all the sunshine. I just worried about the hula girls, and he laughed. 'Marry me,' he said suddenly. I looked at him uncertainly. 'Marry me, when I get back. I love you Alice; you are the only girl I have ever loved.'

"It was a bitter-sweet Christmas, full of joy because we loved each other, and so, so sad that we knew he'd be leaving as soon as the festivities were over. I saw him off at the railway station and ran alongside the train as it pulled out from the station. Then he was gone, and to be honest, I wondered if I would ever see him again.

"The months passed. I received regular letters from Kenny and I could feel the tension rising with each one. The build-up to the bombs was taking place and Kenny told me how everyone was beginning to get worried, but he was trying to put a brave face on things.

"All that changed after the first test at the end of April. He wrote to tell me how all the men had got down on their knees to pray; it was the most frightening experience of his life. He wrote over and over of how much he loved me. Kenny wrote that all the men were getting knock-backs from their girlfriends and he begged me not to do the same.

"These were scary times; there had been some newspaper reports about the effects of the bombs on the men. I was walking home one day and some of my former classmates were sitting on a wall sniggering. When I asked what was up, they showed me a newspaper article about Christmas Island.

"I didn't read it all, but they were saying things about babies and that how soldiers wouldn't be able to have any. I walked off in tears. The thought of never having babies filled me with dread. Kenny must have sensed the change in me from my letters, and his replies became more and more desperate.

"I wrote back to reassure him that I still loved him. I knew I'd made the right decision as soon as he stepped off the train. My heart just melted when I saw his condition and I knew then that I could never love another man no matter what, even if he wasn't quite the same man I had known before he went away.

"His personality had changed in subtle ways. He was quieter, more thoughtful; he looked as though he always had things on his mind. He was only 21 years old, but he acted as though he was much older. He was also very insecure. He kept asking me if I had been seeing someone else while he was away. I told him that was rubbish.

"But there was something going on inside him that I couldn't understand. From being very gentle, he was suddenly very hot tempered. I could usually calm him down, but one day he just exploded after went for religious instruction. I had decided to become a Catholic in preparation for our marriage. On the way home on the bus this guy was looking at me funny and Kenny got mad and thumped him. He had never been like that before. I thought he had really hurt this guy. I managed to drag him away. I grabbed him fiercely to make him see sense.

His eyes cleared, and then he burst into tears. It was bewildering.

"Kenny said he needed a job and started work in a paper-mill factory, but he found it impossible to settle down. He resented authority and couldn't stand being confined. He was like a pressure cooker, and one day he blew. Some guy was giving him a lot of chat at work and Kenny hurled himself across the room and had him by the throat before he could blink. There was a near riot, and Kenny lost his job.

"He was lucky not to be prosecuted. I thought he could get into serious trouble if something wasn't done. Finally I told him that if he didn't stop we were finished. That calmed him down. In those days there was no help for people like Kenny and we just sort of struggled on. We coped. He grew calmer; the storm subsided; the demons went away.

"We had no money but we decided to go ahead and get married anyway, and Kenny seemed happy as we made all the preparations. I made my own outfit and everyone pitched in to help.

"The ceremony at St Margaret's Catholic Church in Johnstone took place on April 23, 1960 and the church was packed. To keep both sides of the family happy we held the reception in the Orange Hall.

"We moved in with Kenny's mother who lived in a large house in Brewery Street, Johnstone. It was a chaotic arrangement as two of his brothers had also moved in with their wives, but it suited Kenny down to the ground. He was still suffering quite a lot from nervous anxiety, which today is called post traumatic stress disorder, and it helped to be with his family. By the time we'd saved enough for our own place, Kenny seemed to have recovered completely.

"As our financial situation improved we decided it was time to start a family. At least that was the plan, but nothing seemed to be happening. I thought there must be something wrong with me so I went to the doctor who carried out some tests. We were so desperate for children that Kenny also went to the hospital for some tests, although he was sure the problem wasn't with him.

"Imagine my shock when the doctor called us back in together to say: 'Mrs McGinley, there is absolutely nothing wrong with you, and you can go away and have as many babies as you wish --- the only problem is you will have to have them with someone else because I am afraid your husband will never be able to father children. His sperm count is too low.'

"Thinking about it now, it was an unbelievable callous thing to say, but at the time we were both too shocked to speak. We wanted so much to have children; it was all I had ever wanted. When we recovered from the shock we demanded to know how this could be so when both our families had lots of children. The doctor just shrugged his shoulders, but then he said a very strange thing to my husband: 'You'll rue the day you stepped foot on Christmas Island.'

"At first I didn't understand, then I remembered those newspaper articles and, I knew. It was so heartbreaking; I was in this terrible position of desperately wanting my own child, yet I couldn't because I knew that Kenny was the only man I could ever love.

"I blamed Christmas Island then, and I blame it now. I blamed it because of the way Kenny had changed and for what the doctor had told me. I loved this man, but we couldn't have children together. They took that away from me. I was never going to have kids.

"In the end we went down the adoption route and we got our lovely daughter Louise. I have never regretted that for one minute. She is a beautiful girl and adopting her was the best thing we ever did. But it still rankles that the opportunity to have children of our own was taken away from us."

Somehow Ken and Alice staggered on through the lean years. Business had all but dried up and selling up had become an inevitability. They knew this would, in many ways, be a relief.

"Increasingly both had become aware that they seemed to be under surveillance: strange cars occupied by shadowy figures appeared outside their home and parked for hours with no obvious intent. Post arrived that had obviously been interfered with; strange noises interrupted their telephone conversations; their home was burgled and confidential papers stolen.

"There were other alarming events that shredded already frayed nerves, like the time McGinley received a summons to attend court on a serious assault charge. He had never been arrested for anything and, much disturbed, took the matter up with the Procurator Fiscal's office where he was told it had all been a mistake.

"Further inquiries revealed that a local firm of solicitors had mistakenly used McGinley's name and address on the charge form. But why, McGinley wanted to know, did the solicitors have his name and address in the first place? The solicitors were evasive, but later admitted they had been commissioned to collect press cuttings concerning McGinley and send them on to "an interested party." The lawyers refused to say who their client was.

Another frustrating problem arose when McGinley's small war pension, awarded for his continuing stomach problems, was summarily withdrawn. He appealed against the decision and during a disclosure hearing McGinley learned that a doctor working for the Pensions Department, who had never examined McGinley, had written across his notes: *"Politically sensitive case. This paranoid appellant is the president of the British Nuclear Tests Veterans' Association."*

McGinley was outraged and naturally kicked up a fuss; his pension was eventually reinstated. The sensation of being under siege reached a head when the British Security Services came knocking on his door.

There were two of them, both male. One was a middle-aged executive type; the other looked to be in his late twenties. They had rung ahead to request an appointment and arrived promptly at the chosen time.

McGinley invited them in and examined their identity cards curiously while his wife made coffee. On the table in front of them was a week-old copy of a newspaper dominated by a picture of Abdelbaset al-Megrahi, the man accused of the Lockerbie bombing.

He had recently been indicted by the US Attorney General and the Scottish Lord Advocate for the bombing of Pan Am flight 103 over the Scottish border town of Lockerbie killing 243 passengers, 16 crew members and 11 people on the ground.

The reason for the visit was because McGinley was certain he had met al-Megrahi --- a year before the bombing.

The encounter took place in Amsterdam at a meeting of a group called WISE, a small but influential anti-nuclear group based in the Dutch capital. McGinley had been invited to one of the group's regular get-togethers and found he was rubbing shoulders with a vociferous cross-section of left-wing intellectuals, environmentalists and nuclear dissidents.

Present also was the renegade CIA spy Norman Stockwell who enlivened the meeting by talking about US covert operations in Africa and Asia. It was during a break in the proceedings that McGinley met al-Megrahi.

He was standing outside the conference hall smoking a cigarette when a mustard-coloured Volvo pulled up alongside. There were two men in the car, and the passenger leant out of the window and gestured him over. McGinley recognised him as one of the spectators who had earlier attended the meeting.

He was a Middle-Eastern man and spoke impeccable English and addressed the Scot as 'Dr McGinley.' He oozed friendliness and asked McGinley if they could meet up again at the next seminar, scheduled for Germany the following month. He was obviously under the delusion that McGinley was some kind of scientist and said he would like to introduce him to some of his scientific friends.

McGinley was quick to disavow him about his academic status, but the man insisted he would still like to see him in Germany. As the man climbed back into the car, McGinley never forgot his parting words: 'We can talk about bombs!'

That was a full year before the Lockerbie bombing and almost four years to the day since the meeting took place. But McGinley recognised al-Megrahi as soon as he saw his picture in the newspapers and on the news bulletins. It shook him so much he phoned the police unit in charge of the Lockerbie investigation.

He recalled: "I was one hundred per cent certain that the man who accosted me in Amsterdam was al-Megrahi. It horrified me to think that this man had mistaken me for a scientist, and that he had wanted to talk about bombs. The fact that he obviously thought I was a nuclear scientist made my blood run cold. I thought it was something the authorities should know about."

The authorities were indeed interested: 24 hours after making the call the two "spies" presented themselves at his door. McGinley recalled how one of them took notes while the other asked the questions. After about an hour they surprised the McGinleys by inviting them for a drink at a local hotel.

During the course of the conversation, the elder of the two men warned McGinley of the need for silence. He said McGinley could probably make a lot of money by going to the newspapers, but that if he did it could "jeopardise everything." McGinley assured the man that he had no intention of going to the press.

The men relaxed and asked McGinley about his campaign and the sort of circles he was moving in. They said they knew all about the WISE conference and its aims. Throughout the conversations, McGinley had the clear impression the pair were building up to something, but never quite got round to saying what it was.

They were particularly interested in the contacts he made abroad and how often he spoke to other nuclear groups. They made some flattering remarks about how he was considered to be very influential among anti-nuclear circles. They asked him how he felt about nuclear power, whether he thought it was a good thing or bad.

After a couple of drinks, the men thanked McGinley and dropped him and his wife back at their home. McGinley speculated on the reason for the visit: "The al-Megrahi incident was certainly of interest to them, but I got the impression they were more interested in the people I was meeting in the course of the campaign. They were definitely on a fact-finding mission to find out who I was in contact with and what we were discussing. They were very friendly and seemed to be sizing me up; I was half expecting them to ask me to keep them informed of future meetings."

McGinley was amused at the idea that Her Majesty's Government might be trying to recruit him as a spy, but the incident unnerved Alice who felt they were becoming increasingly out of their depth. Alice yearned to get away from it all.

They sold Pitcairlie House and moved back to Johnstone where, Alice insisted, they would make a fresh start. It was a forlorn hope. No sooner were they settled than her husband was embroiled in another entanglement with officialdom, this time with an even more formidable opponent than 'James Bond': the Treasury Solicitor.

THE CORONER'S CLERK

The Treasury Solicitor sounds innocent enough. The title conjures up an image of a fusty lawyer armed with a pen and wig, beavering away in a back office concerned only with the collection and disposition of ownerless properties on behalf of the Exchequer.

In actual fact he is a little-known attack dog of government whose primary function is to cling on to governmental purse strings with Rottwieler determination. The Treasury Solicitor's Office encompasses a 600-strong highly professional legal team that was officially defined in 1661 as "the solicitor for negotiating and looking after the affairs of the Treasury."

It has sweeping, some say Draconian, powers, enabling it to delve into every aspect of a case with impunity, and is accountable only to the Attorney General. In the early 1990s this formidable force was suddenly turned on the nuclear veterans who were enjoying considerable success in persuading War Pension Tribunals to find in their favour.

Some of these tribunals had caused considerable embarrassment to the government by awarding pensions to nuclear veterans whom they deemed to have been 'affected by radiation.'

Some mandarin in the Civil Service clearly decided that enough was enough: The Treasury Solicitor was unleashed and set about hi-jacking inquests and pension tribunals. Their mission was to take control of the evidence and present it in a way favourable to the Government line. And it seems they didn't care how they did it.

McGinley obtained first-hand experience of their methods when he got a call from a very frightened coroner's clerk. The man said he had been carrying out inquiries into the case of a former sailor who had been on board HMS Diana, the ship that sailed through the mushroom cloud of an atomic explosion off the Australian coast in 1956.

This was potentially a very embarrassing case for the Government after a pathologist found traces of a radioactive substance lodged in the sailor's body which was being confidently blamed for the man's death from a rare form of bone cancer.

During the course of his enquiries the coroner's clerk, a punctilious police constable, was carrying out interviews of doctors and other officials involved in the case when out of the blue he received a telephone call from a Treasury Solicitor who briskly informed him "the Crown" was taking over the handling of the case.

When the clerk protested he was brusquely told by the lawyer to "step aside and forget about the case." The clerk was troubled and eventually complained to the coroner. Nothing was heard for several days, but then came another phone call – this time in the middle of the night.

The call was made as the bleary-eyed PC lay in bed with his mistress. The caller simply told the man, who was married with two children, the affair was 'known about' and that he was damaging his future job prospects.

The flabbergasted constable didn't recognise the voice, but he was understandably rattled. He was certain his wife knew nothing about his affair, ands his girlfriend was equally certain that none of her circle were in the know.

The constable concluded he was being shadowed and that it had something to do with his run-in with the Treasury Solicitor. He decided to tip McGinley off because he was convinced the forthcoming inquest was being nobbled.

McGinley travelled to see the man, but in the absence of on-the-record evidence from the clerk there was little that could be done. The inquest duly found no evidence to link the sailor's death with his involvement in nuclear bomb tests.

This odd story might well have been dismissed as the paranoid ramblings of a man literally caught with his trousers down, but for a startling coincidence involving the same Treasury solicitor.

Again it involved an inquest, this time into the death of Harold Graham Dovey, a former AWRE technician who had witnessed several atomic explosions in Australia.

Mr Dovey had died of rare form of cancer, multiple myeloma, which has been linked with radiation exposure. As in the previous case, the coroner's clerk was a local police constable who had been asked to investigate the circumstances surrounding Mr Dovey's death.

The man from the Reading Police force confirmed he, too, had been taken off the case by the same Treasury solicitor.

He made the following statement: "I was making routine inquiries at the Department of Health and Reading Area Health Authority when I received a phone call from the office of the Treasury Solicitor.

This man asked me, in a not too friendly way, why I was making inquiries into the Dovey case when he, the Treasury Solicitor, had all the relevant information. I told him it was my job to do so. He replied that it was no longer my job and he effectively sacked me from the inquiry.

I protested, but it was made known to me in no uncertain terms as to my future job prospects if I attempted to interfere. Obviously I cannot say too much about my personal feelings in this matter. Suffice it to say, I thought it was wrong."

Both statements were later given in confidence to Liberal MP David Alton who demanded the Attorney General Sir Michael Havers, and the Lord Chancellor, Lord Hailsham, investigate the claims. He said: "There is something very sinister about this affair. It is scandalous that police officers carrying out their normal duties can be intimidated in this way."

Despite the protests, no inquiry was ever made into these matters. The Dovey inquest went ahead, but this time the jury returned an open verdict which was hailed as a victory for the veterans.

And what happened to the Treasury solicitor? Within weeks he was shunted aside and was last heard of working for the criminal injuries compensation board.

The implications of these disquieting events were not lost on McGinley. He was beginning to realise that 'dirty tricks' had been the stock in trade of successive governments ever since the bomb tests had taken place. Witness statements and first-hand testimony from nuclear veterans and civilian workers suggested something very sinister was taking place, but it was difficult to prove a widespread conspiracy.

Despite the setbacks, progress was being made by the veterans and although the 'smoking gun' that would prove their case was still elusive, even the most diehard cynics could hardly doubt the link between ill-health and the atom tests.

Bowing to pressure, the government began to quietly introduce rule changes to award war pensions to veterans who had certain types of cancers. And there were plans to draw up a Green Paper that would have compensated the veterans through the social security system, without embarrassing the government too much. It was a solution of sorts, and something that McGinley and the veterans would have accepted.

But an unexpected development sent the campaign off in an entirely new and unexpected direction: a veterans' meeting in Newscastle was gate-crashed by a tall, raw-boned Scot who, without preamble, threw a black and white photograph on the table in front of Mr McGinley: "That's what you should be looking at," the man said before disappearing into the night.

McGinley and the rest of those present examined the photo. It was of a little boy, in a white shirt, bow tie and grey shorts, sitting on a tricycle. The lad had no hands or feet and his large, luminous eyes stared out from a grossly-misshapen head. It was a pitiful picture and everyone was struck by the eyes that conveyed a mute appeal.

A search party was sent out to look for the mysterious stranger, but he was nowhere to be found. It was some weeks before they finally tracked him down. His name was Murdo MacLeod, a crofter from Lewis, the largest of the Hebridean islands off the far northwest coast of Scotland.

Thirty years earlier he had been a civilian truck driver and adventurer who managed to get himself attached to the British Army in the Maralinga proving grounds where he witnessed several nuclear bomb tests.

During his year-long tenure, he became William Penney's personal driver and often took the scientist out to the test sites. When it was all over he returned to Scotland where his son John Alexander was born. It was John's face that stared out of the picture. The face opened up a disturbing new chapter in the campaign.

MURDO'S STORY

Able Seaman Murdo MacLeod decided to jump ship at Fremantle, 20 miles along the coast from Perth in Western Australia. He and his buddy Wally McIver had had enough of the old MV Thuyssen. She was a rust-bucket of uncertain parentage which had somehow survived the war and now she shipped coal and scrap metal. They didn't like the captain, a mad Dutchman, so decided to strike out on their own.

They'd heard of big gold strikes in the Outback, and wanted some of the action. They were young and it seemed like a good idea at the time.

They picked up rumours of gold prospecting in the north-west territory, but when they headed north they found nothing, and when they went west they found less. After a couple of months their money ran out and decided to try their luck mining for opals mining in south Australia, on the edge of the Great Victoria Desert.

It was at a place called Coober Pedy. Rumour had it there had been some sensational finds. It was just the thing they had been looking for. They acquired a battered old Land Rover and headed for the digs

In 1956 Coober Pedy was like an Australian Klondyke, attracting hordes of adventurers, all scraping the harsh desert surface for the bright blue gemstones reputed to be lying around just waiting to be picked up. It was so hot, its inhabitants had to live like troglodytes underground in man-made holes and trenches; water and other supplies had to be carted in from great distances.

Murdo got a job as a truck driver while Wally dug trenches. It was tough work, but they were both tough men and they decided to get on with things until better days came along.

The best part of Murdo's job was the weekly run to collect provisions and water from Watson Siding, an isolated railway junction in the middle of the desert about 40 miles west of Coober Pedy. The freight train, when it came, arrived in its own good time, and Murdo often had to wait for hours before it turned up. Murdo soon got to know the local aborigines who regarded the junction as an important meeting place.

He recalled: "It was a place where they rested and held meetings to discuss things. They'd probably been doing it for thousands of years. I think it was a holy place as well. They would often sit on their haunches in circles and sort of chant for hours at a time. As the months went by I became familiar with most of the little tribes that used the spot and even started to pick up some of the lingo. They were nice, dignified people. Simple, I suppose. But noble as well. They were called the Tjarutja and they told me that this was their land, but that I was very welcome to stay."

One day Murdo arrived at the crossing to find the aborigines in an extremely agitated state. He recalled: "They were all wound up and kept pointing into the desert. Charlie, one of the elders explained that a large party of men, soldiers, had arrived on a train in the early hours of the morning. The whole lot had then taken off into the desert.

"'Where to?' I said.

"Charlie pointed down a dirt track that led into the desert. Then he started stamping his feet and shaking all over. He was obviously trying to tell me something, but I was blowed if I knew what."

The mystery was solved a couple of hours later when the freight train with the water and provisions arrived. As the water was transferred to a bowser in the back of his truck, Murdo got talking to one of the drivers. He told him about the soldiers and how nervous the aborigines were.

Murdo recalled: "The driver said there had been talk of a big new army base far out in the desert. It was supposed to be at a place called Maralinga. 'Maralinga means thunder field,' he said. 'It's one of their sacred sites. That's why they're so agitated. They don't like people interfering with their spirits.'"

The next time Murdo went to the crossing there was no sign of the aborigines. They had just melted away into the desert. But there were plenty of signs of other activity. The ground, normally just featureless desert, had recently been churned up by a lot of heavy traffic. There were large tyre tracks and heavy boot prints everywhere. A lot of men and equipment had clearly landed at this remote outpost. And as far as Murdo could make out they were all heading in one direction: the place the aborigines called Maralinga.

Murdo was intrigued and asked around when the next freight train drew in, but other than the fact they were mainly British soldiers, no-one seemed to know anything. The guardsman on the train told him it was all 'hush-hush' and that he shouldn't ask questions.

This, of course, only made Murdo want to find out what was going on even more. He could sense an opportunity. Soldiers, lots of them, and equipment; he could smell there was money to be made. Things at Coober Pedy had not gone to plan. He never found a single opal lying around. He realised he wasn't going to make a fortune there. It was time to move on. He discussed it with Wally that night and they decided to head off to Maralinga and find out what it was all about.

Murdo recalled: "A week later we took off into the desert with just a few days supplies in the back of the Land Rover. We didn't really know where we were going; we just followed the rough road which went more or less in a straight line west. Just before sundown on the first day, we saw a large aircraft flying quite low and heading into the desert just south of us. We took a left into the brush and followed. The plane seemed to come down about 20 miles ahead.

"We camped for the night and headed off in the morning. The terrain became harsher as we travelled. It was all low scrub and saltbush. I couldn't imagine why anyone would want to go there and was beginning to think we had got it wrong. We came across this huge flat plain of white limestone stretching away to the north as far as the eye could see.

Slap in the middle was a town of tents and wooden huts that didn't appear on any map I knew off. On the edge of the town was an airstrip. We followed the road until we came to a sort of border post. Two guards ran out waving their guns and shouting at us to get out of the vehicle.

"We put our hands up, just like the cowboys, and then we burst out laughing at the thought. This seemed to break the ice because one of the soldiers suddenly grinned and put his gun down. We were taken to a guard house while we waited for an officer to arrive.

They wouldn't answer any of our questions, but one of the lads, a Geordie, said they were all sick of the heat and the flies. I remember saying to him that he should try living in a rabbit hole in an opal mine, and he laughed. Eventually this officer arrived. He took one look at us and barked: 'This is a restricted area. You could have been shot. Who told you to come here? What's your business?'

"'Whoa, whoa,'" I said. 'We're only looking for work.'

"The officer said it was a military camp and off-limits to civilians. It looked as though we were going to get the bums' rush until I mentioned the aborigines and how upset they had been.

"The officer looked sharply at me. 'You speak aboriginal?'

"'Sure do,'" I replied with more confidence than I felt. 'Like a native.'

"The officer considered this for a while before saying, 'And what do you do?'

"'I'm a driver, Sir, says I, hoping to impress. 'A good one. Been driving in the desert for years.'

"He grunted and nodded toward Wally. 'And you?'

"Wally said he was a labourer with a good strong pair of hands. We told the officer, who turned out to be a captain, about our adventures gold prospecting in the bush and how we had ended up in Coober Pedy.

"Our voices were drowned out at that moment as another aircraft, a large freighter rumbled in toward the airstrip. 'Well, there's certainly plenty of work,' said the officer more to himself than anything else. He seemed to come to a decision.

"'Sergeant,' he barked. 'Give them a cuppa while I decide what's what.' With that he jumped into his Jeep and drove back off into the main camp. 'You're in,' said the sergeant cheerfully. 'But you might learn to regret it.'

"It was a funny thing to say, and I asked him what the camp was all about. Suddenly the sergeant lost his good humour.

"'One thing you've got to learn about this place is that you never ask questions,'" he said, very sternly. 'Start being nosey and they'll come down on you like a ton of bricks. You got that?'"

The two men were taken into the camp where they were put to work with a contingent of about 40 civilian workers who did general labour duties, building huts, roads and runway repairs.

Murdo was put on border duties, mainly because of his knowledge of aboriginal, and spent his time patrolling the outer limits of the camp that separated the area from the rest of the featureless desert. They were warned several times about the need for secrecy and the dire consequences of talking to "outsiders" about what they had seen.

Murdo learned to keep his mouth shut, and his eyes and ears open. And it wasn't long before he found out what Maralinga was all about.

Its official, that is to say British, name, was the sinister-sounding X200. It was a 450-square mile area of flat saltbush and desert that bore ample traces of the ocean that once covered it. Wave marks stretched into the distance and there were millions of fossil shell fragments.

X200 was the place chosen to be the test site for a series of atomic bombs the British planned to detonate later in the year. As the time for the tests approached, Murdo was assigned a job as a driver, taxiing sentries and officers on patrol far out into the desert in search of aborigines who wandered into the area. Many did, and Murdo's knowledge of the language was a great asset in persuading the gentle people to leave.

His pal Wally, meanwhile, was given a job labouring with the construction workers who were rapidly building the new town which would eventually house thousands of servicemen.

Gradually the small town took shape. There were main streets with comforting, homely names like London Road, and Belfast Crescent. A post office, a hospital, several chapels, and a cinema were thrown up in double quick time.

In due course a football pitch was added as well as a barbers shop, two beer gardens, laboratories and workshops. There was even a VIP dining room with a grand piano which the officers gathered around to smoke cigars and enjoy a beer. The three-mile airstrip doubled as a cricket pitch and the entrance to the terminal was planted with white flowers flown in from England.

Murdo enjoyed himself immensely in the months before the testing began. He revelled in the pioneering spirit of the place. Unlike many of the arrivals he was already hardened to the tough and remorseless conditions. His specialist knowledge of the terrain soon made him indispensable to the soldiers of the royal engineers who toiled far out in the desert preparing suitable test sites.

A civil construction company was used to carry out the work at main camp, but Murdo, as far as he knew, was the only civilian allowed near the forward areas where the bombs were to be tested.

The scientific staff began arriving in July 1956, flown straight into X200 rather than train via Watson Siding. Murdo's services were increasingly in demand as teams of scientists demanded transport up to the forward areas to check out the lie of the land.

Murdo recalled the days with fondness: "I wasn't worried about the bombs going off. In fact I was looking forward to seeing them. In the meantime I enjoyed driving round the desert and talking to the officers and I was interested in the preparations at ground zero in a place called One Tree, about 12 miles north of the town.

They had built a little town there where everything seemed to be in miniature. There were even dummies inside the houses to make it look as though real people were sitting at home having tea or a meal."

Half-way through September 1956 there was a flurry of activity. Air traffic increased and there was a general air of expectation. Murdo was busier than ever ferrying assorted boffins out to One Tree and other sites. He remembered one man in particular. He arrived in the company of two very senior officers and an armed guard.

Murdo took a keen interest in the new arrival: "He was obviously a big-wig, the way they fussed around him. I learned later he was Sir William Penney, the top scientist, the man in charge of the whole shebang. He was pudgy, a bit on the heavy side, and he stood apart from the others.

"I remember him looking into the desert, the sunlight gleaming off his spectacles. It seemed to me he was lonely. But he must have had a sense of humour because there was a poster cartoon of him hanging in the officer's mess. It showed him carrying a little bag with the words, 'atoms, plenty of 'em', written on the side."

Penney's arrival signalled the beginning of a series of four large atomic explosions between 27th September and October 22nd. The first, a Hiroshima-sized device detonated from a tower, was witnessed by Murdo from his Land Rover about 8 miles away. With him were two scientists, both clothed from head to toe in white protective overalls, complete with gas masks.

Murdo said: "I was dressed as I always was, short-sleeved shirt and shorts, but I didn't think anything of it. I just thought, they must know what they are doing. I distinctly remember the ground shaking as the bomb went off. It was just after dawn and the sky was still dark, but suddenly the whole place lit up like it was noon.

"It was an amazing sight. I just stared at it open-mouthed. It was red and black and I remember thinking how dirty it looked. Funnily enough I wasn't scared; I just marvelled at it.

"Even when I was told to drive toward the explosion, some time later, it didn't twig that I might be in any danger. The mushroom cloud had dissipated by the time we arrived near ground zero. The scientists hopped out and very quickly collected some instruments and brought them back to the Jeep in special bags. Then I was told to high-tail it back to base. It was quite exciting."

He spent most of the following day running different groups of personnel into the contaminated areas. The awesome power of an atomic explosion was all too evident as he drove around the scorched landscape, raising clouds of dust wherever he went.

Surplus cars, trucks and other equipment had been seared and twisted into almost unrecognisable shapes. He particularly remembered a Centurion tank that was fused into the red desert sand. Hastily constructed huts and concrete bunkers had been blasted out of existence. The desert near ground zero had been turned into a sea of glass, while a pall of sand and dust drifted about.

A task he took no pleasure in was helping round up the fear-maddened animals that had been tethered on the outer edges of the explosion area for the scientists to examine. Many of the unfortunate creatures, including rabbits, chickens, sheep and goats, had struggled free in their terror and had to be pursued across the smoking landscape. Those he did catch were in a pitiable condition, their eyes scorched from their sockets, flesh burned from their bones. All had to be bagged and taken back to base.

Later that day, Penney decided to view the bomb site. Murdo was assigned to drive him and his escorts into the contaminated area: "He was, of course, in full protective clothing like the rest of the scientists. He didn't speak much to me, but he was very courteous. He asked me very politely if I wouldn't mind taking him to a spot where he could have a good look at the crater. We stopped on the top of this hill about 300 yards away and he got out. He must have stood for an hour, binoculars in his hands, just staring down into the crater."

Over the next four weeks Maralinga shook and rumbled to the tune of three more massive atomic explosions. The bombs were detonated soon after dawn, collection and retrieval of instruments and equipment just before noon. Later in the year scores of so-called 'minor trials' were held in which small nuclear devices were set off. These never made much of a bang, but the scientists seemed a lot more nervous when entering those areas.

Murdo wondered about that, as he wondered about a lot of things...like the strange and disturbing story he overheard about the human beings who had supposedly been brought up in a truck to within two miles of the fourth, and last, of the 'big bang's, at One Tree site.

This story was told by three Australian Sappers who arrived back from the range ashen-faced and in need of a drink. They had been checking instruments at One Tree when a truck had pulled up in an isolated spot away from all the activity. Just behind was a Land Rover containing two stern-faced civilians.

The driver of the truck jumped out and joined them in the following vehicle which then sped off back to the camp. The three Australians were curious and went over to have a look. As they got near they were stopped in their tracks by a cacophony of moans and howls emanating from the truck.

At first they thought the vehicle might contain animals, but all soon agreed the sounds came from human throats. 'Unearthly sounds' was how one of them described it. It made their hair stand on end, added another over a drink in the beer tent later.

The men got to within about 15-feet of the truck and could clearly see movement inside. But they decided not to investigate further; they were just too afraid of what they might find. Later when they returned to the area to collect their equipment, the truck was in the same place, but no sound came from it.

It was a disturbing tale, and one that gave Murdo a deep sense of unease. It wasn't made any better when later the three Australians abruptly disappeared. According to one of the squaddies they had been sent for in the night and hadn't been seen nor heard from since.

The incident added to the sense of gloom Murdo was beginning to experience about Maralinga. Other incidents only served to heighten this sense of foreboding. Like the day he found a dingo mother which had just given birth to six pups in the contaminated area.

None of the pups appeared to have any eyes and most were missing limbs. The mother, whose fur was hanging limply from her flanks, barked feebly at Murdo as he approached, but was too weak to run away. Murdo destroyed them and buried their bodies in the sand.

Then there was the time he came across a patrol that had a rounded up a small family of aborigines who had wandered into the prohibited zone. The little family, comprising three adults and two children appeared to be in a bad way. Their feet were cut and blistered and there were running sores on their legs. They were upset because the soldiers who found them had shot their two dogs.

Murdo learned the family had been found camping in one of the bomb craters. He was ordered to take them back to camp. On the way they vomited profusely and were obviously in a bad way. They told him they had lost two members of their family out in the desert and that there were more sick people wandering about.

The family was later sent to Darwin, a major town in the north. When Murdo asked after them, a sergeant major informed him brusquely the family had been taken to the 'leprosarium,' a large leper colony on a little island just offshore.

Murdo spent more than a year at Maralinga by which time he had had enough. He'd had enough of the heat and the dust and the desert; he'd had enough of fear-maddened animals and burnt-out buildings and sick human beings. Maralinga had become a cursed place for him and he longed for the green grass and rolling hills of Scotland.

He wanted to feel a cold, salty wind on his face...and most of all he wanted rain, clean, sparkling rain. Murdo decided he was going to leave and he told Wally at the earliest opportunity. Wally wished him luck, but said he was going to stay on for another year to save more money

Later that month, with dire warnings from an officer of what would happen to him if he disclosed any of Maralinga's secrets, Murdo joined a small troop of soldiers and civilians bound for Adelaide. Wally came to see him off: "Wally had been a good mate, we'd been through a lot together and I was sorry to leave him behind," Murdo said.

"I could understand him wanting to stay on because the money was good and we'd both saved quite a bit. Wally said he wanted enough to buy a garage business when he got home. But I just wanted to get away. We shook hands and I left. I never saw Wally again and often wonder what happened to him."

In Adelaide, Murdo managed to get himself a job as a deckhand on a large tramp steamer bound for Liverpool. But before he left he bought himself some fresh clothes and then visited a barber and steam room in the centre of town.

"I felt the need to get shut of all the dust," he explained. "I had my head shaved and later I just sat in the steam booth for about an hour with the heat turned up full blast. When I came out I looked like a lobster, but I felt clean. It was good to change into my new clothes and I put my old ones in a bin. I retain in my mind a very clear memory of a little pile of red dust on the floor of my lodgings where I'd changed out of my old clothes.

"My ship took its own sweet time on the crossing to Liverpool, which was just fine by me. I was in no hurry and I enjoyed watching the dolphins that played alongside the boat as we steamed out of Adelaide.

"It took me more than six weeks to get home. Lewis never looked more beautiful. There were little fishing boats in the harbour and the air was tangy with fish and salt. I felt clean for the first time in over a year. It was good to be home."

With the money he had saved, Murdo bought a small croft in the tiny hamlet of Bac and settled down to the life of a simple shepherd. "I didn't want to do anything else," he said. "I'd had enough of travel and foreign parts."

Later he met Margaret, from Stornaway, and they married. The couple settled into the life of crofters and wanted for nothing. Soon Margaret was pregnant and the couple looked forward to having a child to complete their happiness. "I wanted a girl; Margaret wanted a boy, but really we didn't care which," Murdo said. "We just wanted a healthy child"

Their son was born one June evening in 1960. Murdo was waiting anxiously outside the delivery room when there was a sudden commotion.

He recalled: "I was waiting in the corridor outside while Margaret was being helped in her confinement by the midwife. She seemed to be in there a long time, but I wasn't too worried. I was anxious to find out what we were going to have.

"Suddenly I heard this crying and it sounded like Margaret. I got up to go to the door, but the midwife came out and shooed me away. Another nurse arrived, and then a doctor. Margaret was still crying, and I knew something was wrong.

"I went to the door again, but was told to sit down by the nurse. After a while the midwife came out carrying a little bundle wrapped in a blanket. 'Is that our baby?' I shouted as she disappeared down the corridor. Margaret was still crying and I was desperately anxious.

"A nurse asked me if I wanted a cup of tea. I said, 'No, I do not want a cup of tea. I want to know what is happening.' The nurse said the doctor would be with me soon. I demanded to see Margaret and at last the doctor came out to talk to me.

"I forget his name, but I took a dislike to him. He said in an almost matter-of-fact way that there was something seriously wrong with our wee boy. He said he wasn't expected to live, that these things sometimes happen, it was God's will, stupid things like that. I said I wanted to see Margaret and he just shrugged his shoulders and said it would be best if she rested, and then walked away. I went into see Margaret, but they must have given her something because she was fast asleep. I stayed with her all night; I didn't want her to wake up alone. You can imagine what was going through my head as I waited."

The next day the couple were told their baby had severe malformations and wasn't expected to survive the day. The hospital chaplain was on hand to christen the child and they agreed to call him John Alexander.

"We were numb with shock," Murdo said. "They said it was best if we didn't see our son, and we just went along with it. In any case Margaret was heavily sedated and I was in despair. I don't know how we got through the next few days."

At the end of the week Margaret was sent home. They expected to hear any day that John, who was in an isolation ward, had died, but the child evidently had other ideas. Not only did he survive, he seemed to thrive and after a while the doctors relented and consented to them seeing their son.

Murdo said: "We were shown into this dimly-lit room away from the main hospital where all the other mothers were. I suppose they didn't want to upset them. The nurse let us be and stood quietly in a corner while we walked over to the crib.

"At first I couldn't see what was wrong with our wee boy. He was all wrapped up in blankets and he had a little woollen helmet on his head. But when Margaret picked him up we realised what a sad sight he was. His face was all twisted; Margaret started crying and John opened his eyes. In my shock all I could think of was how big his eyes were. He seemed to be looking at us, but I knew that was impossible. We stayed with him for about an hour and in all that time he never made a sound."

On the way home, Murdo and Margaret decided they were going to keep their son. They had been resigned to giving him up because of what the doctors had been saying. But after seeing him and holding him, they had quite simply fallen in love with him.

They informed the hospital the next day, but to their consternation the doctors said they didn't think John would ever be able to go home. Murdo angrily demanded to see a consultant, but was told bluntly that not only couldn't John go home, but there was to be an inquiry into how the child's condition had come about.

Mrs MacLeod was later questioned at length about what had happened during her pregnancy: what she had eaten, had she had any falls, had she taken any drugs? The questions became more and more intrusive.

"They were almost making out like it was our fault," Murdo said. "It just didn't make any sense. Margaret had never taken so much as an aspirin during her pregnancy. I didn't have a clue what they were getting at."

Murdo decided to tell the doctors about his experiences at Maralinga: "I'd pushed it to the back of my mind, but as soon as I saw John I thought of those wretched dingo pups I found out in the desert after the bomb blast. I don't know why, but I was suddenly convinced John's condition was because of the bomb."

He voiced his fears to a doctor and was frustrated when the man showed little interest. The doctor took notes, but said he was unable to say one way or the other if they were connected, adding that he 'rather doubted it'.

Murdo insisted, however, that it be looked in to, and the doctor reluctantly agreed to take it up with his colleagues. Meanwhile John continued to improve and he was moved to the hospital's geriatric unit (it was felt his presence would be too upsetting on the baby ward) where he soon became a firm favourite with the old folk.

Murdo said: "We wanted to take him home, but the doctors thought it would be best if he stayed on at hospital. They said he would be subjected to ridicule from other children if he was allowed out. We didn't like it, but the doctors said John still needed a lot of treatment and it was best if they kept an eye on him.

"We bided our time because we wanted what was best for him. But we yearned to take him home. John was such a bright, happy little boy. He used to crawl all over the ward, getting up to mischief and making everyone laugh. As soon as we walked into the ward he would scoot over to us and throw his arms around us, and he used to cry when we left. I begged the doctors to let him come home with us, but they always seemed to find some excuse for him to stay."

During this time Murdo was surprised to receive a summons to the hospital to see a consultant who had been sent up from London. Murdo was expecting a talk about his son and, hopefully, be given news about when he could take him home. Instead, he found himself being effectively chastised for bringing up the A-bomb tests.

"I was greatly surprised," he said. "This man questioned me quite severely about why I thought the bomb tests had anything to do with John. I told him about the animals and the fact I had no protective clothing at all and that I couldn't think of any other reason why John was born the way he was.

"The consultant got very impatient with this and told me in no uncertain terms that 'all that' had nothing whatever to do with John or what had happened to him. He told me I must just wipe all that from my mind. He repeated that several times. He tried to make me feel foolish, as though it wasn't my business to be worrying about 'all that.' The man even accused me of scaremongering and it wouldn't help anything if I carried on talking like that. I was most surprised by his attitude. After all I was only trying to get to the bottom of why my son was born the way he was."

Murdo was in for an even bigger surprise a few days later when he was again summoned to the hospital.

"I was shown into this room with all these people sitting round a table. I didn't know most of them, didn't know where they had come from. It was like going before some sort of tribunal and I was on trial. One of the few people I did know, a doctor, told me that John's condition was so serious that it was doubtful he would ever be allowed home. I was told it was in the child's best interests if the local authority took responsibility for him. I started to protest, but another man chipped in and said that everything would be taken care of. A special place had been prepared for John on the mainland where he would get all the care and attention he needed."

A document was produced for Murdo to sign. He found himself staring at an official form, a care order, effectively relinquishing the MacLeod's from all parental rights to their son. Confused and with the anger boiling inside, Murdo demanded to know the reason for the sudden change in attitude. He pointed out that assurances had been given they would be able to take John home at some stage.

The vague replies he received made him even angrier: "They wouldn't give me a straight answer to anything. I felt we had been messed around for long enough. I was suddenly very afraid we might never see our wee lad again. I remember shouting at them that we loved our son and meant to have him with us, no matter what they thought and I remember throwing the document at them across the table. 'I'm not signing that,' I said and walked out.

"When I got home I didn't tell Margaret because it would have been too upsetting. I did tell her it might be longer than we thought before we could have John with us."

In fact it was more than a year before the family were united. During that time Murdo was involved in an almost constant battle with the authorities who said they wanted to keep John for what seemed an almost endless series of tests.

Murdo recalled: "I was convinced they were hiding something from me. Looking back now I am more convinced than ever. At one stage they even admitted to me there was nothing more medically that could be done for John, yet they still wanted to carry out tests.

"Why? I asked myself over and over again. They even took him to Edinburgh for some reason and didn't even tell us. I realise now that what they were doing was wrong, but what could I do? I knew nothing about the law and I mistrusted lawyers even more than I did the doctors. All I could do was keep battling away at them, insisting they let John come home."

The turning point came when Murdo's local community decided to rally around to help. They'd heard about little John and began to lobby local politicians to do something about him. The pressure finally brought results and John, at last, was released into the care of his parents.

They took John home in triumph and the whole village turned out for a celebration. John was given pride of place at a big party and all the children came to wish him well. Far from ridiculing him, they all fought over who was going to be his best friend.

The MacLeod's hugged each other and cried as they watched John at the table surrounded by all his new friends. John sat smiling, loving every minute of it. Murdo said: "Some said he looked like a little old man, but we loved him. I knew we had done the right thing in bringing him home."

But John was still a very sick little boy and they were warned something would take him sooner rather than later. John Alexander MacLeod, died in his mother's arms at two o'clock on the morning of December 20, 1963. He was three and a half years old and his death, according to the certificate, was due to a brain haemorrhage.

The whole village turned out for his funeral. Prayers were said in local churches, and children in the village school were given the morning off. Bells pealed as the small funeral cortege made its way to the little hilltop cemetery at the end of the village. There, buffeted by the clean, wild Atlantic winds, little John, a victim of 'God's will' was laid to rest.

CHILDREN OF THE BOMB

John MacLeod introduced a new dimension to the nuclear veterans' campaign. The idea that men, who may have been exposed to radiation many years ago, could father 'mutant children' (as some of the more lurid sections of the press later dubbed them) had something of a Hollywood 'B' movie ring to it.

McGinley decided to contact other BNTVA members to try to gauge the extent of the problem. He was staggered by the results. A pattern emerged showing that throughout the late 1950s and early 1960s hundreds of deformed, crippled and sick babies were born to the wives and partners of test veterans.

The records later showed that more than 750 children suffered various genetic disorders. Incidences of cancer, blood disease, Down's syndrome, spina bifida and other crippling illnesses were well above normal levels. Whole families were affected; it was almost like a biblical plague, and yet no-one had sounded the alarm. How had this scandal gone unnoticed for so long?

A very prominent Welsh politician, whose sister's husband had spent two years on Christmas Island, provided one answer. He said his sister was so overwhelmed by grief at what had happened to her family that she was simply unable to talk about it. He said her husband, a soldier, had died of pancreatic cancer at the age of 39.

He recalled: "My sister and her family have suffered most dreadfully. When her husband was diagnosed with cancer he was treated appallingly. The Army treated him like a pariah because he blamed his presence on Christmas Island for his illness, and the doctors made him feel like a fool. Neither he nor his wife was given any help or support. She nursed him until he died. And he died a very bitter man because of the things that had happened to his children."

The couple's first child, conceived soon after he came home, lived only for an hour. The child had no top to its head and was deformed. The next child seemed to be OK, but the joy was short-lived. Blood tests revealed the baby, a son, had an incurable type of leukaemia. He is being kept alive on drugs, but his mother has been told it is only a matter of time. As if that wasn't enough, their third child, a little girl, was born with a hair-lip and cleft palate.

Many other families of veterans displayed a similar reluctance to talk. It went a long way to providing an explanation why the scandal had remained concealed for so many years.

These people simply had no desire for their agony to be resurrected once again, especially in the columns of a newspaper or the flickering light of a TV screen. Nevertheless, enough people decided the time had come to speak out.

Archie Ross, who was at Grapple Y had been skeptical about the possible adverse health effects. He just did not believe the bomb was responsible for the cataracts on his eyes, or the terrible suffering endured by his malformed daughter.

It took a remarkable coincidence and a bit of detective work to convince him. Overnight he turned from doubting Thomas to believer. His conversion began with a telephone call to an old RAF colleague whom he had not seen since they were together on Christmas Island in 1958.

Mr Ross recalls: "I was 23-yrs-old and newly married and I faced the prospect of a year under canvas on this fly-blown desert island. But I didn't have much time to moan. I arrived on November 4th 1957 and four days later I witnessed the most impressive and terrifying device I will ever see, the detonation of the hydrogen bomb.

"But I had great trust in my superiors and also in the British Government and scientists. I believed they would never send men into a situation that was suspect, or dangerous, or untried without being certain it was all safe, sound and secure.

"I served my time reluctantly, but with ever hopeful prospect of returning home safely to the new adventure of married life. I wished and worked like all the other men who worked with me, the time away. Having spent all but three days short of a year, I returned home in November 1958 to as near a normal life as possible in H.M. forces, and went about my life.

"On 11th April 1960, my wife gave birth to a little girl, Julie, and the grief of finding this tiny tot malformed was indescribable. The cause? No-one could say; no-one understood. The doctors said it was an act of God, but a few people suggested it could have been as a result of Christmas Island.

"I was totally, but totally unconvinced. As far as I was concerned there was absolutely no reason for it to be Christmas Island. There was nothing wrong with me. I was unaffected. Julie's condition was simply hard luck. An accident. An act of God.

"In any event, we were far too concerned about our daughter to be worried about why she had been born that way. Our tiny child, at the age of two years, commenced a series of 16 major operations, ending at the age of 17.

"The people at Great Ormond Street Hospital for sick children were marvelous. They were so kind to our little girl who hated operations, who arrived sometimes twice a year pale-faced with fear, who tried to smile, desperately and bravely, hoping the operation would be cancelled, but still going through with it.

"There was a lot of talk of thalidomide at the time, but never about Julie. We were on our own; there was no comfort in knowledge, nothing to blame. No-one knew what caused Julie to be malformed.

"Then things started to go wrong with my own health. At the age of 45 I began to have very itchy eyes. At the age of 47, my eyelashes began to grow into my eyes. At 48 the nuisance became an ordeal. Then a young doctor noticed skin adhesions in my right eye. It soon developed into my left eye. He sent me to a specialist who told me he didn't know what was causing the problem and that he had never seen it in anyone of my age.

"The specialist asked me questions and he became very interested when I mentioned Christmas Island. He said bright, flashing lights could have caused my problem. He told me of the nuclear veterans association and advised me to contact them. I felt I would be better advised seeking another specialist, which I did. To my surprise he also advised me to contact the association, so I did.

"I spoke to the British Nuclear Tests Veterans' Association and I told them I was extremely sceptical. They suggested I should contact one or two of my old comrades from Christmas Island. I was impressed by the fact they did not try to force opinions on me, so I decided to do a bit of detective work.

"After many weeks I located one old chum from Christmas Island who was still serving with the RAF. He had travelled with me to the island. We shared a tent, worked together and travelled back together.

"When I telephoned, he was not at home, so I introduced myself to his wife whom I'd never met. Without divulging any of my problems I enquired after my old comrade. 'How's he getting on these days?' I asked.

"'Very well indeed,' came the reply.

"'It's years since I last saw him. Is he still fairly fit?'

"'Oh yes, he's OK...except for the fact he's been experiencing eye trouble since he was 40.'

"'Really? In what way?'

"'Cataracts. First one eye, then the other. He is waiting for another operation now.'

"'Good grief,' I said. 'I am sorry. Is everyone else OK?'

"'Yes, we have two sons both of whom are healthy,' she said. 'Have you any children?'

"'Three,' I replied. 'The eldest one unfortunately was malformed at birth, but after a traumatic youth she really has turned out to be a super lass and I am extremely proud of her. She has adjusted very well.'

"'How strange,' came the reply. 'Our first child was deformed and died soon after birth.'

"Her reply hit me like a bombshell. After 27 years of many painful and miserable experiences with Julie, the penny finally dropped. It was just too much of a coincidence; the atomic bomb had to be responsible for her suffering.

"I felt myself becoming very angry. I thought of all the fine, healthy, strong young men who were sent out to the bomb tests. Those fit, trusting young men. Young men who were never given a choice. They trusted their government. They trusted their superiors. They trusted the scientists. And most of us trusted in God.

"The reward? A long, lingering, wasting death for many. Leaving wives with children. Many of those children have died. Many of those children are deformed. I was appalled and sickened. There was no doubt in my mind. The atomic bomb was responsible and we had been conned and lied to for 30 years."

Many more came forward from every corner of the country with similar heart-wrenching stories.

In the tiny village of Llanymddyfri, near Swansea, Mrs Margaret Basey, had never doubted the insidious effects of the bomb tests. She spoke after she put her 'baby son' to bed. Her 'baby' was Stephen and he was a fully grown man aged 22 years.

He had been born with crippling physical malformations and was severely mentally handicapped. Stephen was unable to perform the simplest of tasks, and needed constant care and attention But with a devotion only a mother can give, Mrs Basey was coping as best she could.

Stephen was born four years after her husband, March Buttivant Basey, who served in the Royal Navy returned from Christmas Island where he witnessed two nuclear tests. He died of multiple myeloma, a bone disease, in 1975 and Mrs Basey had been left to care for their son alone.

As in the case of John MacLeod, the authorities wanted to step in. Mrs Basey said: "When Stephen was born they wanted to take him away from us. They said he would be better off in an institution, but we chased them. I told them if anyone was going to look after him, it was me. They weren't very happy, though.

"I hated those people. My poor late husband had been such a healthy man; strong as an ox and he was so gentle and kind. But he'd changed when he came back from those tests. Disease coursed through his veins and his spirit was broken. They didn't care.

"He hardly ever talked about the bomb tests, but I knew they'd changed him. He'd become moody and irritable, completely unlike the man I knew before. He seemed to be crumbling inside and I was very worried about him. When I became pregnant, I thought it would change things. I thought we could go back to the way we were before. But then Stephen was born, and March just got worse.

"I tried to talk to him about why Stephen was the way he was, but March didn't want to discuss it. I spoke to the doctors telling them there had never been any illnesses in either of our families, but they just shrugged their shoulders and said it was one of those things.

"When March got the cancer he lost the will to live, really. The cancer was the last straw. It was a nasty cancer and he suffered a lot. I did my best for him, but the spirit had gone. The only time he spoke about it was just before he died. He told me his sickness was the result of the bomb tests and he also believed our son's condition was caused by the same thing.

"He was totally convinced about it. He told me not to believe anything the doctors said and to fight for all the help I could get. He said he knew he was dying and that he was sorry for everything, and then he died."

"I've never forgotten what he said. There's just me and Stephen now and he is our son. I don't mind looking after him. He goes to a special school during the day, but he always comes home to me in the evening. He is just a big baby really, and I know he would be heart-broken if he was parted from me. I admit we could use some help, but Stephen gets all the love he needs at home. He wouldn't get that in care."

Sid Harris a hotel owner from Blackpool cries bitter tears; he cries tears for the boy who wasn't able to. His only son Trevor couldn't cry because disease affected the ducts in his eyes, making it impossible for him to shed a tear. When the pain got too bad, all he could do was rock back and forth while he cried inside.

Trevor died at the tender age of 12. Mr Harris, who witnessed three nuclear explosions during service with the RAF on Christmas Island, said: "Trevor was born with an extremely rare disease, a form of cancer that affects the bone and the blood. It's so unusual there were apparently only 12 cases in the world. It caused my son's bones to literally crumble to dust, and I had to watch him while he suffered. There was nothing anyone could do.

"I don't think Trevor had a pain-free day in his short life. It really was a terrible disease and he was always in pain. The more I saw him the more angry I became because no-one could tell me why he was suffering so much. Everyone wants to blame someone or something for this sort of thing. But I must admit I went along with the doctors who said it was probably just pure chance. I'm not so sure now.

Former army motor mechanic Ken McCormack lived with death and disease in his family since witnessing Britain's first A-bomb at Monte Bello in 1952.

He recalled: "I always blamed the bomb, but no-one would believe me. I have always been convinced it ruined my health and that of my family. I have never been so sure of anything in my life. I have suffered a series of heart attacks, but the loss of our eldest son Peter hit me hardest of all. He was born soon after I returned to Britain and contracted a rare form of kidney cancer to which he eventually succumbed at the age of 28."

Mr McCormack was so convinced the bomb caused his son's cancer that tried to get the words 'radiation induced cancer' on his death certificate. Of course the doctors wouldn't comply.

He recalled: "They said they were unable to do that because they did not know what caused Peter's cancer. The nearest they could get was that it was an act of God. But I am sure it was because of my radiation exposure. I know I was contaminated because of the nature of my work.

"I was stationed about seven miles from the explosion and part of my job was to measure radiation levels in samples recovered from the shore near the test site. The instruments I was handling were highly radioactive, the Geiger counters went off the scale, but the only protection I had was a pair of gloves. I was never told about possible dangers. Like the rest of the men I just did as I was told."

His wife Muriel lost two other children through stillbirths. "They never let me see those babies because they were so badly deformed," she said. "They never even told us what sex they were. There is something very wrong with this family, yet neither Ken nor I have had any history of bad health in either side. It is as though we have been cursed; I find it hard to understand what has happened to us."

Denise Grove was born with no muscles down the left side of her body. It was a mystifying illness which baffled the best medical brains in Harley Street and consultants in the world famous Great Ormond Street hospital. "The doctors didn't want to touch me," said Denise. "They had no idea what was wrong with me and didn't want to do anything for fear of making things worse."

But as she grew, it became clear something would have to be done. "There were no muscles in my neck, my left arm, or leg. I was all lop-sided. I just flopped all over the place."

Finally a surgeon was found at the Orsett hospital in Essex who was willing to take on Denise. "I think he regarded me as a bit of a challenge. He was a wonderful man and he became a good friend. All I can remember of my childhood is being in hospital, that's all I ever knew. The surgeon tried everything he could think of. He would try one operation, and if it didn't work he'd try another. Then it would be back to the drawing board."

In the first 10 years of her life, Denise had six major operations and more than a dozen minor procedures. She was cut open, stitched up, then cut open all over again. Gradually Denise was rebuilt. Muscles were grafted into her neck so she could hold her head up, and her left arm was strengthened. False ligaments were put in her leg which stretched with her as she grew.

She suffered agonies on the way and had to wear big red surgical boots and a plastic brace which she had to wear day and night. Her childhood was a nightmare of taunting children and cruel stares. As she entered her teens, the doctors said they'd done all they could and that only exercise would now help her recovery.

"I never had any boyfriends," she said. "I lacked the confidence. I worked out a technique where I walked beside my girlfriends and got in the same step as them, so people wouldn't notice my limp. I was often in despair about the cruel things that had happened to me. I used to cry out and I kept wondering why I was born like this. It's been awful going through the years with people asking, 'What's the matter with you?' and my having to say, I don't know.

A lot of people thought I had polio or some other disease. Some people used to shy away from me because they thought it might be contagious! In the end I used to invent things like I was run over by a car, or had had a heavy fall. Anything to stop the questions."

Denise's dad Fred Barker, a former Sapper in the Army told her he had been stationed on Christmas Island when a hydrogen bomb was tested. Denise, his first child, was born less than two years after he returned.

"Dad said he'd always blamed himself for the way I was, but I told him not to worry. It's the Government that should pay for putting so many men in harm's way in the first place. It couldn't possibly be his fault. He was only following orders. I don't know what the future holds for me. I am still a very slow walker and I get very tired, and I am still very weak down my left side. I always have to think about how I walk and have to tell myself to move my left leg in front of my right. I am scared I will end up in a wheelchair."

Mrs Valerie Billing, from Ripon North Yorkshire, was still recovering from the shock of being told her baby daughter Claire had been born with a deformed leg, when the doctor asked her if she had ever been exposed to radiation.

She recalled: "I expected to be asked what sort of pills I had taken, things like that. But I wasn't even sure what radiation exposure meant. How could I, a housewife from Ripon, be exposed to radiation? The doctor said they were considering every possibility because they had absolutely no idea why Claire was born that way. He said radiation exposure was just one of many possibilities. I told him in no uncertain terms that I'd never had so much as an X-ray."

Mrs Billing may not have been exposed to radiation...but her husband Robert had. He was present at three H-bomb explosions on Christmas Island in 1957-58. It was his job to drive an Army land rover taking scientists out to the test sites to collect samples.

He said: "The scientists were covered head to toe in white protective suits and gas masks. All I had on was a pair of shorts and a bush hat to keep the sun off. I must have been contaminated and it looks as though I have passed something on to Claire. There can be no other possible explanation. I think it's very significant that one of the doctors asked my wife if she had been exposed to radiation. Of course she hadn't...but I certainly had."

Gerald Gollop from Wiltshire was serving with the RAF on Christmas Island when he witnessed two explosions. "One of them nearly took the island apart," he recalled. Mr Gollop's health was fine...but his wife had to be sterilised after given birth to two badly deformed babies soon after Mr Gollop returned. The first child, a girl, born in 1960, was so badly deformed, the doctors wouldn't let the couple see her. The child lived for just five hours. Their second child, born six years later, was also deformed, but stillborn "We went through hell," said Mr Gollop. "I always thought there might be a connection with Christmas Island, but the doctors just said it was an act of God."

Young Paul Noble was nicknamed the "matchstick boy" due to a strange illness that made his bones so brittle they would break at the slightest knock. The young man by the time he was 19 years old had broken his legs more than 200 times and suffered innumerable broken arms and collar bones. His mother Margaret said: "We first noticed the disease when Paul began to toddle. As soon as he bumped into something, or just fell over, he would break a bone. He was permanently in plaster throughout his childhood. He had so many he didn't even seem to mind the pain. Paul can't do strenuous exercise apart from swimming. The muscles in his legs are completely wasted."

Doctors offered no explanation for Paul's condition other than, 'It's one of those things', and they didn't seem to make a connection when his dad John, a former Army Sapper, told them he had been out to Christmas Island where he witnessed five nuclear explosions. Mr Douglas of Leslie, Fife, said: "I always had a gut instinct about Paul; I always thought there was a connection with the bomb tests. But who was I to argue with the doctors? They just wouldn't listen."

The case histories piled up. The story had turned into an oddyssey of epic proportions and one that was growing by the day. In just a week thirty-two of those families independently told of the most appalling problems with their offspring. Between them they had a total of 57 children who had either died, been born deformed or suffered other crippling diseases and illnesses.

On the face of it, it was overwhelming evidence that something was seriously wrong with the children of the men who took part in nuclear bomb tests. Their stories resonated with truth.

These were decent, ordinary people with no particular axe to grind or political point to make. They were deeply patriotic and loathed to criticise the services they once so proudly represented.

But they were resentful of the indifference of the Ministry of Defence and the Government to their health problems which they were convinced had been caused through witnessing nuclear bomb tests.

They were also angry at the posturing of ministers whose only experience of atomic bombs had been gleaned from the newsreels. They felt they had been fobbed off, talked down to and treated like troublesome children.

Most felt no surprise that other servicemen's children had been affected. For they had long harboured the suspicion that the atomic bomb was finally reaping its grim harvest.

The story hit the newspapers and there was uproar. Scores more veterans told of problems with their children. But the official guardians responsible for the nation's health were not impressed.

The Cancer Research Institute and the Medical Research Council both agreed that radiation-induced genetic disorders were entirely possible. Laboratory experiments on mice and fruit flies had proved that conclusively.

But most experts dismissed the reports as 'alarmist' and were quick to point out that, two per cent of new-born babies suffered some form of genetic disorder. An article in the prestigious *New Scientist* magazine dismissed the reports as 'biased' because the men had 'selected themselves' by volunteering information about problems in their children.

Professor Joseph Rotblat recognised a familiar pattern in the expert's responses. In an interview he warned about the 'established scientific caucus' who were more concerned about protecting their government-funded grants than delving into the tricky waters of radiation-induced genetic effects. "It's all about money," he said. "You are not going to get anyone to endorse this. They'll use Neel and Schull."

Neel and Schull were two scientists commissioned by the US Government to study the effects on children born after the bombings of Hiroshima and Nagasaki. After a lengthy five-year investigation no evidence of genetic disorders was found in the offspring of survivors.

Despite these official assurances, few people were persuaded. The strictly formal Japanese community shunned survivors of the bomb as being "unclean." Marriage was often impossible; many families left the city to start a new life elsewhere. Those that did escape eradicated all evidence they had lived in Hiroshima.

A 1965 survey of atomic bomb survivors asked couples if they had experienced "adverse discrimination" in marriage. Of those in the unmarried 35-39 age group, 21.4 per cent reported discrimination. It was hardly surprising, therefore, that few reported incidents of damage to their offspring.

But the Hiroshima/Nagasaki cohort were not the only radiation exposed groups to be studied. Early radiologists who absorbed relatively large cumulative doses such as the New Jersey radium dial painters who in the 1910s and 1920s ingested radioactive materials in the workplace all suffered illness and early death. Uranium miners and patients treated with radiation were other affected groups.

Ionising radiation, the same as produced by atomic bombs, was well known to cause biological changes in both humans and experimental organisms. Academic papers available at the time showed that animals exposed to even very low levels of radiation could produce genetically damaged offspring.

As long ago as 1943 distinguished New York scientist Herman Muller won a Nobel Prize for his research into the genetic effects of radiation and it was generally accepted in scientific circles that radiation could induce mutations in the offspring of animals exposed to radiation.

Other research contained clear and unambiguous warnings about the genetic effects of radiation. World-renowned geneticist Dr D.G. Catcheside hammered home the point in a paper entitled 'Genetic Effects of Irradiation with reference to Man,' which he presented to the British Medical Research Council in February 1947.

He wrote: "All organisms investigated viruses, bacteria, fungi, liverworts, flowering plants, drosophila and other insects and mice, show genetic effect as a result of ionising radiations. It is therefore most probable that induced genetic changes, mutation and chromosome changes alike will be induced in man."

This made the long-term medical studies of the A-bomb's victims a high priority, for unlike victims of conventional bombings, their bodies' responses to the effects of the bombs could take decades to appear. All of this makes it even more surprising that Neel and Schull found no evidence of genetic mutation in the offspring of survivors.

In August 1956 Neel and Schull formerly presented their results at the First International Congress of Human Genetics in Copenhagen. Later that year they published them in a paper, tentatively named "The Children of Hiroshima", but published as "The Effect of Exposure to the Atomic Bombs on Pregnancy Termination in Hiroshima and Nagasaki."

When the final 1,241-page report was published, they found themselves under attack from the wider scientific community who accused them of not being able to substantiate the results. Two of their most vociferous critics were Stanley Macht director of the Department of Radiology at Washington County hospital in Hagerstown, Maryland, and Philip Lawrence chief of familial studies unit of the Division of Public Health Methods, in the Public Health Service in Hagerstown.

Macht and Lawrence in October 1951 launched a survey of radiologists and other physicians to detect possible genetic effects of radiation. They sent out 8,000 questionnaires, about half to radiologists and half to physicians in medical specialties unlikely to involve exposure to radiation. The questions asked the doctors how many years they had been regularly exposed to radiation through X-Ray diagnosis, radium therapy or use of radioisotopes and whether they had ever been exposed to levels greater than accepted tolerance levels.

They also asked them to describe their reproductive history, number of children, miscarriages, congenital defects and stillbirths. The doctors wanted to find out if there were any anomalies present in their immediate families or those of their partners.

The Macht and Lawrence results indicated that the offspring of exposed fathers had higher rates of abnormalities. These abnormalities were visible in the first generation of offspring, and although the mutations were statistically relatively small, they were alarming enough to warrant further investigations.

Neel and Schull were quick to dismiss the findings, claiming they had the "holy Grail" of research material in the survivors of Hiroshima and Nagasaki. Their reassurances were accepted by most scientists. But further research once again put them on the back foot.

Paul de Bellefeuille, a Canadian Paediatrician who re-analysed the Neel and Schull data found significant genetic effects in some groups. He published two papers debunking the findings, and even suggested that Neel and Schull had attempted to conceal genetic effects in some groups.

De Bellefeuille decided to analyse the offspring of parental pairs in which one parent was heavily or lightly exposed and the other not exposed at all. This analysis revealed significant effects for sex ratio, stillbirth, neonatal death and total loss. He concluded that his new analysis brought out definite indications of genetic ill-effects of atomic radiation, at a high-level of statistical significance.

Neel and Schull also came under attack in Japan. Professor Sudao Ichikawa, a specialist in radiation genetics at Saitama University, claimed the study was deliberately biased. He did his own calculations and discovered he could make Neel and Schull's information show significant levels of genetic disorders in the children.

In a statement, he said: "It was obvious the figures had been juggled to produce the right answers."

Little of this important research reached the wider public. This considerable body of evidence should have alerted the British scientific establishment to the fact they were wrong to put so much credence on Neel and Schull. But they chose to ignore it

Prof Rotblat thought he knew why: "The problem is that most scientific and medical institutions, especially in this country, rely heavily on government funding for their research. That would be removed at a stroke if the 'wrong' research was produced. Scientists learned a long time ago not to rock the boat. Money always rules the roost."

Dr Anver Kuliev, head of genetics at the World health Organisation in Geneva was one of only a handful of established scientists willing to go on record in support of the veterans. He said new studies, were being carried out whose initial findings suggested there was indeed a link between radiation exposure and genetic disorders.

The Tory government, as usual, was unmoved. A written statement from Adam Butler, a junior Defence Minister was terse and to the point: "Of course we are sorry for these unfortunate children. However it must be said that as there is no evidence that servicemen had received a radiation exposure other than that of normal background radiation, it is unlikely, therefore, that their children would have been affected."

Later that year the long-awaited study into mortality rates among the veterans was published by the National Radiological

Protection Board. Fronted by distinguished scientist Sir Richard Doll, the report was maddeningly inconclusive.

On the one hand it found that mortality rates were roughly similar among the veterans and a control group of ex-servicemen who had not attended the bomb tests, and a similar pattern emerged for cancer rates. But although the report also identified a possible increased risk in test participants developing leukaemia, this was dismissed as a "chance finding."

The MoD's response to a rising tide of criticism of the report from various academics and organisations was to commission a second study by Doll and his team, which it was estimated would take at least another two years. The plight of hundreds of sick children of nuclear veterans was completely ignored.

With public interest beginning to wane, the veterans lobbied individual MPs for support. Most Tory MPs, the party in power, refused to endorse the veterans (with the exception of Winston Churchill, grandson of the war-time leader and a handful of others), while those in the Labour and Liberal ranks whole-heartedly gave their support. The Labour Leader Neil Kinnock gave a "categorical pledge" to hold a full judicial inquiry into the bomb tests once Labour was returned to power. The rest of the putative Labour government, including a young Tony Blair, his deputy John Prescott, Margaret Beckett, David Blunkett and Jack Straw also solemnly promised to help the veterans.

The Ministry of Defence was eventually forced to issue another statement admitting that radiation could cause genetic damage, but added the confusing rider: "As far as radiation damage is concerned, it is known that for a given dose, the risk of causing genetic damage is markedly less than the risk of causing cancer."

The statement was ridiculed. Distinguished Birmingham epidemiologist Dr Alice Stewart, who had already produced a study showing that atomic veterans had suffered a higher than normal rates of cancers, accused the government of trying to fudge the issue, adding: "The clear link between radiation and genetic effects has been well established for many years."

Another scientist, Dr Rosalie Bertell, head of cancer research at the Rothwell Park Institute in Buffalo, New York, also condemned the MoD's statement. Dr Bertell, who was in England to present evidence at a public inquiry into the Sizewell B nuclear plant said: "The nuclear powers have been covering up the genetic effects of radiation since Hiroshima."

The row rumbled on, but the government refused to budge. One Tory minister admitted privately: "We can't accede to these demands there is no telling where it will end." And there lay the problem with the veterans' campaign: it was in some ways too successful. They had won the argument and secret plans were in the pipeline to compensate them through the social security budget. But the added dimension of the veteran's children would open the door to unimaginable payouts. So the government dug its heels in and counted on the media and by default the public, growing bored with the story. But just when they thought the issue had gone away, the nuclear agenda was kept in the headlines by new revelations about the notorious Sellafield reprocessing plant which for 30 years had been the dark heart of Britain's nuclear bomb making industry.

THE DARK TOWER

On the wild and windswept coast of Cumbria in the far north west of England stands the giant Sellafield nuclear plant glowering on the horizon like a modern-day manifestation of the Dark Tower in Tolkein's *Lord of the Rings.*

There is something about Sellafield that inspires supernatural awe. When it was built in the 1950s it was so remote that it was a dawn to dusk journey just to travel the 350 miles from London.

Even today the last 40 or so miles can only be accessed by the A595, a winding country road that hugs the shoreline of the Irish Sea as it meanders through valleys and towering rocky outcrops. For miles there is little sign of habitation until quite suddenly after a bend in the road the giant plant leaps into view.

There is an almost palpable sense of foreboding about the place, and up close it seems to thrum with a dark energy. Legends of death and disease are woven into its fabric, and the deadly menace of its discharges extends for miles along the once pristine coastline of the Irish Sea.

People who live in this remote corner of England have learned to live and even welcome Sellafield for the wealth and prosperity it has brought. They have made a pact with the nuclear devil in return for a more equitable life.

Sellafield was built in the late 1940s on the site of an old Royal Ordnance factory, and the local population, mainly farm workers, looked upon the activities with some interest.

The huge influx of building workers, mainly Irish navvies, bussed in to dig the ditches and foundations, were looked upon with suspicion, while the vanguard of young pipe-smoking, duffle-coated scientists was regarded with the same awe as an invasion by alien beings.

Lured from Oxford and London to take part in the pioneering work, these brilliant young men were housed in a guarded, purpose-built hostel next to a derelict Georgian mansion brooding among trees in the village of Holmbrook.

Living accommodation was three concrete blocks containing single rooms, said to compare favourably with a luxury hotel. A communal block contained a bar, a billiards room, shops, an assembly hall and a dance floor. Peacocks sunned themselves on the roof while dominating the skyline, the mighty square-topped 400-foot towers of Sellafield looked like unworldly monuments awaiting their statues.

The daily ritual for workers entering the site was straight out of science fiction. They entered through guarded gates and were required to remove all their clothes and don fresh ones. On leaving they had to go through a series of showers and then enter a machine which clanged "like a demented fire engine" if it detected any radioactivity.

Outside the closely-guarded gates of the plant, green vans toured the narrow lanes as scientists tested water, soil and vegetation.

Atomic energy development was the most exciting job in Britain at the time and the young scientists revelled in the allure of being at the cutting edge of a new scientific dawn.

The serious business of producing plutonium began in 1947 when the plutonium production piles were built. The system was cooled by air flow rather than water and was considered revolutionary at the time.

The site was given a new name, Windscale, and work progressed at a brisk pace. By 1952 production of plutonium commenced and by March of that year the site operators opened up the reactor vessel and gazed upon the first plutonium produced in Britain.

It was a singular achievement, and the precious cargo was soon heading for Aldermaston to be installed in Britain's first atomic bomb.

There was much rejoicing and the scientists became the "nuclear knights" of the realm invested with Arthurian acclaim and prestige. Their stock rose even higher when Britain's young Queen Elizabeth II formally opened Britain's first nuclear power plant on the nearby Calder Hall site in October 1956.

The new station was hailed as a world first and amazing things were promised. The new "super-fuel" would soon transform energy supplies.

Word got round that a single ton of uranium would release as much energy as four million tons of coal, making nuclear power "too cheap to meter."

Holiday jets and cruise ships would soon be powered by nuclear engines; harbours could be blasted out of the coastlines by "controlled atom bombs", and even household appliances such as kettles and washing machines could, in theory at least, be powered by "nuclear atoms."

None of these things of course ever came to fruition, but it was necessary to whip up the patriotic fervour to mask

Windscale's primary objective: to produce the fuel for Britain's atomic weapons.

As the arms race intensified Britain was desperate to stay in the running. More and more demands were made on Windscale, to produce enough plutonium for Britain's bomb makers at Aldermaston.

The workload became too much and the system began to creak. The first ominous sign occurred in May 1956 when a steel component in the furnace with its deadly charge of uranium fuel shattered.

An immediate repair was essential to prevent a massive release of radioactive gases. The only way to repair the damage was by entering the "basement" of the furnace via the concrete channel that links the furnace to a deep pond used to store the spent fuel rods.

But even with protective suits, no man could spend more than 25 minutes in the chamber. Meltdown was only averted by 251 volunteers working in quick-change relays.

Details of the incident were kept secret and the crash production of plutonium for Britain's nuclear bombs continued unabated. It finally proved too much for the system. In October 1957 Pile No. 1 blew its top and an uncontrolled fire raged for two days and nights.

According to official reports a problem was first identified at 2pm on October 10 when radiation monitoring equipment identified activity in an air sampling filter.

Other measurements were taken from various areas of the site before Pile No 1 was examined by health physics officials. The sight through a viewing window must have made their hair stand on end: the heart of the pile containing the uranium was glowing white hot and vast quantities of radioactivity were being released.

Amazingly the plant's bosses tried to keep things "in-house" and no warnings were issued. As Pile No 1 spewed radioactivity into the air, local people went about their business as usual; mothers pushed their babies in prams along the streets, shops displayed their foodstuffs in the windows and young children played in their gardens.

While this was going on Windscale managers were in a panic. No-one seemed to know what to do and for a while the site resembled a film set for the Keystone Cops.

Guards from the on-site Atomic Energy Authority police were issued with protective suits and respirators, and ordered to guard the perimeter. But the sight of these unfamiliar figures, reeking of rubber and grunting incoherently into facemasks sent their Alsatian guard dogs wild, the result being they immediately attacked their masters.

As the guards and dogs ran hither and thither over the site, the managers were desperately trying to find out what was happening inside the furnace. An old periscope from a submarine was used to look inside the furnace while a contingent of men were despatched to strip a nearby building under construction of its scaffolding.

Scores of men, working without protective clothes, used the scaffolding to push thousands of highly radioactive fuel elements out of the stricken reactor pile. Others wrestled with burning graphite as the furnace began to glow red hot.

They worked through the night but the pile carried on burning and the scaffolding glowed white hot and melted. They soon became exhausted and most had far exceeded the radiation limit. Other volunteers were bussed in from outside.

After two days, and with the fire burning out of control, the decision was taken to try to put the fire out with water hoses. This was a highly risky procedure which could have culminated in a huge explosion.

But the bosses decided they had no choice; only then was the local police force alerted and evacuation procedures put in place. Luckily the feared explosion never materialised and the situation was gradually brought under control.

But by this time the word was out and a ripple of panic spread throughout the surrounding communities. Local media representatives arrived at the gates of the plant and their ranks were soon swelled by hundreds more who swept up from Manchester and London to report on the "Plant of Doom."

Windscale managers felt as though they had been transported back to the French revolution as the clamouring mob besieged the gates to the plant. The situation was not made any better by the all-pervading stench of thousands of gallons of sour milk dumped by local farmers in fields after officials warned their cattle had been grazing on contaminated land.

With the world now watching, the government was desperate to play-down the incident. Press releases spoke of only "minimal" releases of radiation and reassured the public that the release of iodine-13, which could cause thyroid cancer, would deteriorate in less than a week.

But prime minister Harold McMillan wanted to bury the issue, and summoned one of the few men he could trust to clear up the mess: William Penney.

Penney, already overloaded with work on the imminent Grapple X H-bomb trial at Christmas Island, rattled through the proceedings with almost indecent haste and "faults of judgement and inadequacies of instruments" were blamed for the accident.

A White Paper, published barely a month later, stated that the "Windscale mishap" caused injury to no-one and did not cause any local contamination.

An early press release suggested that most of the contamination was blown into the Irish Sea, although this was later amended when it was admitted there were two distinct plumes, one that carried fallout toward the north-east and the second south-east over densely-populated areas of England.

Contamination eventually reached western Europe. Penney insisted that much of the evidence presented to the inquiry be presented in secret because of national security considerations. The effect was to put a cloud of distrust over the site. And there was much to be suspicious about.

Joseph Corrie, a Sellafield worker who helped put out the fire later died from bone cancer. His widow Sheila told an inquest her husband had worked at Sellafield since 1947.

On the day of the 1957 fire she said: "He had been working right underneath the fallout. They were told the following Monday to wash all their clothes, but he had worked all day in those clothes. Someone told him he was contaminated."

She said her husband's illness started with pain in his back and ribs and was in "terrible pain." Sellafield's chief medical officer Dr Geoffrey Schofield said he carried out tests on Mr Corrie's liver, lung and bones. These showed levels of plutonium in the organs between five and 10 times that in the general public. He added that the quantities of plutonium were "extremely small."

The eight-man jury at Whitehaven returned an open verdict on Mr Corrie's death.

Nuclear scientist Joseph McMaster was enjoying a day off at Seascale with his family when the fire broke out. He, his wife Stella and baby daughter Lynn were all exposed to radioactive fallout as they enjoyed a brisk walk along the coast.

Mr McMaster recalled: "On the day of the accident I remember seeing this plume of black smoke coming from one of the reactor stacks and thinking, God, I hope that's not what I think it is. But no warning was given for days, so we thought things were all right and continued to walk; we enjoyed a picnic in the sand dunes while all the time fallout was raining down on us. No-one told us."

Over the next 24 years the couple were to bury three of their four children. Daughter Lynn died of a rare form of leukaemia, linked to radiation exposure, when she was still a teenager. Second daughter Jill died of a similar sickness a few years later. Mrs McMaster later gave birth to twin girls one of whom, Judith, died after three days. Doctors said her lungs were not properly formed. The Ministry of Defence rejected out of hand any connection with the Windscale fire.

Twelve miles up the coast from the plant is the village of Maryport which experienced a sudden sharp spike in Downs syndrome births in the aftermath of the 1957 fire.

Very high levels of radiation were found on the beaches which many believed caused the problem. Researchers found that on average 164 babies a year were born in Maryport during the 1970s. Figures show you would expect one Down's syndrome child for every 1,600 live births to women in their twenties.

On that basis one Down's baby would be born in Maryport every 10 years. Yet in the same period eight Down's babies were born to women with an average age of 25.

Another extraordinary cluster of Down's babies was linked by two Irish doctors with women who were at school together in Dundalk, across the Irish Sea from Windscale. The authorities dismissed both claims as "fanciful".

But the slow drip, drip of cases was starting to build and in 1983 the dam burst. A Yorkshire TV documentary revealed that childhood leukaemia in the Seascale area was 10 times the national average.

The programme struck a chord and dovetailed neatly with the claims being made by the nuclear veterans. It soon transpired that many men who worked at the plant, now renamed Sellafield because the Windscale name had become so toxic, had fathered children with a range of genetic disorders.

The controversy reached fever pitch when it was discovered doctors had been secretly "harvesting" the dead bodies of stillborn children and those killed in road accidents for tissue samples to test for radiation uptake.

This hugely controversial research, carried out by West Cumbria Health Authority, also studied samples of foetal tissue and placenta without the consent of parents. The discovery of a document signed by the local District Medical Officer stating it would be "inappropriate to disclose results to parents", added fuel to the flames.

But these "baby experiments" were only the tip of the iceberg. It turned out that pathologists had been collecting bones and body parts from dead and stillborn children for decades and sending them to America for a so-called "sunshine experiment."

Apparently thousands of body parts had been shipped from all over Britain, and other parts of the world, to a research centre in Chicago were tests were carried out on the uptake of Strontium 90, a key ingredient of nuclear bomb tests fallout.

The body parts had been gathered without the knowledge or consent of the parents. The existence of this experiment was at first flatly denied by the British Department of Health. But an American doctor made worldwide headlines by disclosing the existence of just such an experiment called "Project Sunshine".

The United States Department of Energy later admitted more than 6,000 dead babies had been harvested for use in fallout experiments without parental consent.

The National Radiological Protection Board, which had resolutely insisted that no-one had been affected by the fallout from the Windscale incident, finally issued a report estimating that 32 deaths and at least 260 cases of cancer could be attributed to the fire.

But there were widespread concerns that this figure was much too low. In 1993, official figures confirmed that in nearby Seascale, the incidence of leukaemia and non-Hodgkin lymphoma (both linked with people being exposed to radioactive material) was 14 times the national average.

Ken McGinley could see clear parallels with the Windscale experience and that of his own veterans. It didn't surprise him that William Penney had been the man chosen by the government to keep a lid on the incident.

He had been writing to the scientist for several years asking him to comment on the plight of the nuclear veterans, but had never received a reply. In 1985, however, an unexpected opportunity arose to bring ex-soldier and scientist together.

THE URINAL DIALOGUES

Lord William Penney, OM, KBE, OBE, PhD, DSc, Father of the British atomic bomb, Fellow of the Royal Society, Fellow of Imperial College and Supernumerary of St Catherine's College Oxford, must have thought he was in purgatory: every time he went to the lavatory, he was joined at the urinals by Ken McGinley, former private in the Royal Engineers, who greeted him with a cheeky, "We'll have to stop meeting like this…"

Trapped and helpless, Lord Penney could only smile weakly as he endured a stream of questions from the loquacious Scot who easily brushed aside Penney's MoD minder, a huge flat-faced individual with beetling brows, whenever he moved to intervene.

The unscheduled 'meetings' were held in the improbable setting of the gentlemen's toilets in a large building annexed to the St James's hotel in central London. The building was the venue for the Australian Royal Commission which had clattered noisily into town for a spot of Pom-bashing, over the conduct of the British during atomic bomb testing carried out in Australia's vast deserts in the 1950s.

Penney had been most reluctant to take part in these proceedings, but had been persuaded by his former masters in Whitehall. Ever the patriot he agreed to be questioned by the Commission, chaired by a colourful and abrasive Australian judge named James McClelland, dubbed 'Diamond Jim' for his sharp suits and sparkling tiepins that brought to mind a Mississippi riverboat gambler.

Penney was not enjoying the experience.

He had prepared a 12-page statement setting out how the bomb tests had been conducted, and how safety considerations had been the number one priority of the scientific team.

McClelland was having none of it and had already lambasted the British government for withholding relevant documentary evidence covering that period of British scientific history.

He suggested the government was dragging its feet and warned witnesses not to trifle with the truth. He had already caused a minor sensation by producing like a rabbit from a magician's hat an official document showing that British scientists had seriously considered using Wick, an island off the northern coast of Scotland, as a possible test site for nuclear weapons.

Parliament was in uproar; Scottish politicians were raising hell.

Penney, according to those closest to him, was deeply affected by many of the allegations that were coming out of the enquiry, such as those about using men as human guinea pigs.

But the stories that upset him most were those claiming that many of their children had been born deformed. These had already prompted him to send at least one letter to a newspaper expressing his concern about the "dreadful problems."

And it was well known he had been devastated over the birth of a malformed baby to the wife of his old Los Alamos colleague Sir Ernest Titterton.

It was March 1985 and McGinley had been in the news almost constantly for two years. His tub-thumping allegations had culminated in part to Penney's presence before the commission.

Under normal circumstances, Lord Penney would have run a mile before agreeing to see McGinley who only that afternoon had been on TV accusing Penney and his political masters of "crimes against humanity".

Unfortunately for Penney, the meetings were unavoidable. At aged 76, he had a condition not uncommon in gentlemen of advancing years: a weak bladder. This necessitated him visiting the toilet at frequent intervals and, to his obvious embarrassment, found his visits coincided with McGinley who, it seemed, had a bladder condition in synchronisation with his own.

Scientists like Penney had good reason to be careful about whom they met. Once feted and admired, they were now being treated like pariahs. The horrors of nuclear war had been brought into sharp focus by the veterans, and the public was baying for blood, especially in Britain which had a long tradition of nuclear antipathy.

Penney's shoulders slumped whenever the slightly-built Scot appeared at his side; it was an ignominious position to be in for a man of his stature.

McGinley, who away from the microphones was a courteous man, was aware of his discomfiture. "I don't mean to bother you Lord Penney," he said during one visit. "I'm not doing this deliberately. It's just that, well...if you've got to go, you've got to go."

Lord Penney, a burly square-set individual, big around the beam and a heavy jaw, had been given a rough ride by the commission who seemed to be holding him personally responsible for all the sins of the nuclear bomb tests.

He was forced to answer some uncomfortable questions and admitted that at least one of the bomb tests had been far bigger than expected. Penney obviously loathed the experience.

Throughout all the pre-publicity, he had maintained a lofty silence, not wanting to add fuel to the debate, hoping all the brouhaha would eventually go away. He had never been known to give an interview about the bomb tests, and he usually avoided questions.

But on his 'comfort breaks' he could hardly avoid McGinley, and McGinley took full advantage: "I bombarded him with questions at every opportunity," recalls McGinley.

"I knew I would never get another chance. I told him about the effects on some of the soldiers and how it had affected their lives. I told him about the widows left behind and the children that had been born deformed. I said it could not possibly be all coincidence.

"He listened carefully and looked distinctly uncomfortable. I don't think anyone had spoken to him like that before. I remember him saying he was "sorry" for what had happened to the men, and that everything had been done to protect them.

"He gave me a copy of the statement he had made to the commission. As far as I was concerned it was full of inaccuracies, but I didn't want to upset him, and his minder was ready to step in at the first opportunity.

"I believe he was sincere in what he was saying, but I also thought he was hiding something and I told him so. Penney just looked sad. That's my last memory of him."

McGinley couldn't know it, but Penney was battling liver cancer to which he finally succumbed in 1991.

Some experts said it was 'highly likely' it was linked to his role in the atomic bomb tests. Some believed it was an apposite end to a life steeped in secrecy and suspicion.

His scientific achievements were monumental, but people like Ken McGinley found it hard to have any sympathy. "The fact is that people like Penney and his ilk destroyed thousands of lives, and I can't really forgive him for that," was McGinley's only comment.

Lord Penney's funeral took place in the village of East Hendred, 20 miles from Oxford, where he and his wife retired to in 1976.

He lived in some splendour in a substantial 17th century cottage in Cat Street with white plaster walls, hand-hewn beams in the ceiling, manicured lawns and substantial of gardens.

As the "Father of Britain's H-bomb" he had been showered with honours and took up several academic positions including Rector of Imperial College.

He remained shy and secretive to the end of his life and rarely talked about the atomic bomb tests that had brought him so much prestige and fame. But he was said to have retained a self-deprecating sense of humour, despite the horrors his work conjured up.

One example of this came at the height of his fame in 1958. Harold Macmillan invited him to a drinks party and asked him how many megaton bombs it would take to destroy Britain, to which Penney replied: "Five or six will knock us out, or to be on the safe side seven or eight," adding with his characteristic grin: "I'll 'ave another gin and tonic, if you'd be so kind."

His old Los Alamos colleague, Professor Michael Moore, believed that Penney never got over the death of his first wife. "I believe this is what drove him to achieve what he did," he recalled.

"He had a naturally sunny disposition which changed after her death. Penney was always marked down for greatness and he never had any of the pangs of conscious about the use of the atomic bomb that most of the rest of us had.

"He was a British patriot through and through, even though I did hear talk that the Americans regarded him as 'one of their own' from the time he went to America to study in the early 1930s.

"Certainly he always went along with everything the Americans said. They trusted him because he was never tainted by any connection with the Communist cause prevalent in Cambridge and other universities at the time.

"They were particularly impressed that Penney had cut off all ties with Hyman Levy, his mathematics tutor at Imperial College, who was a well-known communist.

"Of all the British scientists, it was Penney that people like Leslie Groves, the director of the Manhattan Project, wanted most to work in America. But Penney would never leave the country he loved."

Penney liked gardening, and could often be seen digging for potatoes in a small vegetable patch to the left of the house. Locals called him "Bill", his wife was known as "Lady P" and they, as you might expect, were pillars of the community.

Before he died, he burned all his private papers and tellingly left a substantial sum in his will to build a play park for local children.

It was later officially opened by his wife Lady Eleanor Penney in memory of her husband. She walked down a footpath through a crowd of villagers and children to open the new Penney Play-park. She cut a ribbon across the gate and unveiled a plaque commemorating the opening. She told the local newspaper: "Bill loved children and always found them much easier company than their elders."

THE ROAD TO CHERNOBYL

The Australian Royal Commission left Britain with its tail between its legs. The "killer punch" that McClelland had cherished never materialised.

After all the windy rhetoric his commission had discovered that 30 badly-leaking drums of radio-active waste were dumped off the West Australian coast; one hundred aborigines walked barefoot over nuclear-contaminated ground because boots they had been given didn't fit; and a 1953 British nuclear test that allegedly caused a 'black mist' should not have been fired.

These were slim pickings for McClelland who was denied a triumphal return to Australia, and even less for McGinley and his veterans to get their teeth into. The Ministry of Defence appeared bomb-proof; there was no exposed flank to attack. Once again the veteran's campaign began to sink in a sea of indifference.

Fate took a hand on April 26, 1986 at 1.23am Moscow time, when an explosion occurred in the No 4 unit of the Chernobyl nuclear power station 18km from the town of Chernobyl and 2km from the "company town" of Pripyat.

It was the most serious accident in the history of nuclear power. A series of blunders by operators involved in safety checks led to the withdrawal of all 211 control rods from the reactor.

This in turn led to a sudden loss of water used to cool 1,661 uranium fuel assemblies that were set in pressure pipes surrounded by 1,700 tons of graphite blocks. This in turn caused a power surge creating a huge chemical explosion which blew the top off the reactor and spewed out vast quantities of radiation.

Conservative estimates put the energy release at around 50 million curies. This represents about 4,000 times as much activity as was released in the 1957 Windscale fire, and a million times as much as 1976 Three Mile Island accident in Pennsylvania caused by a partial meltdown in a nuclear reactor.

But because of mismanagement and a lack of monitoring equipment no-one on the site at first appeared to realise the wreck of reactor No 4 was leaking vast quantities of radioactive substances into the environment.

In the immediate aftermath about 150 people on site suffered from radiation sickness and 31 died of a variety of causes, including radiation, burns and falling masonry.

In the surrounding population most people were protected from the immediate effects because they were indoors (most in their beds), although many lived in wooden buildings which did not give as much protection as more conventional European dwellings. A woman, who was in her garden at the time, did experience symptoms of radiation sickness (sudden vomiting and extreme tiredness) within hours of the explosion.

More than 30 separate fires were caused by the explosions and there are many stories of heroic actions by the men who dealt with the immediate aftermath of the disaster.

Within five minutes the paramilitary fire brigade serving the station arrived on the scene. This was very soon reinforced by the Chernobyl town brigade who immediately attacked the fire on the roof of the turbine hall.

Without a thought for their own safety, and with no protective clothing, the fireman successfully prevented the fire from damaging unit No 3, which was separated from No 4 by just a wall.

There was no telling the consequences if that the wall had been breached. The main, and most dangerous, core fire was dealt with by 6.35. Six of the firemen were later to die of acute radiation sickness, and many others were severely affected.

In the early hours after the explosions, the health of those on site was the principle concern of the emergency authorities. Evacuation of the town of Pripyat didn't begin until noon on April 27.

However, iodine preparations had been given to children at school on the morning of April 26, and to the rest of the town in the afternoon.

At first the well-paid company workers were stoical about what was happening. They calmly went about their business as usual. But by the late afternoon something akin to panic was beginning to set in.

Long queues formed outside emergency stations where the iodine was being distributed, and there were reports of people burning their mouths and even poisoning themselves through lack of instruction.

As the day wore on water carts began spraying the streets and stalls selling vegetables and other foodstuffs were removed.

The enormity of the disaster became more evident as night fell and the sky glowed red in the distance. At daybreak, the authorities finally ordered the evacuation of the town.

Food was left on tables and washing left on lines as more than 47,000 people began a mass exodus; within 18 hours the town was deserted.

In the days following all people within 10km of the plant had been evacuated, and by May 7, all within 30km, a total of 116,000 people from 186 settlements. The huge movement of people was swollen by the evacuation of tens of thousands of cattle as well as sundry other farm animals.

Meanwhile the shattered remains of No 4 reactor continued to burn. Tons of graphite ignited, while molten metal fissioned out of control, releasing dangerous isotopes that were sucked up into the smoke, adding to the radioactive soup above the plant.

Helicopters dumped huge loads of lead, sand and boron onto the plant in an unsuccessful attempt to staunch the conflagration. Water could not be used because it would have reacted with the graphite which would have created a huge cloud of deadly carbon monoxide.

The authorities realised the only option they had was to try to contain the fire until all the flammable material ran out. Meanwhile an enormous radioactive plume began to drift toward Pripyat --- and beyond.

Of course, none of this was known to the outside world and at first the Soviets did their best to conceal it. The first the West knew of something untoward was when the Swedes detected abnormal levels of radioactivity outside their nuclear power plant at Forsmark.

The monitors revealed five times the normal radioactive emissions. Similar reports came from other parts of Sweden as well as Finland and Norway. Sweden after hours of searching confirmed the radiation was not coming from their country.European wind patterns soon revealed the source of the radiation pointed in one direction: the Soviet Union.

When the Swedes and other Scandinavian countries demanded an explanation from Moscow, they were initially met with denials and silence. But after several hours, an expressionless newscaster on Moscow television read a statement from the Council of Ministers, which was dour and uninformative even by Soviet standards.

In full it read: "An accident has taken place at the Chernobyl power station, and one of the reactors was damaged. Measures are being taken to eliminate the consequences of the accident. Those affected by it are being given assistance. A Government commission has been set up."

The news made sensational headlines all over the world. The more Moscow tried to conceal what had happened, the more hungry the West came for information regarding it.

Stories of a huge movement of people and animals on a biblical scale were irresistible. Newspaper editors and broadcasters scrambled for news of this mighty exodus.

Scientists, doctors and nuclear experts where wheeled out to give their opinions on what had happened, while assorted, soothsayers, religious cranks and other doomsday merchants predicted the end of the world.

Despite the best efforts of the Moscow censors, more details of what had really happened began to emerge. Finally President Gorbachev, in the spirit of glasnost, decided to open the door and let the outside world in.

He issued a decree whereby nothing was to be hidden, nothing covered up. Film was released of the helicopters above the smoking reactor ruins desperately trying to damp down the flames and footage was released of queues of evacuees being monitored for radiation at the roadside. The Novosti News Agency was given full powers to release information to Western scientists and news organisations.

One story immediately stood out among many: the heroism of the fire-fighters who had doomed themselves to certain death by entering the nuclear maelstrom without a thought for their own safety.

And one man in particular was hailed the "hero of Chernobyl". He was Lieutenant Colonel Leonid Telyatnikov, head of the Pripyat fire brigade who was one of the first on the scene.

According to Novosti it all began for Telyatnikov at exactly 1.32am when he received a telephone call telling him there was a fire at the nuclear power plant.

He immediately dressed and rushed to his car. Driving toward the plant he had to weave round fiery debris that littered the road. As he got closer to the plant he saw a bluish glow from the remains of what had been reactor No 4.

He realised this was no ordinary situation. Telyatnikov knew he and the rest of the fire fighters were "entering the gates of hell", but he knew what had to be done. They were the only ones who could prevent the fire spreading to reactor No 3.

At the gates, the radiation sensor had frozen at a radiation reading higher than existed in Hiroshima after the atomic bomb.

Telyatnikov and his 27-man crew pressed on nevertheless, even though they knew it was now a suicide mission. They stared up in horror at the reactor room where flames were leaping more than 50 feet into the air, and at tiny figures scurrying in panic in the exposed upper levels.

Several times Telyatniknov climbed to the 120-foot top of the blazing building to direct operations at the very heart of the blaze. He stayed there until the roof collapsed and the flames were finally extinguished.

He and his incredibly brave crew carried on until they were finally relieved by fire fighters from Kiev. The firemen along with paramedics and power-station guards who were injured were flown to Moscow's hospital Six where they were put into an isolation ward and enclosed in sterile plastic bubbles.

About 300 people, suffering from radiation sickness and damage to skin and lungs were later treated at the hospital. But within the first few days, 22 died following a terrible pattern of vomiting, bleeding, black blisters, hair loss and high fever, before lapsing into a coma from which they never recovered.

All over the Soviet Union the fire-fighters of Chernobyl were being treated to the kind of acclaim usually reserved for war heroes.

Two of the fire team that died were given posthumous medals. Telyatnikov, aged just 35, and a father of two, was the only survivor given permission by the authorities to talk about his ordeal.

In a screened interview from his hospital bed, speaking hardly above a whisper, he said: "The fire was raging, devouring everything. The reactor's mouth was pouring out a death-carrying breath. But we had no choice but to stay. It was our duty.

"We didn't know how many people were trapped and we had to stop the fire spreading to the other reactors. We found eight survivors, naked and huddled in the lavatories, miraculously still breathing.

"We stayed for three hours in the choking, blinding poisonous atmosphere and one by one my men began to buckle. I saw my comrade Vladimir Tisschura writhing on the ground and after that Nikolai Vaschuk swayed and fell flat on his back. Then a third man fell. Bravest of all was Vitali Golopa who was only 25.

"He plunged into the radioactive pool beneath the reactor to pull the plug and drain off the contaminated water. He died soon after..."

The outside world was just as enthralled by their bravery as in the Soviet Union. Messages of support and offers of medical and technical help poured in.

Ken McGinley, still pushing his own nuclear agenda back home, wasn't going to let the opportunity pass. As far as he was concerned he and the Chernobyl firefighters were "brothers in arms" and he persuaded his local council and fire service authority in Renfrewshire to strike two bravery plaques in honour of the heroes of Chernobyl.

But he wasn't content to send these prestigious awards via the diplomatic bag: he decided to travel to Chernobyl to personally deliver them. But he was told that was impossible. In those days the Soviet Union was still a closed society for foreigners, and even ordinary Soviet people were not allowed to travel inside their own country without permission.

In any event, the hero fire fighters were in an isolation hospital in Moscow, and virtually the whole of Ukraine and Belarus had been declared a disaster zone.

But McGinley was not to be denied: somewhere he had read the Chernobyl fire-fighters were admirers of British soccer. Using his local contacts he persuaded the players of Celtic and Rangers, Scotland's premier soccer teams, to sign two footballs which McGinley said he wanted to present personally to the heroes of Chernobyl.

One bright morning he walked up the imposing driveway of the Soviet embassy in Kensington Palace Gardens, London, and knocked on the door. A startled security guard eventually showed him into an imposing reception room dominated by a large, ornate desk.

Sitting behind it was a dapper little diplomat who had carefully placed McGinley's two soccer balls into the 'In' tray (they had been removed from McGinley to be security scanned).

With a quizzical expression he listened to the Scotsman's request to personally deliver the objects to the heroes of Chernobyl. He looked at McGinley, then at the footballs. Finally he reached for the telephone.

Within a week the Soviets granted a special visa for McGinley to make the trip as the "honoured guest" of the Soviet people. Soviet President Mikhail Gorbachev, who had taken a personal interest in directing events at Chernobyl, apparently authorised the trip after speaking directly to the British newspaper magnate Robert Maxwell who wanted the story for his newspapers.

Maxwell, a well-known eccentric and business buccaneer, lived up to his billing by personally telephoning McGinley at his home to inform him: "You are going to Russia!" McGinley was taken aback when the tycoon went on to ask him how long he had been a member of the Communist Party!

The bemused Scot recounting the call later said, "I told him I was a Catholic, and that seemed to satisfy him."

Within a fortnight McGinley landed at Moscow's Sheremetyevo international airport to the sort of reception usually given to a visiting world leader.

He was met by various apparatchiks from the Moscow Mayor's office who whisked him off in some splendour in a convoy of sleek Russian Zil limousines to his hotel, where a dinner had been prepared in his honour.

After a visit to the Bolshoi ballet and the Moscow State Circus he was taken to see Telyatnikov and the rest of the Chernobyl survivors at Hospital Six.

The third floor of the hospital had been set aside for dozens of survivors of the Chernobyl disaster who were cocooned in isolation units. For the most part the victims lay motionless in beds, covered in creams and sterile sheeting that swathed their bodies including their heads.

Only their eyes were uncovered as they stared up at the ceiling. There was little hope for some as they quietly waited for death. For others, those that had handled radioactive equipment, extensive skin grafts were the only answer. And, of course, they all faced the near-certainty of contracting cancer later in life.

Half a million people, mainly women and children who had been evacuated to safe areas in the countryside, faced the same uncertain fate although the State authorities insisted it was just a precautionary measure.

McGinley, who bizarrely was greeted as 'Dr McGinley' wherever he went, was bombarded with assurances from various scientists and government officials that the radiation plume had only touched the city briefly when there was a sudden wind change, but there was little residual fallout.

Kiev was now considered safe and the scientists were keen for him to encourage the large numbers of foreign students and tourists who had fled in panic in the immediate aftermath of the disaster to return.

Before he knew it McGinley was escorted to the airport and two hours later touched down at Kiev's Borispol airport. In keeping with his new-found status as international envoy he was placed in glorious isolation at the front of the plane, while the rest of the passengers were herded to the back.

He was the first off the plane and soon on to a smart little mini-bus (his fellow passengers disembarked from the rear onto an open cart pulled by a tractor) and was whisked through customs controls without the usual formalities.

The first thing he saw on stepping out of the terminal building was a tanker truck spraying water across the forecourt. In the distance another tanker was similarly spraying the approach road.

McGinley walked across mats foaming with detergent through the arrivals hall, and was "swept" by a uniformed official with a radiation monitor before being escorted to his car.

On the approach road to Kiev, his car passed a large crowd of schoolchildren, the girls with gaily-coloured ribbons, and the boys wearing sashes, all lined up in regimental fashion waiting to board a convoy of buses. He was told they were being taken to summer camps far away in the mountains "for their own safety."

Five miles from Kiev, the car was stopped at a checkpoint while a soldier sprayed the car tyres with detergent. All along the route huge convoys of military vehicles rumbled north toward Chernobyl, laden with sand and cement. It was explained these were for the vast concrete tomb being built around the stricken reactor.

Kiev city, usually a bustling metropolis of some three million people, was spookily quiet. The sidewalks were mostly deserted and what traffic there was seemed to scurry like beetles between buildings as though to avoid the invisible enemy in the air.

The city's entire transport system had disappeared almost overnight as more than 1,000 buses, trucks and cars were commandeered to help in the huge evacuation of Chernobyl and the surrounding villagers.

Only a few days before, loudspeaker announcements all over the city had ordered the bewildered population to stay indoors and shower every day. No fresh vegetables were to be eaten and milk supplies had to be dumped.

McGinley's small entourage pulled up at the impressive six-storey Dneiper Hotel, and stepped into an eerily silent world. The cavernous foyer echoed to his footsteps as he made his way to the reception desk where a single clerk stood nervously to attention.

McGinley and an official cum minder from Intourist, the State travel agency, and a couple of journalists were the only guests in the hotel, and that night they dined in splendid isolation in the huge dining room beneath magnificently ornate chandeliers. As they ate, a ceaseless convoy of tankers, spraying water, patrolled the roads and pavements just outside.

McGinley was later joined by Mr Nikolaj Lavrukhin, First Vice Chairman of the Kiev City Soviet. A very important man indeed, but who now seemed tired and dispirited.

Mr Lavrukhin was at pains to assure that all danger from Chernobyl had passed. He produced radiation charts and figures. He said radiation levels had now dropped from a dangerous 0.5 in the early days of the disaster, to a safe 0.06.

He was joined by Mr Victor Dobrotvor, Soviet head of culture and tourism for Ukraine, who arrived with an entourage of three. He frankly admitted that the bottom had dropped out of the tourist trade for Kiev.

In an aggrieved voice he said a total of 61 parties representing more than 1,800 people had cancelled their holidays because of Chernobyl. Mr Dobrotvor was at pains to impress upon McGinley that all danger had now passed and that people shouldn't be afraid of coming to his great city. "Even the grass cut out in the fields is being stored and checked for contamination," he said reassuringly.

McGinley realised by now that his importance and status had somehow been grossly inflated and that the "Chairman of the British Nuclear Test Veterans' Association" had different connotations in the Soviet Union. But who was he to argue?

He decided to sit back and enjoy the experience. He recalled: "I'm not sure who they thought I was, but they obviously believed I had a lot of clout. I think Robert Maxwell must have given me star billing. It was obvious they were working to a very well rehearsed script with the objective of getting the message across to the outside world that all was well in Kiev."

Their reassurances would have been more convincing but for the fact that as they spoke a tanker passed outside, spraying the pavement and spattering the window of the room they were talking in with water.

Mr Lavrukhin looked up as the tanker swung by and burst out laughing. The moment broke the ice, and Mr Lavrukhin and his party threw away their well rehearsed scripts and relaxed. Mr Lavrukhin talked about his family and how they had all been caught up in the panic to evacuate the city.

He said he received a call in the early hours of the morning informing him there was an emergency at Chernobyl. He wasn't given too many details at that point; just that there had been a large explosion.

As soon as he put the receiver down, it rang again. It was his boss who told him to report to the town hall at once. Before he could get out of bed, the phone rang again. It was the Ministry of the Interior in Moscow demanding information.

He ran to his car with just an overcoat over his pyjamas. At the town hall everyone was milling about, unsure of what to do. His boss was already there and was on the phone to people in Chernobyl. The chief of police and the fire officer ran in and were instructed to make all haste to Pripyat.

The blood drained from their faces when informed the nuclear power station had blown up.

Mr Lavrukhin said everything after that was just a blur. His job was to prepare for the possible evacuation of the whole city; an enormous task which kept him preoccupied night and day for three days.

Everything depended on the wind. If the winds swung toward Kiev, then everyone, three million people, would have to be evacuated; a virtually impossible undertaking but one which, nevertheless, had to be prepared for.

This would mean somehow telling the populace something of the emergency on their doorstep without causing widespread panic. On the second day, the winds did indeed swing toward Kiev and the first phase of the evacuation began.

All the schoolchildren, roughly about 200,000, were bussed out of the city and dispatched with all speed south to pioneer camps.

Lavrukhin's own family, his wife and two daughters of school age, were evacuated in this first wave as they lived north of the city and therefore closest to Chernobyl. Mr Lavrukhin was overwhelmed by the responsibility: Not only did he have to deal with the possibility of the mass evacuation of the city...he also had to deal with the huge influx of people from Chernobyl and the surrounding area.

The following day McGinley was taken on a short trip outside the city limits to see the efforts being made to bring back normality.

Heading north out of Kiev there was evidence of the vast evacuation that had taken place. Municipal buildings and community centres were crowded with evacuees: so many that in some areas makeshift shelters had been hastily constructed on the pavements.

Leaving the city limits, things became even more chaotic. Fields surrounding the Ukranian capital had been turned into large encampments, with wooden and canvas structures supplying the bulk of living space. Many tents had been set up by the side of the road, and further tented camps had sprung up in wooded clearings.

Large convoys of trucks, tractors, buses, battered old cars and even a few horse-drawn carts were all parked up on the sides of the road. Groups of mainly young men stood around in surly groups. Check points, were positioned at intervals on the side of the road heading away from the disaster zone.

These were manned by up to a dozen people, each brandishing radiation monitors or jet-sprays hooked to their backs. Everyone passing through was swept and either passed 'clean' or directed to join the ragged queues at hastily erected tented clinics.

All that was left behind was a vast wasteland abandoned by its inhabitants as they fled the invisible enemy that spread like a dark stain from the stricken Chernobyl reactor.

BETRAYAL

McGinley's eyewitness accounts of events in the Soviet Union made banner headlines. But the publicity generated by the Chernobyl incident was a mixed blessing.

Abroad, the veteran's stock had never been higher. It encouraged ex-servicemen from across the globe to come forward with hair-raising accounts of their own experiences.

A group of former Soviet generals revealed that thousands of troops had been deliberately irradiated after an atomic bomb, twice the size of Hiroshima, was dropped near the provincial city of Orenburg in 1954.

Hundreds were said to have died in the immediate aftermath and the pilot and co-pilot of the TU-34 that dropped the bomb both died of leukaemia.

A startling report alleged that an experimental town in Kazakhstan had been "nuked" to test a new nuclear bunker system doubling as a subway. According to information passed to western scientists the bunkers survived the blast, but hundreds of luckless "volunteers" who had been herded inside the maze of tunnels died horribly after the fireball sucked all the oxygen from the air in the tunnels.

Elsewhere a huge explosion in 1957 at a nuclear bomb factory in the Ural Mountains caused the evacuation of an entire region. Hundreds of survivors were said to have been carted off to a town near the city of Penza where military doctors used them in radiation experiments.

French ex-servicemen also contacted their British "brothers in nuclear arms" to talk of their experiences in the Algerian desert and Polynesia in the Pacific. France exploded more than 200 nuclear devices and hundreds of soldiers were now complaining of ill health.

But like Britain and the Soviets, the secrecy surrounding the test programme and the difficulty of scientifically proving a link between radiation and illnesses that often emerged decades later prevented them from gaining compensation.

In Britain, the death of William Penney in 1991 marked a watershed. Any hope the veterans had of compensation seemed to die with him. There was a different mood in the country as Britain entered the 1990s.

It was a time of unprecedented economic growth and prosperity. People were obsessed by celebrity and the celebrity lifestyle. The nation embarked on a gigantic spending spree and considerations about the environment and other issues were brushed under the carpet.

Society appeared indifferent to the horrors of the past, and the nuclear bogyman didn't seem so scary any more.

The British Nuclear Test Veterans' Association, its membership inexorably dwindling by the death (natural or otherwise), began to fall into disarray. Lack of progress in the campaign led to rows, in-fighting and arguments about what direction the organisation should take.

Ken McGinley's position as chairman for the first time was being challenged. Sheila Gray, his long-time secretary said: "People used to think he was God, and his word was law. They were not so sure any more."

In a bid to revive flagging morale, McGinley launched an action in the European Court claiming his human rights had been violated by the British government.

Appearing before nine European judges in 1997 he argued the case that the government had concealed vital documents; he claimed the lives of veterans had been ruined by being forced to witness nuclear tests at Christmas Island and that the government had used them as guinea pigs.

It all had a tired, familiar ring to it and with no new evidence to go on, no smoking gun, the court action failed. It was another bitter blow and it left the campaign with nowhere obvious to go.

Many veterans abandoned the fight. Others vowed to carry on, but there were few options left open. Ken McGinley strove to keep the issue in the public consciousness.

He wrote to the famously-abrasive actor Sean Connery asking him to consider performing a voice-over for a proposed documentary on Christmas Island. The actor said he was prepared to consider it, and McGinley managed to get an Australian soap actor to agree to play the starring role. But the project failed through lack of interest.

McGinley introduced a royal angle by revealing the Duke of Edinburgh had visited Christmas Island in 1959 on board Britannia. (The Queen's consort apparently hopped off the boat for an hour or two to have a look at the troops and watch a native dance. But he was careful not to eat or drink anything until he was safely back on board.)

But although these activities garnered some publicity, they had little impact. The Conservative government, the Ministry of Defence and the British public were unmoved.

Happily a revival of fortunes seemed on the cards when Tony Blair's Labour Party swept to power in 1997.

Blair and most of his government had all pledged their undying support for the nuclear veterans during the long, lonely years in Opposition. Sitting Labour MPs and prospective candidates had ruthlessly used the nuclear veterans to embarrass the Tories.

They had all joined Blair in supporting a Private Member's Bill in 1990 which would have handed justice to the veterans and their families. The Bill, championed by Labour MP Bob Clay, was "talked out" by Tory backbenches to howls of protest from Labour MPs

Unfortunately the Labour Party wasn't so well disposed toward the veterans once in power. A letter of congratulation from McGinley, and a gentle reminder of Labour's earnest promises in Opposition, was sent to Tony Blair as soon as he had his feet under the table at 10 Downing Street.

There was no response.

A follow-up letter several weeks later again was ignored. It was only after several more letters had been sent that Blair replied; the news was not good. Tony Blair said that although he was "sympathetic" toward the veterans, he wrote: "Unfortunately independent scientific studies do not support the payment of general compensation."

The veterans were outraged, but the Blair administration was as intractable as the Tories had ever been. Veteran campaigner Jack Ashley, a Labour Peer and long-time supporter of the veterans, pleaded: "Most of the Cabinet supported the veterans in opposition. The least they can do is to support them now when they have the power to do something about it…"

But Tony Blair was unmoved, and his equanimity was still unruffled even when an extraordinary story emerged about his own involvement in nuclear bomb testing. Apparently when he was a little boy, he was exposed to radiation from an A-bomb test in Australia.

The story begins on October 11, 1956 when young Tony, aged three and big brother Bill, six, were at home in suburban Adelaide with their mother Hazel. She was a 33-year-old housewife, married to husband Leo who was a lecturer in law at the University of Adelaide.

Mrs Blair was a shy, introverted woman who wasn't keen on the social side of life in this far-flung corner of the Empire. According to Bill Blair his mother missed her home in the UK and felt lonely and isolated.

In the absence of any real friends, she devoted herself entirely to the well-being of her young family. She stayed home most days, and was watching Tony and Bill playing on their tricycles in the garden (an activity the two Blair boys enjoyed doing most), when a large, reddish-brown cloud stretching from horizon to horizon moved toward Adelaide.

It transpired later the cloud enveloped much of the Blair's neighbourhood as well as large parts of the city. A radio report said it was a sand-storm. What it didn't say was that mixed in with the sand was a deadly seeding of radioactive isotopes.

Unexpected wind changes had apparently blown the dust from Maralinga, 350 miles to the north east of Adelaide, where the British government had detonated an atomic device.

Experts at the local Giles Weather Station, run by the British, had calculated that prevailing winds would gently sweep the radioactive cloud across the less populous desert regions of the northern territories. But things had gone wrong.

According to Hedley Marston, one of Australia's foremost scientists, unforeseen wind shift blew part of the radioactive mushroom cloud across Adelaide, contaminating much of the city and the eastern seaboard.

Using a home-made filtering device and Geiger counter set up on the roof of a laboratory, Marston recorded huge levels of radioactive Iodine, Caesium and Strontium-90 in the air over the city.

He was furious when these measurements were officially denied, and accused the British government and William Penney (who was in personal charge at Maralinga at the time) of covering-up the incident.

Marston claimed he had measured radioactive iodine levels up to 5000 times higher than normal in the thyroids of sheep at two locations near Adelaide, enough to contaminate the food chain.

According to Marston, strontium-90, linked to bone cancer, and leukaemia was being ingested by children, via cows' milk; government policies at the time guaranteed a half pint of milk daily to every Australian schoolchild.

In papers published after his death, he complained to his friend, the nuclear physicist Sir Mark Oliphant: "I am more worried than I can convey about the expensive quasi-scientific pantomime that's being enacted at Maralinga under the cloak of secrecy. And even more so about the evasive lying that is being indulged in by public authorities about the hazard of fallout.

Apparently Whitehall and Canberra consider that the people of northern Australia are expendable."

Marston later accused the Atomic Weapons Test Safety Committee and the British and Australian governments of lying. The presence of iodine-131 in animals, he warned, would result in increased cases of human cancer of the thyroid gland.

His outspoken criticisms meant he was ostracised by both Australian and British scientists who accused him of scaremongering. He had his equipment confiscated, and his research grants evaporated over-night.

Marston, who died in 1965, was posthumously vindicated in 1985 by the Australian Royal Commission who found that most of his calculations were correct.

When the Blair's returned to the UK, health problems beset the family. Tony Blair was just 11, when a stroke deprived his father of speech for many years, and soon after his sister Sarah was hospitalised for two years with rheumatoid arthritis. His mother contracted thyroid cancer and was dead at the age of 52, after a long battle. It is well known that Tony Blair later suffered heart problems.

British medical researcher and toxicologist Dick Van Steenis who had access to much of Marston's papers wasn't surprised. "Adelaide was plastered with radioactive fallout from 11 to 16 October 1956 comprising plutonium-239, americium-241, iodine-131, strontium-90 and caesium-137," said Van Steenis. "Tony Blair's mother died of thyroid cancer following that exposure."

Dr Van Steenis, who studied medicine in Adelaide, further claimed: "All the medical conditions could have been triggered by exposure to radioactivity. And, as a youngster in Adelaide, drinking local milk Tony Blair is very likely to be at risk of bone cancer himself, almost certainly with a residue of strontium-90 in his bones and bone marrow. It is a hell of a catch-22 for the British prime minister. He has never denied the impact of the Maralinga tests on his family. He has never denied that radioactive fallout was ultimately the cause of his mother's death. But he would not acknowledge it, because to do so would strengthen the legal case against his government for the compensation entitlements of British and Australian veterans."

Bill Blair described the impact of the health problems in the family in a newspaper interview. He described his mother as a "very brave woman, adding: "She was in hospital for considerable periods. It was traumatic for all of us. Her death had the effect of ending a particular part of the family story. A year or so before she died, hoping the illness had gone away, she and my father bought a house that they began to renovate. She never got to live there."

Her death affected his brother Tony "very much ... I think people have tended to underestimate the role my mother played in forming Tony's view of life. From Tony's perspective, I believe it was a combination of things that gave him the drive to succeed. The death of his mother affected him every bit as much as his father's stroke."

Tony Blair, for whatever reason, has chosen to ignore the possibility his family may have suffered. His spokeswoman when pressed for a comment derided it as "a silly season story", and refused to comment further.

As the new millennium approached, the veterans received an unexpected windfall in the shape of a generous donation of £50,000 from distinguished British author Catherine Cookson.

This enabled them to fund a study by Dundee University into blood diseases among the veterans. The research uncovered evidence that many more veterans were stricken with blood cancers than NRPB studies had suggested. The Dundee research was backed up by death certificates and medical records, and blew a very big hole in Government's entrenched position that veterans were not harmed by their participation in the tests.

But the NRPB, which by then was conducting its third study into the health of test veterans, was not impressed and issued a statement denouncing the research as 'unscientific.' It was a familiar mantra.

In 2000 Ken McGinley decided to step down as national chairman of the veterans association. He announced he would never give up the battle, but after 18 years he wanted to spend more time with his wife and daughter.

In truth he was exhausted by the internecine in-fighting that had broken out within the ranks of the association. Many members were openly voicing their disappointment about the way the organisation was being run, and of course the lack of progress being made.

McGinley was replaced by John Lowe, a mild-mannered former national service seaman who had witnessed the first Grapple tests at Maldon Island in 1957. He was joined by Jeff Liddiatt, who served with the RAF in Maralinga from 1959-1960.

Between them they managed to fill the vacuum caused by McGinley's departure and prevent the organisation from imploding. They decided to adopt a quieter approach to the campaign, working behind the scenes to persuade MPs from all parties to support the cause. It was an uphill struggle.

SICK FAMILY SYNDROME

It was 2002, and figures released by the veterans showed they were dying off at the rate of three a month. They were limping into extinction. It took a brainwave from Fleet Street legend Richard Stott to put them back on the agenda.

Stott, who had edited three national newspapers during a distinguished career, had always been a supporter of the nuclear veterans and had used his newspapers to campaign on their behalf. One of his particular bailiwicks was the fate the children of the veterans, something that tended to be ignored by the rest of the media.

A campaign by one of Stott's newspapers back in the 1980s had uncovered the scandal of the "Atom Bomb Kids" which identified hundreds of children as being affected by their father's participation in the atomic bomb tests. Stott now wanted to find out if the "curse of the atom bomb" had reached across to the next generation.

Reporters launched a new investigation. Newspaper files and other research materials stretching back 20 years eventually identified 350 families of nuclear veterans who had complained about health problems in their children.

What was the fate of the grandchildren? Letters were sent; phone calls were made; reporters knocked on doors. The results were astonishing: 115 families of nuclear veterans were identified who had health problems in 169 of their grandchildren.

Their testimonies were shocking. Sicknesses such as leukaemia and other cancers were way above average; deformities, miscarriages, stillbirths and congenital illnesses were rife. Skin disease, eye problems, deafness and mental health issues were commonplace. It was as though the gene pool of entire generations had been contaminated.

Statistician John Urquhart, a government adviser on radiation issues, was asked to analyse the figures.

He calculated the leukaemia rates in the grandchildren were six times the national average. The number born with deformities and other crippling diseases were ten times the norm, and the figure for Down's syndrome was seven times more than expected.

Seemingly, something terrible was happening in the families of nuclear veterans. A new pandemic was at work: a sick family syndrome threatening untold generations with disease and early death.

Prof Joseph Rotblat was among the first to comment: "This confirms our worse fears about what can happen if the DNA is damaged by radiation. These figures are extremely alarming. They should be published and discussed."

Richard Stott excoriated the Government in an article in the mass circulation *Daily Mirror* newspaper: "How many more generations of the damned will our politicians allow to suffer before they accept the calamities of their predecessors and the consequences of their own cowardice?" he thundered. "In a very few years there will be no nuclear test veterans left, old soldiers are fading away fast now."

There was an outcry. MPs tabled Parliamentary questions. A Commons motion demanding compensation for the victims and a thorough study of the new evidence was backed by 80 MPs.

Norwich Labour MP Dr Ian Gibson won the backing of MPs for an emergency Commons debate. He told the House: "For many, many years I have known of the hazards of radiation. I have met many people who were involved in the nuclear tests. I can see that they and their families are suffering from exactly the same long-term effects, in some cases lethal. From my knowledge of the atomic bombs on Hiroshima and Nagasaki, there is a direct similarity in terms of genetic effects across generations. The problem is that the Government refuses to see what I regard as the clearest evidence."

Veterans from all over the country converged on Parliament to listen to the emergency debate. Ken McGinley was persuaded to come out of retirement to add his weight, and was treated like a hero.

Hundreds stood outside waving placards. They had arrived in buses, cars, invalid carriages and even motor-cycle sidecar. They came on foot, on crutches and in wheelchairs. Many would have crawled there if no other transport had been available.

In the crowd was Shirley Denson whose RAF husband Eric died so tragically and Archie Ross with daughter Julie.

Since her experience in the pensions court, Mrs Denson had become one of the MoD's most implacable opponents. With her long hair flowing behind her, she had morphed into a Boadicea figure moving determinedly through the throng, chivvying the huddled pensioners and keeping up spirits.

At a noisy rally in a Commons committee room, Richard Stott and Dr Gibson, sharing a platform with John Urquhart and internationally-renowned nuclear expert John Large, gave rousing speeches and were rapturously cheered.

During the emergency debate that followed, defence minister for veteran's affairs Dr Lewis Moonie floundered during intense questioning from MPs. In a bad-tempered debate he promised the latest evidence would be sent to "experts" for review.

The veterans were in ebullient mood. They believed they had the Government on the run. Many thought it was only a matter of time before victory was theirs. Dr Gibson said he had the ear of Tony Blair and was trying to arrange a meeting to discuss compensation. Was the long fight over at last?

Unfortunately the Ministry of Defence didn't see it that way. After sitting on the dossier for several weeks, Mr Moonie replied. In a lengthy statement, he predictably questioned the scientific basis of the study, and produced a blizzard of statistics.

He wrote: "I have to say that our considered view is that the scientific basis of the study is highly questionable…the study is based on 350 families of British nuclear test veterans. It has to be said that the 350 families form a small sample group, given that there were in the region of 20,000 test veterans. Based on the average family size in the UK in the intervening years, it could be assumed that test veterans would have had about 50,000 children who would subsequently parent around 100,000 grandchildren…"

Mr Moonie continued in a similar vein for six pages, before finishing: "I do not believe that the information presented in the dossier provides evidence that would lead us to review our policies on war pensions."

In the wake of this, Tony Blair pulled out of planned discussions. It was another crushing blow for the veterans, and there were howls of protest from all sides of the political divide.

Labour MP Dr Ian Gibson joined forces with Tory MP John Baron and forced a parliamentary debate. Representatives from the National Radiological Protection Board, now calling itself the Health Protection Agency, agreed to attend the meeting.

But the new organisation, under the thumb of the Ministry of Defence, was as intractable as the old. The same old arguments where wheeled out: no evidence of radiation exposure; statistical studies found no discernable difference in the health of test participants; the men were never in any danger…

The press lost interest, the MPs ran out of words and the initiative once again slipped away from the veterans.

Somehow the campaign staggered on, kept alive by Shirley Denson and Dennis Hayden, a veteran of the Australian bomb tests, and a few other stalwarts who formed a breakaway group which fought increasingly fruitless skirmishes with the Ministry of Defence.

They were derided as "Sunday afternoon revolutionaries" in some quarters for their zeal in trying to keep the campaign in the news agenda, but they ignored the jibes and carried on regardless.

Meanwhile the suffering of the innocents continued unabated. As the politicians argued, a tiny baby boy was being laid to rest in a corner of windswept country graveyard in Swansea.

Around the small white casket were his mother, grandmother and great-grandmother. The infant was called Joshua and he never had a chance to see the world: he was stillborn at 25 weeks, a tragic signal that the genetic scourge had jumped to the fourth generation of British servicemen who took part nuclear bomb tests 50 years earlier.

Joshua's family decided to bury him next to his great-grandfather John Condon, an RAF serviceman who died of leukaemia, aged just 24.

Mr Condon died of leukaemia two years after he worked on the Valiant and Canberra bombers used in the H-bomb tests at Christmas Island. He was stationed at Burtronwood, the giant bomber base near Liverpool, as the bombers returned "red-hot" to the UK, and it was his job to strip down the highly-radioactive engines.

Very soon he fell ill, and was diagnosed with the incurable blood disease. His widow Margaret was left to bring up their one-yr-old daughter Diane alone.

Seven years after her husband died, Margaret was also diagnosed with leukaemia. Astonishingly it was the same rare form of the disease that had killed her husband. It was only when she made enquiries at the hospital that treated him that she learned his illness may have been linked to radiation exposure.

But she was still at a complete loss to understand how she could have contracted the same disease until told she may have been contaminated by washing her husband's overalls which he brought home after work.

Mrs Condon wrote to the Ministry of Defence, and was reassured that her husband had never been contaminated, and it followed, therefore, that she could not have been affected.

But tragedy struck again when their daughter Diane developed a cancerous tumour and her unborn baby was aborted. She was given chemotherapy treatment and appeared to have beaten the cancer, but miscarried twice more before giving birth to a healthy daughter, Rebecca.

The family were relieved that Rebecca was fit and well, until she became pregnant at 18. At about 23 weeks she went to the doctor because she was concerned about not being able to feel her unborn baby moving. Tests revealed the devastating reason: the baby was dead.

A reason was never given for the child's death, but the family believe they know. Rebecca's mum Diane, has no doubts: "We all know the reason. There was never any illness in the family before my dad contracted leukaemia. But now it is just one thing after another. It just seems to go on and on."

It is of course impossible to establish whether there is a connection with Mr Condon's exposure to radiation and the tragic series of illnesses in his family. But the Condon case is by no means unique. Evidence of trans-generational genetic disorders pepper the files of the nuclear tests veterans association.

A prime example of a "nuclear family" is that of Archie Ross. Since returning from Christmas Island he has suffered cataracts which doctors confirmed were almost certainly caused by ionising radiation.

As we have seen, soon after he returned to the UK, his wife gave birth to Julie who had a range of physical disabilities that persist to this day. But Mr Ross also had another daughter, Tracy, who was born perfect.

The family was again thrown into turmoil when Tracy married and gave birth to a Down's syndrome baby, Jacob. The odds against these events occurring naturally are incalculable. But no official study has ever been proposed to investigate this dreadful phenomenon.

MARK OF THE BOMB

In 2006 the veteran's campaign was given an unexpected boost from the other side of the world. Seemingly out of the blue, a new scientific technique established that exposure to A-bombs could leave a fingerprint in the DNA of the victim.

New Zealand servicemen who witnessed the Grapple series of tests at Christmas Island had without fanfare commissioned a study by Professor Al Rowland of Massey University to examine this novel concept.

They asked him to investigate if sailors, on board two ships that steamed through fallout zones, had suffered genetic damage. Rowland said that after the passing of 50 years he wasn't sure there would be anything to find. But after meeting the NZ veteran's charismatic chairman Roy Sefton, he said he would give it a go.

Rowland concentrated on new scientific tests which looked at translocations, the exchange of genetic material, between different chromosomes. Translocations show evidence of genetic damage and are therefore important indicators of cancers and other illnesses.

Under strict scientific disciplines, blood was taken from 50 of the NZ nuclear veterans for comparison with 50 servicemen who had not been at the tests.

The study identified crucial differences: the veterans had far more cancers and skin problems. And the level of translocations in veterans was three times higher than in the control group.

When the results were published they couldn't be faulted. The study was successfully peer reviewed by respected scientific journals. Rowland was unequivocal: this was proof that servicemen had been exposed to radiation from the Grapple bomb tests.

The news was a huge boost to the flagging fortunes of the British veterans, especially when even the MoD was forced to admit it couldn't fault the procedures used by Rowland.

The breakthrough was a remarkable testament to the tenacity of Roy Sefton who set about gaining support for the study after he became ill.

He was just 17 when he was sent to the Pacific aboard the frigate Pukaki which, together with its sister ship Rotoiti, was to monitor British H-bomb tests for the New Zealand government.

By the time he was 30, Mr Sefton could hardly walk and his joints ached that much there were times he couldn't touch anything without feeling pain. But he soon discovered he wasn't alone.

At least six of his shipmates died in their 20s, from cancers associated with radiation poisoning. Professor Neil Pearce, a distinguished epidemiologist analysed the health records of the New Zealand veterans and found a small, but significant increase, in death rates. He also discovered the men died from cancers typically associated with radiation.

During the Grapple Tests Pukaki spent months patrolling the seas around Christmas Island. Because fresh water was so scarce, the crews often bathed in rainwater as they chased the rain-storms following the explosions. And they ate locally-caught fish and produce from nearby islands.

Mr Sefton was convinced the crews' health problems were caused by fallout. But the British government denied there was any link with the tests. Sefton, observing how the British veterans were getting nowhere with their claims, decided the New Zealand veterans would go it alone.

They raised the $250,000 needed to carry out the complicated and costly genetic tests on the veterans. But even then Professor Rowland was sceptical: "I had my doubts that we could find out anything about something that occurred 50 years ago. But the alternative was to do nothing and I felt that if we lived in a responsible society we at least should give it a try."

Professor Rowland had access to a new technique that had been used on Chernobyl victims and nuclear workers, but never before on nuclear veterans. Rowland started selecting 50 veterans of the nuclear bomb tests and 50 controls, matched perfectly for age, lifestyle and even drinking and smoking habits. It was a painstaking task that took many years.

The results were astonishing: signs of damage in the chromosomes, the structure that contains the DNA, in the nuclear veterans, was so marked that Professor Rowland had no hesitation in signifying that this was caused by radiation. Each pair of chromosome has its own colour. A colour switch would mean a sign of genetic damage known as a chromosomal translocation. The more translocations you have, the greater the risk of developing cancers.

Professor Rowland found the translocations in the nuclear veterans were three times the number of translocations in the controls. The results were higher than the Chernobyl victims, in fact they were the highest Rowland had ever seen.

His conclusion: "Our view is that this was caused by radiation because the frequency is so high and we have taken into account every other known confounding factor. We are left with only one option: this group was damaged because the men took part in Operation Grapple."

While the British government digested this unwelcome news, the rest of the world bowed to the inevitable.

The nuclear nations, including, America, Russia, France and China announced they would pay compensation to their nuclear veterans. Even the Manx government, the Tynwald, agreed to pay 12 veterans living on the island £8,000 each for the physical and mental anguish they had suffered through their participation in the bomb tests.

Britain now stood uniquely alone in its stubborn refusal to acknowledge the veteran's claims. Rather than concede defeat, it dismissed the evidence of the Rowland study as "too small".

But the Rowland evidence could not be discarded so lightly, and a high-powered firm of London solicitors decided to mount a legal challenge.

In the past the Ministry of Defence had blocked legal moves against it by saying any action would be time-barred because the bomb tests occurred outside the legal time limit. Rosenblatt solicitors decided to challenge this in the courts. If successful, it would open the way for a multi-million pound compensation claim by the veterans.

It was a high-risk strategy and the firm stood to lose millions, but it pressed on nevertheless and 1,010 veterans were chosen to fight the case in the High Court, with nine 'lead' cases as the stalking horses. And they believed there was really only one man capable of leading the fight. It was the man who started it all, and he was the only one who could finish it.

Ken McGinley prepared for the showdown like a veteran gunslinger. His clothes were laid neatly out on the bed in his hotel room two miles from the Royal Courts of Justice: grey slacks, with a cheese-cutter crease; crisp, blue cotton shirt; shoes shined and buffed so you could see your face in them. Tie: blue and red diagonal striped, and a dark blue blazer fresh from the dry-cleaners. On both his tie and blazer was a badge topped by a crown. On the bottom were the words: All We Seek is Justice. In the middle, the mushroom cloud of an atomic explosion in full deadly bloom.

He dressed with care, brushed his hair and regarded himself in the mirror. Satisfied, he took the lift and walked across the foyer of the hotel and out of the doors. A taxi pulled up immediately: "The High Court," he instructed and settled back in his seat.

After a three week trial, Judge Mr Justice Foskett stunned the Ministry of Defence by casting aside the time-barred ruling, opening the way for massive compensation claims by the veterans.

There were wild scenes of jubilation outside the court. And it was a personal triumph for Ken McGinley who armed with just the contents of his brain and a photographic memory easily saw off the best efforts of the Ministry of Defence with all its vast legal clout and inside knowledge.

The hugely expensive barristers had him in the witness box for two days, but hardly landed a single blow. McGinley, adroit as ever, even had the judge smiling as he explained with characteristic Celtic bluntness his role in the 30-year battle: "I saw it as my job to speak on behalf of all the veterans; to put my head above the parapet; to get as much publicity as I could for the cause. Today, you call it 'spin', but to me it was nothing but the unvarnished truth."

The judge was fulsome in his praise of McGinley:

> He was an engagingly frank and open witness who had lost none of the combative instincts that had obviously led to him becoming the champion of those he felt had been short-changed by various Governments over the years. He was an older, wiser and more restrained man than the man seen on some of the video clips I saw and as quoted in some of the newspaper cuttings that were put to him relating to things said some 20 years or more ago. There will be many who, over the years, have achieved some of the highest offices in countries throughout the world about whom the same story could be told.

It was a glowing endorsement of the achievements of the former sapper from Johnstone. Judge Foskett urged the two parties to get together "in the hope that serious efforts toward a settlement will take place at an appropriate time." Like most observers he clearly felt that both protagonists had fought themselves to standstill and the time for reconciliation had arrived.

But as the champagne corks popped outside the Royal Courts of Justice, the horse trading between the Ministry of Defence and Rosenblatts over settlement issues was not going well.

The exact details of these negotiations are unclear. According to the MoD, a proposal for a substantial cash payment was on the table, but was rejected. According to the veteran's legal team no formal offer was ever made, so there was nothing to reject.

There were angry exchanges on both sides which spilled over into parliament with one MP describing the "Oh yes we did; oh no we didn't" antics as a "pantomime." In the end in a fit of pique the MoD announced its intention to appeal the Foskett judgement. With unlimited resources from the public purse it could afford to do so.

In January 2011, the case came up in the Appeal Court and it was a fiasco for the veterans. The three presiding judges were not as accommodating as Judge Foskett and they allowed the MoD's appeal.

The frustrating see-saw legal system of British justice catapulted the veterans back into limbo. It was a bitter blow for the veterans, and with little choice left, the decision was made to take the battle to the Supreme Court.

March 14, 2012. 9.59 GMT.

The end when it came was swift.

Lord Wilson of the Supreme Court, the highest court in the United Kingdom, stepped up to the rostrum and delivered the coup de grace: "I consider that each of the appeals should be dismissed," he intoned, like a priest reading the last rites. "I consider that the actions have no real prospect of success."

The veterans had lost by 4-3 he said, adding: "Putting aside the law for one moment, all seven members of the court would wish to record their personal sympathy for the veterans. It must be bad enough for the nine veterans, and the other claimants, to learn that they have lost this final round, but to learn that they have lost by the narrowest possible margin must make it even worse."

The judgment was received in silence by the small band of nuclear veterans and widows outside the Royal Courts of Justice in the Strand. Most had had enough of sympathetic words. There had been many disappointments, but this latest really did feel like the end. There were no champagne corks popping that day as the routed army of cold war warriors quietly dispersed and melted away.

The Ministry of Defence relished the moment. Jubilant Andrew Robathan MP, the latest in a long line of defence ministers for Veterans Affairs, immediately fired off a gleeful letter to all members of parliament informing them of the decision.

The Supreme Court ruled by a majority decision that all nine lead cases were statute barred and declined to allow the claims to proceed. Perhaps of greater significance is that ALL (his emphasis) the Justices recognised that the veterans would face great difficulty proving a causal link between the illnesses suffered and attendance at the tests. The Supreme Court described the claims as having no reasonable prospect of success and that they were doomed to fail.

The triumphal tone of the letter was the final kick in the teeth for the veterans. Their legal team struggled to put a brave face on the disastrous result. There was talk of regrouping and taking the fight to the European courts. But just getting to Strasbourg to fight the battle normally took at least three years, and time was not on the side of the veterans. It was their darkest hour.

The verdict came as no surprise to Ken McGinley. He rightly guessed that his triumph before Judge Foskett was a false dawn. Despite the celebrations, he knew in his bones that it had not been enough.

After 30 years of struggle he had still not found the 'smoking gun', the knock-out punch…the one piece of crucial evidence that would finally nail all the lies. And he also knew the British people had wearied and grown tired of the nuclear veterans.

He had noted the empty press benches (the various proceedings had engendered little interest from Fleet Street's finest); the heady and intoxicating oxygen of publicity had evaporated. After the Supreme Court ruling he had few words left to say and he slipped quietly away, anxious only to return home to his wife in Johnstone.

THE DOG IN THE NIGHT-TIME

There is a famous Sherlock Holmes short story, "Silver Blaze", which focuses on the disappearance of a racehorse and on the apparent murder of its trainer by an intruder. The tale is distinguished by Holmes deducing that the mystery hinged on what he called: "the curious incident of the dog in the night-time."

In the story a puzzled Inspector Gregory of Scotland Yard points out that the dog did nothing in the night-time, to which Holmes replies: "That is the curious incident." The point being made of course is that the dog didn't bark because it knew who the intruder was.

Sherlock Holmes doubtless would have found the "curious incident of Grapple Y" just as intriguing. For like the dog, the lack of fanfare or fuss when this most important of bombs was detonated, was notable to say the least.

This, after all, was Britain's ever biggest bomb. If ever there was a case where the dog should have been barking loudly and urgently, this was it. But the government of the day treated it as a matter of little importance. In fact the silence was deafening.

The press, was also uncharacteristically subdued. Instead of trumpeting it to the heavens, the following anodyne article that appeared in the *Times* (The government's traditional mouthpiece) on April 30, 1958 was typical of the way the incident was reported at the time:-

A British nuclear device was successfully exploded at a high altitude over the central Pacific yesterday. It was announced last night that Mr Aubrey Jones, the Minister of Supply, had received a report from Air Vice-Marshal Grandy, task force commander, Christmas Island. It was stated scientific measurements were being collected for accurate evaluation, and that early indications were that fall-out would be negligible.

Considering that Grapple Y was the culmination of Britain's H-bomb tests which the year before had been afforded banner headlines and spread across acres of newsprint as a "dress rehearsal for the death of the world", this was a remarkably muted response.

The official record of the event was also notable for a complete lack of drama. Group Captain William Edmund Townsend of the Royal Australian Air Force, one of several official observers specially flown to Christmas Island for the Grapple Y test, reported:-

After breakfast, we were taken to witness the shot. It was learned this was a "clean" hydrogen bomb. The air burst precluded any water or dust being drawn up from the surface which may give possible radioactive fall-out and it was not anticipated that any fall-out from this bomb would occur.

He makes his glimpse of Armageddon sound like a stroll in the park. It is interesting to note, however, that Townsend reports he "learned" that it was a clean bomb; in other words he was acting on information received rather than what he observed.

There is no mention anywhere of the storm clouds that gathered after the burst, much less about any ensuing rain. Like the dog in the night-time, Townsend, a dyed-in-the-wool establishment figure later awarded the CBE, was curiously silent on that score.

In the absence of an inquisitive Sherlock Holmes, Grapple Y faded unheralded into history; an event of little consequence.

It was 50 years before it was brought blinking back into the daylight when John Large, a consultant nuclear engineer internationally respected for his work in assessing the risks posed by nuclear explosions, identified Grapple Y as a possible cause of contamination on Christmas Island.

His interest was aroused after one of the few photographs of the bomb was published in a scientific journal. It was a classic picture of a nuclear explosion complete with majestic mushroom cloud. But what made it unusual was the stem of the cloud which was oddly striated with a series of tooth-like ridges round the edges.

Large was convinced this was caused by the explosion sucking up large amounts of sand and sea water into the stem. This, of course, was contrary to the accepted wisdom that the bomb was exploded too high in the air to cause fallout. Large made a study of all the available photographs of Grapple Y together with rare video footage and reached the conclusion that the bomb exploded much lower than had been admitted by the Ministry of Defence.

He calculated, from a series of "timed, sequential photographs of Grapple Y" that the detonation height was 1,500 metres, and not the official height of 2353 metres. Large suggested that the troops could have been contaminated by the resulting fallout.

It was a convincing argument that was given a cameo role in the various court hearings. Unfortunately its importance was overshadowed by the Rowland Report which usually received star billing.

It was only after the debacle of the Supreme Court hearing that Grapple Y was re-examined as part of a general review of all the evidence to see what could be salvaged from the wreckage.

The review was undertaken on an *ad hoc* basis by Ken McGinley and a small group of researchers from the Open University who were looking for evidence which might be useful to nuclear veterans fighting for pensions through the notoriously slow Pensions Tribunals system.

The Australian tests, the so-called "dirty bombs" that had grabbed all the headlines in the 1980s, were once again examined, but there was little fresh evidence about these tests: it had all been said before, so it was decided to put the Christmas Island tests, of which little was known, under the microscope.

These tests had made only sporadic appearances in the headlines, and Grapple Y had made the least impression of all. Even in Lorna Arnold's seminal work on the hydrogen bomb tests *Britain and the H-Bomb* published in 2001, Grapple Y is given the least billing. But she did make one very interesting observation: buried away in her account of the bomb is a passage about the task force commander Air Vice Marshal Grandy reporting to his political masters in Whitehall:-

> Immediately after the shot the weather had deteriorated and had there been any further delay the operation could not have taken place during the rest of that week. As it was, cloud conditions reduced the number and quality of the photographs obtained.

She doesn't say precisely what the "deteriorating weather" was but, Penney's deputy, Bill Cook, reveals another strong clue in an interview he gave to the *Bulletin of Atomic Scientists* published not long after he returned from Christmas Island. The magazine's correspondent notes:-

> When the test took place Cook showed no sign of excitement. On one crucial occasion when the weather was highly doubtful he carried on seemingly unworried...when it was over, his characteristic smile broke, but only later did he admit that he had been concerned.

Does the weather being "highly doubtful" mean that it rained? And if it didn't why had he been "concerned?" But these clues were slim pickings and too obscure for the nuclear veterans to make anything of.

Much more was needed. It was decided to probe deeper, and further signs of "suspicious behaviour" by Grapple Y were soon forthcoming.

A trawl of *Hansard*, the official parliamentary record, revealed that Grapple Y had been the subject of a fierce debate back in 1991. This followed allegations that something had gone wrong with the April 28, 1958 explosion, and that troops had apparently been caught in a deluge of heavy rain.

This had been denied by the Ministry of Defence, but Sapper Arthur Thomas told in an interview for a TV programme: "Suddenly over the loud-speaker system came the order to get under cover quickly and to clear the open ground. Apparently the wind had changed and the fallout cloud was heading back to Christmas Island. I dashed to my motor vehicle and sat in the cab compartment, closed the doors and windows and remained there for half an hour. Shortly afterwards, however, the wind direction reversed and the men were ordered back to their positions."

Another soldier's account of what happened is even more dramatic. Tom Birch told the *Dispatches* programme: "The explosion and the enormity of the cloud left me speechless. I thought, my God what the hell's going on? We were all quite amazed, you were frightened; all sorts of emotions came out.

"As I walked back to the Port Camp I suddenly became aware of a very thick black cloud approaching inland from the sea. It was as black as pitch. The cloud came over part of the island then retreated back out to sea again. By that time we had all been showered in rain which was as big as ten-pence pieces.

"We all ran like mad to get away from the rain. Lots of men were caught out in the open though. Immediately after the detonation there was panic among the boffins. From the way they were acting it was clear that something had gone far wrong. The whole thing appeared abnormal, unusual."

The importance of whether or not it rained after the blast was not lost on Labour MP Jack Ashley who went on to ask specific questions in Parliament about the height the bomb exploded, protective clothing worn by the men, and the allegations of rainfall. His questions obviously hit a raw nerve judging by the tetchy reply from Defence Minister Archie Hamilton:-

I must say at the outset that the irresponsible and sometimes misleading allegations made by the "Dispatches" television programme, from which the right hon. Gentleman drew many of his points, were based on a series of factual inaccuracies. The unfounded allegations made by the programme can only add unnecessarily to the concern and anxiety of those who participated in the nuclear test programme and their relatives.

After brushing aside doubts concerning the height the bomb exploded, the protective clothing worn by the servicemen and the distance they were from the blast, Hamilton really gets into his stride. In a high dudgeon he professes to being "mystified" by the allegations about whether or not it rained after the blast:-

The Dispatches programme alleges that there was heavy rain off Christmas Island on 28 April 1958 which substantially increased the amount of radioactive fallout. All that I can say is that shortly after the test extensive environmental monitoring did not measure any deposition of radioactive materials from the detonation. On the basis of that evidence therefore there could have been no exposure to internal contamination as a result of inhalation.

It is interesting that Hamilton does not actually say that it didn't rain, just that there was no radioactive fallout. He goes to great lengths, over six pages, to rubbish the points raised by veterans over the years, but the crucial question of whether or not it rained is dodged.

The same pugnacious stance (and evasiveness) was evident in the reaction of another defence minister called upon to answer similar allegations nearly 15 years later.

Labour MP Dr Lewis Moonie was in combative mood when he replied to a letter sent to his department in 2003 by Labour MP Siobahn McDonagh. She had written to Moonie demanding answers to questions raised by her constituent Shirley Denson, whose husband had piloted one of the sampling aircraft that flew through the mushroom cloud created by Grapple Y.

In a seven-page reply Dr Mooney insisted that Mrs Denson's late husband had never been placed in any danger while carrying out his duties:

The Canberra aircraft used for sampling had pressurised cabins which prevented the ingress of air...and no significant levels of contamination were ever detected...

But when the question of rainfall is raised Dr Mooney is as indignant as Hamilton:

Some of the assertions made by Mrs Denson have been raised by members of the British Nuclear Tests Veterans' Association before on many occasions over the years. The Ministry of Defence has addressed these points time and again but the BNTVA chooses to lend credence to certain misapprehensions.

When he finally gets round to answering the question, Mooney shows he is every bit as nimble-footed as Hamilton. The following passage quoted verbatim from his letter is a master-class in dissembling:-

Environmental recordings for Main Camp on Christmas Island for the date of the trial and subsequent days showed that sticky paper and air samples were below the level of detection for contamination, and also that there was no rainfall. The first measurable rainfall at the Main Camp following the detonation occurred on 2 May 1958. There is a meteorology report giving observations of precipitation 5km from station 2057Z, which was a surface wind monitoring position, two hours after the detonation. However, environmental testing on Christmas Island during and after the Grapple operations showed no measurable fallout on the island. AWE Aldermaston has no evidence to show that water contaminated with radiation was precipitated out over the island.

This is a murky statement. In the first sentence we have Dr Mooney stating quite clearly that there was "no rainfall." In the second sentence he states "measurable rainfall" was recorded four days after the blast. Then in the third sentence he blurs the issue further by stating there was "precipitation" two hours after the detonation.

Dr Mooney is being disingenuous. Precipitation means rainfall, which means it did rain soon after the Grapple Y explosion as eyewitnesses have testified. Dr Mooney obviously had no intention of addressing that issue for he quickly moved on to say that environmental testing showed no fallout over the island after the blast.

It is interesting to note that Dr Mooney refers to only the Main Camp while making his observations about there being no rain. What he didn't say was that it was irrelevant whether it rained over Main Camp or not because there were few troops there to be rained upon.

Most of the men were evacuated to various mustering areas miles away as a safety precaution against the possibility of the bomb-carrying Valiant aircraft crashing on takeoff from the airfield, which was next to the Main Camp.

Why has the British government been so afraid of acknowledging that it rained? If there was no resultant radioactive contamination why bother to deny it? Was something being hidden?

Rainout is well known in scientific circles as being a particularly pernicious form of radioactive contamination. It was first observed about 30 minutes after the Hiroshima bomb as a "black rain" which was discoloured by tar and other materials in the wooden buildings set alight by the explosion. Its ability to hold its strength and not be dissipated like dry fallout is well known. A notorious example was observed in the township of Troy in upstate New York in April 1953.

What became known as the "Troy Incident" began at the Rensselaer Polytechnic Institute when a group of students entered a laboratory for their radiochemistry class. They were startled to note that all the Geiger counters used in their studies were registering radiation many times the normal rate.

Their tutor took the students on a tour of the campus and discovered similar high readings. High concentrations were found in the gutters and drains which were overflowing because of the previous night's heavy rains.

The school contacted the U.S. Atomic Energy Commission's Health and Safety office in New York City. Further measurements were taken and it was found that gamma radiation on the ground was a hundred times normal; beta ray radiation was even higher and hot spots were found in gutters and puddles.

The explanation was soon forthcoming: there had been an atomic bomb test conducted in the Nevada desert two days earlier. The mushroom cloud had reached 40,000 feet into the atmosphere then drifted 2,300 miles across the United States in a north-easterly direction. It passed over Utah, Colorado, Kansas, Missouri, Illinois, Indiana, Ohio and Pennsylvania before being caught up in a storm that dropped rain on upstate New York, southern Vermont and parts of Massachusetts.

In recent years the discovery of a leukaemia cluster in the Troy area has been confidently attributed to the incident.

Had a similar but much more localised incident taken place on Christmas Island? The only way this could be answered was by examining the environmental records and meteorological reports for Christmas Island at the time of the Grapple Y blast.

This was impossible during the time Hamilton and Mooney were making their statements because the relevant documents were buried deep in government archives, and not available for public consumption.

But things changed. The Freedom of Information Act which came into force on January 1, 2005 allows a general right of access to information held by public authorities.

It has been used to great affect to winkle out embarrassing information hidden away in government archives. Tony Blair is said to have remarked ruefully that it was one of his biggest mistake to introduce this legislation because of its propensity to reveal what politicians would like to stay hidden.

And so it proved in this case. A series of information requests were sent to the Ministry of Defence. And after a period of stonewalling, a raft of new material finally tumbled out of the archives. It proved to be the tipping point for the veteran's campaign.

The first tranch of material to be released was the original weather charts relating to conditions over Christmas Island for the 24-hour period covering April 28, 1958. The blizzard of data clearly showed what all the politicians had been dancing around for years: there WAS rainfall in several areas in the hours following the explosion.

The charts reveal it rained between the following times: 2025-2037; 2136-2148; and 2155 to 2230. Bearing in mind the detonation took place at 1905, the charts show that at precisely one hour and 20 minutes after Grapple Y it rained for 12 minutes; 59 minutes later it rained for another 12 minutes, and seven minutes after that it rained for 35 minutes.

Notable on one chart was a comment: "large rainbow over the Port Camp at 2200 hrs." This is just short of three hours after the shot. The charts are also peppered with the arcane symbols which weathermen use to denote rainfall: an inverted isosceles triangle with dots on the top.

Thousands of men were gathered in the Port Camp area at the times it rained, and this was the clearest evidence yet that there was rainfall over the area after the Grapple Y explosion, despite all the obfuscation by the Ministry of Defence.

But this crucial evidence was just the curtain-raiser. The Meteorological Office in Bracknell, Berkshire later released a report entitled "Weather and Winds During Christmas Island Nuclear Tests."

This 10-page document was originally sent from the Director General at the Met Office, in response to a request by a senior official (his name is redacted) at Aldermaston. The official had requested meteorological data for Christmas Island for the period of the nuclear weapon tests 1957-58.

The report begins with the observation that the rainfall at the Main Camp on Christmas Island, "occurred only on 8 November 1957, and 22 August 1958 and then only as light showers." No sign here of rain after Grapple Y, which was 18 April 1958.

But confusingly the report continues: "Although there is always the possibility that heavy showers fell elsewhere."

We now know from the Met charts already discussed that it did indeed rain elsewhere, especially in the Port Camp area.

Any lingering doubts are finally dispelled when the report makes it clear that not only did it rain, but that the rainfall was actually *caused* by Grapple Y.

This revelation is repeated twice in the report; the first is in the main text which states that two hours after the blast, "precipitation reached the surface in a shower possibly caused by the bomb." The second, and even clearer reference, is in Appendix 1 of the report which states: "Precipitation in sight, more than 5 km from station, reaching surface. Cumulonimbus from bomb."

Cumulonimbus is an extremely dense, vertically developed cloud extending to great heights, usually producing heavy rains, thunderstorms, or hailstorms. Just for the sake of pedantry cumulonimbus is Latin for "rain heaps."

This is prima facie evidence that Grapple Y created a thunderstorm which deposited rainfall on areas where servicemen were gathered thus exposing them to rainout.

According to the Meteorological Office, rain that originates above a radio-active cloud causes areas of heavy contamination just downwind of a nuclear blast. All the evidence suggests this phenomenon is precisely what occurred after Grapple Y.

The 50-year cover-up was beginning to unravel. But this remarkable document had not yet relinquished all its disturbing secrets. Buried in the text is a passage strongly indicating that servicemen were *deliberately* exposed to radioactive fallout.

This sinister possibility is revealed in a passage discussing wind directions recorded during the whole period of the Christmas Island tests, 1957-58.

The report, illustrated with charts and graphs, shows the prevailing winds during the bomb tests always blew away from the island, and certainly away from areas where the majority of men were billeted. But then the text takes a sudden startling turn:-

except for the period up to about 9 hours after the test at 1905 GMT on 28 April 1958 when the winds were light, and near to being southeasterly. Since the airfield and the camp were almost due northwest from the explosion, the winds on this occasion were examined in more detail.

So, Britain's biggest ever bomb was detonated at the only time during the H-bomb testing programme when the winds were blowing over the island and directly toward the Main Camp where the majority of troops were living.

This immediately gives the lie to the official announcements in Parliament and elsewhere that nuclear bomb tests were only ever carried out when the wind direction ensured fallout was taken away from inhabited areas.

Clearly this was not the case for Grapple Y. But it gets worse. The weathermen then go on to calculate precisely when the fallout would arrive at the main campsite:-

Assuming particles were released at 2.4 km, 22.3 n miles to the south-east of the camp (direction about 142 degrees), it appears that those with fall speeds of about 1/3 m/s could have reached the camp at 2100 GMT (1200 local time). Heavier particles released from the thermonuclear cloud at greater altitudes could have arrived at the camp later.

Remember, this report with all its disturbing implications was compiled in response to a request from an Aldermaston bigwig on November 13, 1985.

This was at the height of the nuclear veteran's battle for compensation with the Thatcher government. At the time servicemen and their organisations were being ridiculed for daring to suggest that the tests exposed them to radiation. They were criticised for making "unfounded allegations", lectured about the safety precautions taken for tests, and were chided for suggesting that anyone was in any danger.

Yet all the time the Ministry of Defence was in possession of a this deeply disturbing document suggesting that not only were servicemen contaminated by rainout, but also that they were deliberately put in the path of fallout.

If this report had been released at the time (as it should have been) it would have caused uproar and doubtless would have led to a complete vindication of the veteran's claims. It would also have focussed attention on Grapple Y, which was something the Ministry of Defence clearly wanted to avoid at all costs.

This last point cannot be emphasised too strongly. In Britain the powerful Campaign for Nuclear Disarmament (CND) had been formed in January 1958, just three and a half months before the Grapple Y explosion.

The movement, which numbered among its members Bertrand Russell, Canon John Collins, the Canon of St Paul's Cathedral, J.B. Priestley, Kingsley Martin and the author Doris Lessing, was formed as a direct consequence of the Bikini atoll disaster four years earlier when the Bravo bomb had gone so disastrously wrong.

When the new organisation was presented to the public in Central Hall, Westminster, in February 1958, more than 2,000 people turned up. This unexpectedly large turnout encouraged the organisers to stage a 50-mile protest march from London to Aldermaston over the four-day Easter Period in early April. They said that if 60 or 70 people turned up, it would be enough to make the national newspapers.

In the event 5,000 people gathered in Trafalgar Square on Good Friday morning, April 4, 1958. They filed through the streets in a two-mile column and proceeded toward Aldermaston.

There was a carnival atmosphere among the throng as they marched down the highway. Students sang folk songs, Jazz bands played, mothers pushed prams; whole families marched together in an infectious spirit of peace and love.

The cause seemed good and brave and it caught the national imagination. On one of the coldest, windiest Easter Sundays in memory, more than 10,000 people shivered in the driving rain outside the barbed wire perimeter of the site, to hear speaker after speaker calling for a ban on nuclear bombs.

The Establishment was rocked to the core and it was hardly surprising that when Grapple Y went wrong it was covered up. And the cover-up continues to this day, as further documents that came to light proved.

THE TRUTH OF CHRISTMAS ISLAND

The Meteorological Office reports had established a credible pathway for the radioactive contamination of troops on Christmas Island.

But although the new information was a momentous advance for the veterans, the Ministry of Defence still had a "get out of jail" card in that there was still no direct evidence that contamination actually occurred.

The mantra by successive defence ministers had never varied. Defence minister Hamilton confirmed it in his speech to the Commons:

Shortly after the test, extensive environmental monitoring did not measure any deposition of radioactive materials from the detonation.

And Dr Mooney reiterated it in his April 2003 letter to Labour MP Siobhain McDonagh, when he stated that

environmental recordings were below the level of detection for contamination.

So despite the rain, and the fact it was caused by the bomb, and that the wind blew it over the island, there was, apparently no evidence of contamination.

It didn't make sense, so further Freedom of Information requests were made, this time for the environmental records, for Christmas Island at the time of Grapple Y.

Thus far the only environmental records released by the government covered the whole Pacific, obviously a huge area encompassing thousands of islands in the general area of both British and American bomb tests.

The islands in the British sphere of influence were so far away from Christmas Island that it was hardly surprising there was little increase in radioactivity recorded.

What the British had conspicuously left out were fallout records on Christmas Island itself. This was apparently for the simple reason the bomb tests were supposed to have been detonated too high in the air to cause localised fallout.

Nevertheless, the FoI requests specifically asked for this data. After some resistance, Aldermaston reluctantly released a hefty 42-page report: "Environmental Monitoring at Christmas Island 1957-1958." Written by four officials from Atomic Weapons Establishment Safety Directorate it was written specifically to reassure politicians about safety aspects on Christmas Island. It began with a warning.

> This document and the information it contains is the property of the Ministry of Defence. It is provided in confidence for the personal information of, and use by, recipients and holders. It must not be communicated either directly or indirectly to, or discuss with, the press or other media, or any other person not authorised by, or on behalf of, Director Safety AWE to receive it.

What didn't they want us to know? Maybe the reason is that the report is a master-class of obfuscation and evasion clearly designed to reassure, yet failing dismally. Even the opening sentence is a falsehood.

> Detonations were permitted only when it had been reliably concluded that the meteorological conditions, *in particular wind directions,* were such that fall-out would be carried away from inhabited areas (emphasis added).

We now know of course that this isn't true: the Meteorological Office report clearly states the winds for Grapple Y explosion were blowing toward areas where servicemen were gathered. So, based on the MoD's own stringent requirements, the shot should not have been fired. The authors of the report were clearly not conversant with the weather reports.

And what are we to make of the next statement?

> Environmental measurements were usually below the limit of detection. On the few occasions when radioactivity above this limit was detected the levels were low, decayed or dispersed rapidly, and did not constitute a hazard or danger to test participants, visitors or inhabitants of the island.

What they are clearly trying not to say is that after all the denials and assurances by ministers to the contrary there *was* radioactive contamination on Christmas Island even if it was "low or decayed." But the next statement contradicts even that slippery assurance when it concedes there was

> a single enhanced measurement of 2.8 microcurie per square metre" found at Main Camp 32 hours after one of the detonations. This was slightly above the recommended limit of 1 microcuries per square metre.

It was in fact nearly three times the recommended limit, which some would argue was a lot more than "slightly above." But this important distinction pales into insignificance when considered alongside the next staggering announcement

A few very high values (up to 300 microcuries per square metre after extrapolation back to one hour after detonation) were recorded from the uninhabited southern parts of the island, none of which was nearer than 8 km from the nearest inhabited area.

In the space of a few short paragraphs we have moved from the definitive "below the limit of detection" on to "slightly above the recommended limit" to arrive at "a few very high values of 300 microcuries per square metre!

Let us be clear: this measurement was 300 times the recommended safe limit which was just 1 microcuries per square metre…by any standards a very serious contamination.

Remember: the Christmas Island bombs were all supposed to have been "clean" because they were exploded too high in the air to cause any fallout. This astonishing document makes a nonsense of all that.

To find such high concentrations of radiation just a few miles from inhabited areas is a very grave situation.

Radioactive contamination does not recognise borders, and if it had already travelled 20 km from the point of detonation there is no reason to suppose it would just stop dead in its tracks when it reached 8 km from the camps, as the authors of the report imply.

But there was more: Further in the text, Grapple Y makes a sudden startling appearance, leaping out of page 7:-

During Operation Grapple Y, the greatest and only significant measured value (of 150 microcuries per square metre) was obtained at the uninhabited site at Vaskess Bay. However, records indicate that subsequent surveys using hand-held instruments did not confirm this high figure.

Grapple Y's "rogue" status" is once again confirmed. It clearly contaminated at least one area with radiation levels 150 times the recommended safe limit.

Vaskess Bay is on the east coast of the island and just a few short miles from several inhabited areas including St Stanislas Bay, Paris, Benson Point, and most important of all, Port London where thousands of men and islanders had been evacuated for safety reasons.

The charge that hand-held instruments didn't confirm the readings taken from the official site is suspect because we are not told what readings they did measure, or when they were taken.

In any event a helpful chart marked Table 4 at the back of the report gives a picture of the pattern of contamination over the island.

Entitled "Results of Local Survey for Operation Grapple Y" it details the fallout readings from 11 different monitoring points. Five sites, including the Main camp and the airfield are declared "below detectable level."

But the other six, which includes Port London and the Joint Operations Centre, record measurable fallout, and some readings are way above proscribed safety limits.

This explosive document graphically illustrates the dishonesty and deceit as practised by the Ministry of Defence and its placemen.

For 50 years successive defence ministers have insisted absolutely that there was no radioactive fallout over Christmas Island after nuclear bomb tests. Yet here we have admissions, set out in official documents, that there was major contamination on Christmas Island following the Grapple Y explosion and others.

Two of the central pillars of the British government's defence of its conduct over the nuclear weapons tests of the 1950s have been destroyed by the information contained in these documents. According to the evidence from the official archives this is what happened:-

Grapple Y, Britain's biggest bomb, unleashed enormous elemental forces over an island already saturated with rain and enveloped by water vapour from earlier downpours. Christmas Island was like an enormous test-tube into which a giant spark was introduced.

The bomb created a violent rainstorm that scavenged highly radioactive fission products from the bomb which were borne by the wind over large areas of the island (as the scientists knew it would) and deposited over areas, like Port Camp, where most of the troops were gathered.

Huge hotspots of radiation formed at various points on the island as the fallout carried by the prevailing wind gradually came to earth. It was inevitable that the men were contaminated, either directly or by swallowing water, and swimming in the lagoons.

The contamination would have entered the bloodstream, eventually reaching vital organs producing various types of cancers. This internal exposure would not have shown up on the external monitors worn by the servicemen.

Exploding Grapple Y may have been a technical and scientific triumph, but it was also an exercise in folly that put at grave risk the lives and well-being of thousands of unsuspecting servicemen.

It was a gamble that paid off for the government. For despite all the evidence there was still no actual proof that the servicemen so callously placed in danger were ever harmed by their experience. The insidious effects of the A-bomb had been cleverly concealed among the huge cohort of 20,000 servicemen who took part in the 21 tests carried out by the government.

But the unmasking of Grapple Y as a rogue bomb changed everything. The veterans could now concentrate their efforts on this one bomb to see if there was a marked difference in their health. And they had the ideal 'control group' to compare them with: the men who attended the other tests.

A total of 3,722 servicemen witnessed the Grapple Y blast. If a study of health problems in the men who attended this test found that higher than normal numbers had been hit by illness than men from the other tests, the important principal of cause (Grapple Y) and effect (higher incidents of sickness) could be established.

The National Radiological Protection Board had already set the precedent when it commissioned a small study by Leiden University into incidents of cataracts reported by nuclear veterans. The study, carried out in 1993 compared 10 veterans who suffered from cataracts with an equal number who didn't.

The idea of targeting one bomb test was not new. American nuclear veterans had forced the Regan government into recognising their claims after a smart US attorney representing the family of a soldier who had died of leukaemia homed in one bomb test codenamed Smoky, conducted in the Nevada desert in August 1957.

He discovered that nine cases of leukaemia occurred among 3,224 men who participated in Smoky. This represented a significant increase over the expected incidence of 3.5 cases. The results were published, and the U.S. government was eventually forced to concede that the increase could have been due to radiation exposure.

There was an instant knock-on effect, and soon all 250,000 American nuclear veterans were included in a compensation scheme that recognised their claims if they conformed to certain medical criteria. If a pattern of ill health could be found in the Grapple Y veterans, the British government would be obliged to follow a similar path.

The British veterans set about tracking down as many published accounts provided by nuclear test veterans over the years, to establish which bomb tests these individuals had attended. The beauty of this approach was it couldn't be dismissed as biased because the men who complained had no idea of the significance of Grapple Y when they told their stories.

As far as they were concerned they were just "atomic veterans" and which explosion they witnessed was irrelevant.

To test the hypothesis, the veterans made a study of the research material carried out into birth defects in the grandchildren of nuclear veterans in 2002.

Although dismissed by the MoD, the importance of this study was that it provided vital information about the "when and where" of the tests the men witnessed. One of the first things they noted was that the majority of veterans who reported sickness in their grandchildren had been stationed on Christmas Island.

John Urquhart was asked to investigate further. He examined the data collected for the grandchildren study and discovered that indeed the majority of the complainants had been stationed on Christmas Island. But a by-product of his study stunned the veterans: 69 per cent of the Christmas Island cohort was present at Grapple Y.

This was a startling result. It was as if the grandchildren had suddenly reached out across the generations to tap their veteran grandfathers on the shoulder.

But was this just a bizarre coincidence, an aberration? Or was it proof of the pernicious nature of Grapple Y? Urquhart erred on the side of caution. He believed the survey was too small to give a definitive answer and said the only way to get a credible picture was to examine the records of all the nuclear veterans who had complained of health problems, and then establish what bomb tests they witnessed.

This was a difficult undertaking because by this time the official records of the BNTVA had been widely dispersed, and much of the material had been lost.

Fortunately, however, McGinley had retained a meticulous record of every nuclear veteran who had contacted him during his tenure as chairman of the BNTVA. These hand-written accounts, in five A4-sized journals, included details of more than 3,000 individuals, roughly a sixth of the total number of men who had attended the bomb tests.

And, crucially, the archive contained information enabling researchers to pin-point the location of the men and the bomb test(s) they were present at.

John Urquhart carried out a detailed analysis of the data contained in the "Y-files" and, together with information from published materials in newspapers and journals, produced a "master list" of 2,409 nuclear veterans who could be positively placed at one or more of the 21 nuclear bomb tests carried out by Britain in the 1950s.

The results were staggering: the response rate for men attending Grapple Y was 1,159 out of 3,722 men at Grapple Y, compared with 1,250 of the 13,206 men who attended all the other tests.

So, nearly 50 per cent of men who had made complaints had been present at Grapple Y. But there was more: cancer rates for Grapple Y men were nearly four and a half times the rest, while there were nearly nine times as many for joint cancer and fertility problems, which included miscarriages, stillbirths and birth defects. Urquhart's study also quashes any suggestion that the results were biased. In a damning summary he concludes

The continuing secrecy of the British government about the true nature of the nuclear tests ensured that the respondents were unaware of whether one particular test was more dangerous than another, thus eliminating any bias due to self-selective response from self-reporting. The great difference in response rates for men attending the Grapple Y test compared with all the other tests strongly suggests an underlying health difference consistent with significant exposure to radioactive fallout from the Grapple Y test.

This is the truth of Christmas Island: On April 28th, 1958 a multi-megaton thermonuclear bomb was detonated off the south east coast of Christmas Island. The bomb created a radioactive thunderstorm that travelled slowly up the east coast of the island contaminating large areas. An unspecified number of men, possibly thousands, were caught in this lethal downpour, and many later paid the price in death and injury.

The authorities were aware of this, but covered it up and shamefully turned a blind eye to the suffering that inevitably ensued.

Men died slow, horrible deaths as a result. Young men, who hardly had a chance of life, died of old men's diseases. Young wives, whose men returned home physical and psychological wrecks, suffered with them.

And when their broken babies were born they could only weep in despair at the haunted look in the midwives' eyes, and the hopeless shake of the doctor's head.

When Grapple Y was detonated the world was in turmoil.

Nuclear war was a real possibility and few could blame the British government for deciding to build its own nuclear deterrent.

Even the cover-up of the Grapple Y incident can be understood in the face of a world gone mad.

But there is no excuse for the continuing secrecy and cover-up that has surrounded the bomb tests. For 50 years nuclear veterans have complained, but successive governments have turned a blind eye to their suffering.

Worse they have cynically ignored compelling evidence, revealed in this book, that many were wilfully exposed to radioactive fallout.

The Ministry of Defence stands condemned for consigning those who tried to expose its wickedness to a life of sickness and penury.

But most of all it stands condemned for its callous indifference to the torment of untold numbers of children who have been sacrificed on the altar of nuclear expediency.

On 9 May, 1989, Margaret Thatcher stood up in Parliament and made the following announcement in reply to a demand by MP Jack Ashley for compensation for nuclear veterans

> As the right hon. Gentleman knows, cases were carefully looked at by a special inquiry of medical people, who did not find cause and effect. I say to the right hon. Gentleman with the greatest respect that the cause and effect that he says has been proved has not been proved, and therefore compensation is not appropriate.

Nearly a quarter of a century on this stringent criterion has at last been fulfilled. The evidence presented in this book shows clear cause and effect.

Britain's nuclear veterans are the victims of a grave injustice. Not only have they been decimated by their participation in the bomb tests, but their offspring have been dreadfully damaged as well.

It is a cruel irony that the children and grandchildren supplied the last piece of the jigsaw that exposed the British government's historical perfidy.

Politicians from all parties are guilty. The evidence was there for them all to see, but they chose to ignore it. They turned a blind eye to the suffering of a generation of brave men, and closed their ears to the cries of their children.

The British government owes the nuclear veterans an apology and compensation where appropriate. Every other nuclear power has compensated its Cold War warriors. It is time for Britain to do the same.

THE END

Printed in Great Britain
by Amazon